PENGUIN BUSINESS

WRITERS ON STRATEGY
AND STRATEGIC MANAGEMENT

J. I. Moore is a founder member of the Business Strategy Network and a senior partner in its consultancy associate. His first degree was in philosophy and his second in business administration. A series of increasingly senior managerial positions in the automotive, farm machinery and friction materials industries (with, successively, Ford, Lely and Trist, Draper) prepared him for teaching business policy at Thames Valley University and, later, at the University of Bath.

This is the book he would have liked on his desk at every stage of his working life.

D1648770

J. I. MOORE

—

Writers on Strategy
and Strategic Management

THE THEORY OF STRATEGY AND THE
PRACTICE OF STRATEGIC MANAGEMENT
AT ENTERPRISE, CORPORATE, BUSINESS
AND FUNCTIONAL LEVELS

PENGUIN BOOKS

PENGUIN BOOKS

Published by the Penguin Group
Penguin Books Ltd, 27 Wrights Lane, London W8 5TZ, England
Penguin Books USA Inc., 375 Hudson Street, New York, New York 10014, USA
Penguin Books Australia Ltd, Ringwood, Victoria, Australia
Penguin Books Canada Ltd, 10 Alcorn Avenue, Toronto, Ontario, Canada M4V 3B2
Penguin Books (NZ) Ltd, 182–190 Wairau Road, Auckland 10, New Zealand

Penguin Books Ltd, Registered Offices: Harmondsworth, Middlesex, England

First published 1992
3 5 7 9 10 8 6 4 2

The acknowledgements on pages x–xi constitute an extension to this copyright page.

The moral right of the author has been asserted

Typeset by Datix International Limited, Bungay, Suffolk
Set in 10/12 pt Monophoto Times
Printed in England by Clays Ltd, St Ives plc

To John Edwards,
Director of the Centre for Enterprise Policy Studies
at the University of Bath,
who made this book possible – and much else besides,
as he must surely know

Contents

—

Acknowledgements   ix
Foreword   xiii

PART ONE
The Shapers and Movers

Preface   1
1. Kenneth R. Andrews   5
2. H. Igor Ansoff   15
3. Alfred D. Chandler Jr   34
4. Michael E. Porter   42

PART TWO
The Consultants

Preface   57
5. Robert D. Buzzell and Bradley T. Gale   59
6. Bruce D. Henderson   72
7. Benjamin B. Tregoe and John W. Zimmerman   81

PART THREE
The Scholars and Researchers

Preface   91
8. Derek F. Abell   95

9. Joseph L. Bower 110
10. Richard G. Hamermesh 120
11. Henry Mintzberg 131
12. Richard P. Rumelt 145
13. Malcolm S. Salter and Wolf A. Weinhold 155
14. Oliver E. Williamson 173
15. Robert A. Burgelman and Leonard R. Sayles 184

PART FOUR
The Developers and Teachers

Preface 193
16. Lester A. Digman 195
17. Jay R. Galbraith and Robert K. Kazanjian 206
18. Charles W. Hofer and Dan Schendel 216
19. John A. Pearce II and Richard B. Robinson Jr 230
20. Arthur A. Thompson Jr and A. J. Strickland III 238

PART FIVE
The Incrementalists

Preface 251
21. James Brian Quinn 255
22. Charles E. Lindblom 263

PART SIX
The Analysts of Decline

Preface 271
23. Kathryn Rudie Harrigan 273
24. Stuart St P. Slatter 281

Index of authors and authorities 299
Subject index 303

Acknowledgements

—

Though I am responsible for everything that follows, many people – newcomers to my acquaintance as well as friends – helped me along the way. Sometimes it was by facilitating the work, as did Graham Pickup of West Educational Publishing, Martin Hanifin and Kurt Strand of Richard D. Irwin, Joseph Bower of Harvard's Graduate Business School, and Roger Martin-Fagg of the Management College, Henley. Some, like Terry Garrison of Henley, Ken Clarke of Bath University, Trevor Hunwicks of Benton International and Chris Pooley of Nuclear Electric, stirred me with ideas and suggestions when my own resources ran low. And some never ceased to encourage me in their highly individual ways: Eric Lewis of Foster Wheeler, by assuming what had yet to be proved; Peter and Lesley Austin, by remaining invincibly interested in even the most tedious of my days; Bri and Joy Thornton, for their respective hectoring and coaxing; and Sue and Robert Pfunder for always being there.

I can only hope that what has been done here justifies their unfailing concern and marvellous generosity.

Ellesborough, 1992   J. I. MOORE

Permission to use the following figures and tables is acknowledged (page references are to the original editions):

Derek F. Abell: *Defining the Business*, 1980. Tables on pp. 176, 184, 190 reprinted by permission of Prentice Hall, Englewood Cliffs, New Jersey.

K. Albert: *The Strategic Management Handbook*, 1983. Figure 16-4 on pp. 16–17, by R. H. Rock and M. Eisthen, reprinted by permission of McGraw-Hill, Inc.

H. Igor Ansoff: *Corporate Strategy*, McGraw-Hill, 1965. Figure 7.2 on p. 116 reprinted by permission of the author. *Corporate Strategy*, McGraw-Hill, 1987. Table 1.1 on p. 27, figures 6.1, 6.2, 7.1 on pages 109, 110, 122 reprinted by permission of the author.

R. A. Burgelman: Figure 9.1 from 'A Process Model of Internal Corporate Venturing in the Diversified Major Firm', published in *Administrative Science Quarterly*, June 1983, reprinted by permission of *Administrative Science Quarterly*.

Buzzell and Gale: *PIMS Principles: Linking Strategy to Performance*, Free Press, 1987. Exhibits on pp. 21, 24, 28, 48, 49, 72, 75 and 81 reprinted by permission of PIMS Associates Ltd.

L. A. Digman: *Strategic Management: Concepts, Decisions, Cases*, 2nd edition 1990. Table 2.1 on p. 37 reprinted by permission of Richard D. Irwin, Inc.

Galbraith and Kazanjian: *Strategy Implementation*, 2nd edition, copyright © 1986 West Publishing Company. Figure 4.2 on p. 51 and Tables 4.1 and 4.3 on pp. 53 and 67 reprinted by permission of the publisher, all rights reserved.

C. W. Hofer and D. Schendel: *Strategy Formulation: Analytical Concepts*, copyright © 1978 West Publishing Company. Excerpts from Table 2.2, Table 2.5 and Figure 2.8 reprinted by permission of the publisher, all rights reserved.

Henry Mintzberg: *Structure in Fives: Designing Effective Organizations*, copyright © 1983. Figure on p. 216 reprinted by permission of Prentice Hall, Englewood Cliffs, New Jersey.

J. A. Pearce II and Richard B. Robinson, Jr: *Strategic Management: Strategy Formulation and Implementation*, 3rd edition, 1988. Figures on pp. 11, 13 and 51 reprinted by permission of Richard D. Irwin, Inc.

Michael E. Porter: *Competitive Strategy: Techniques for Analysing Industries and Competitors*, copyright © 1980 the Free Press. Figures 1.1 on p. 4 and 2.1 on p. 39 reprinted with the permission of the publisher, a division of Macmillan Inc.

Michael E. Porter: *Competitive Advantage: Creating and Sustaining Superior Performance*, copyright © 1985 the Free Press. Figures 1.3 on p. 12 and 2.2 on p. 37 reprinted with the permission of the publisher, a Division of Macmillan Inc.

Malcolm S. Salter and Wolf A. Weinhold: *Diversification through Acquisition: Strategies for Creating Economic Value*, copyright © 1979 by Malcolm S. Salter and Wolf A. Weinhold. Figures 1.1 on p. 8 and 3.1 on p. 61; Table 6.1 on p. 114 reprinted with the permission of the Free Press, a division of Macmillan, Inc.

Stuart Slatter: *Corporate Recovery*, Penguin Books 1984. Figures 3.3, 5.1 and flow chart on p. 75 reprinted by permission of Penguin Books Ltd.

A. A. Thompson and A. J. Strickland: *Strategic Management*, 5th edition, 1990. Figures and tables on pp. 5, 35, 42, 44, 85 and 219 reprinted by permission of Richard D. Irwin, Inc.

Every effort has been made to trace copyright owners. The publishers apologize for any errors or omissions and would be grateful to hear from copyright owners not here acknowledged.

Foreword

—

No sector within the extensive field of business literature has received more attention in recent times than what has come to be called strategic management. And few have seen so many changes of direction, perspective, emphasis – even name, during so short a period. But whether it has been termed general management, business policy, corporate strategy, long-range planning or corporate management, the sector has always addressed the same issue: the determination of how an organization, *in its entirety*, can best be directed in a changing world.

This book aims to help the reader become better acquainted with some of the most influential contributors to the sector. Of course, selections from among so many candidates may always be faulted, but anything less than an encyclopedia would be open to the same criticism. What is proffered is a necessary, but not sufficient, introduction to strategy scholarship. The hope is that the reader will be stimulated to study more deeply and widely, and will then discover that the foundations laid here have provided a sure structure on which to base a greater understanding. However, though all students want to become managers, the converse does not appear to be true. So, for these more cursory readers the hope is less ambitious: that they find the book useful to dip into – in order, at the very least, to avoid being upstaged in competitive discussion!

The format is the same as that of its companion work, *Writers on Organization*. Both books seek to set out the significant elements of each writer's thinking within a few pages. In composition, however, they differ. This book makes more use of figures, tables and diagrams – principally because its writers, with few exceptions, find it difficult to communicate their ideas without them. And it incorporates many more quotations. These, it must be acknowledged, tend to interrupt the flow of sentences. But they do make the reader familiar with what the author actually said – for good or ill.

Both books are essentially engaged in distillation; and such a process may be thought incapable of doing justice to what could have been a lifetime's grinding labour. Worse, it might be said to trivialize by simplifying. As before, the endeavour here has been to show developments within a writer's corpus of work, and connections between it and the literature as a whole – even at the risk of being repetitive. Nevertheless, the overall dangers implicit in what has been attempted must be recognized. The serious student would be well advised to go back to source material before delivering himself of a scholarly interpretation.

Textual interjections have been kept to a minimum, being indulged in only when they have seemed necessary for clarity's sake, or to be more informative. The singular exceptions are the brief prefaces to each section. In these some licence has been taken – as should be perfectly evident. But then the business of grouping writers in this way is, in itself, somewhat arbitrary. To take just one example: Kenneth R. Andrews could have been placed in at least two other sections. However, it is considered that his outstanding early contribution to theory justifies the choice which has been made.

Regrettably, some cautionary words must be said about language. It is a sad characteristic of any scholarly work which acquires a public reputation that some phrase, some label, some pithy definition gains a general currency and simultaneously loses the precision its originator prescribed for it. And this, it seems, is especially true of business literature. Terms like cash flow, synergy, learning curve, parameter, charisma, interface, matrix organization, paradigm – along with so many others – have, every one, suffered just such a devaluation in their passage from academic thesis to ordinary conversation. If blandness is the price that scholarship has to pay for popularity, then we are all the poorer: practising managers, because serious arguments can founder over semantics; and students, because they can be tripped at any step along that route which is measured with assessments and examinations by someone more diligently critical than themselves.

In preparing the book, this 'sad characteristic' and its hazards have become only too apparent. So, wherever it has seemed right, an explanation has been given as to how writers have meant their terms to be used. It may make for tedium in the reading; but it should add rigour to the discussions which, it is to be hoped, will follow.

Finally, the reader will note that some career information about each writer has been included. While accuracy has always been striven for, events may already have outdated some of what is said here. Moreover, since one or two experts have proved to be shyer than their fellows, the accounts of their other achievements are less complete than is ideal.

PART ONE

The Shapers and Movers

Preface

No single person can be said to have invented corporate strategy. Just as military strategy did in the eighteenth century, it 'emerged' during the 1960s, as the consequence of a series of apparently disconnected events, and the articulation – principally – of three people.

Among the events one can name are the impetus given to business thinking by the strategic studies of the USAAF, when some of the personalities involved[1] returned to civilian life in 1945; the business policy teaching, with its emphasis on the role of the general manager, at Harvard Business School; the steady movement of management education (in the US) from a preoccupation with the internal (e.g. with so-called management principles) towards an external orientation best exemplified by the arrival of the marketing concept in the early 1950s; and the influence of systems thinking brought about by scholars such as L. von Bertalanffy.

The three people were Kenneth R. Andrews, Alfred D. Chandler Jr and H. Igor Ansoff. They are 'principally' responsible for moving and shaping much of what has happened since because they were the first *formally* to delimit the area of strategy in terms of concepts, definitions, and methodologies.

They were, of course, utilizing the individual insights of some remarkable men.

---

1. Perhaps the most notable of these was Robert McNamara, who became, in turn, Chairman of Ford Motor Company, Secretary of State under John F. Kennedy, and President of the World Bank.

As early as 1955, for example, Peter F. Drucker was making the distinction, in *The Practice of Management*, between tactical and strategic decisions; not perhaps quite in the way that we do today; but close enough for us to recognize certain similarities when he says that the latter include 'all decisions on business objectives and on the means to reach them'. Moreover, as everyone is aware, he was the first writer to ask the crucial question, 'What is our business?'

Perhaps only the members of his gifted Harvard team[2] can know what Andrews, their *primus inter pares*, owes to them; and what they owe to him. What we do know, however, is that *The Concept of Corporate Strategy*, which elevated their renowned teaching-by-coaching method to an entirely different intellectual plane, was described by them as 'his pioneering volume'.

Ansoff has always made acknowledgement to the influence of other thinkers and practitioners on his work; and never more generously (considering his decision not to adopt one of their main findings!) than to Richard M. Cyert and James G. March.

And always, in the general background, is the prodigious figure of Herbert A. Simon.

Ostensibly, of the three, Chandler was perhaps more influencing than influenced. Indeed, it is wonderful to observe how often his work has been referred to, throughout these thirty years, by contemporary and successor alike. The popular view is that his reputation rests upon the famous dictum that 'strategy follows structure'. And, assuredly, it started there. But, we would argue, the long-term significance of what he did (especially if our critique of his methodology is valid) rests upon two other contributions: (1) that he created *en passant* the very concept of structure – which, of course, is not to be confused with organization – thus opening up a new area of research and scholarship; and (2) his definitions (of industrial enterprise, administration, strategy, structure, and so on).

Michael E. Porter's inclusion as a shaper and mover should be no surprise to those who have come to strategy in the last ten

2. Among whom can be numbered Edmund P. Learned, C. Roland Christensen, William Guth and Joseph L. Bower.

years: for scarcely a modern textbook can be found which does not include his five-box schema. Yet they may not realize the magnitude of the change he has wrought. Before him – and despite strategy's emphasis on the need to see the firm as it fits into the world about it – the focal point was the firm. To be sure, there was much talk about the environment. But it was as an abstraction. Case studies were rarely accompanied by an industry note. And even more seldom were there data on suppliers or potential entrants. What Porter gave us was the firm's proper setting: its industry; and a structured way of looking at it.

It is true that he has raised as many questions as he has answered. (For instance: What constitutes an industry? How does one define an exit barrier? Why is it called a 'generic strategy'? And are there not four rather than three of them?) But then is this not the fate of all innovators? He has changed the nature of the debate; and never more interestingly than when, by implication, he argued that competition was better avoided than sought.

1

Kenneth R. Andrews

—

From early in the century Harvard Business School set itself to enhance the technical competence of businessmen and managers; and, in the process, created – many would argue, perfected – that most powerful and dramatic teaching vehicle, the case study. Nearly forty years ago a group of accomplished teachers in the School wrote and compiled the forerunner (*Policy Formulation and Administration*, now in its ninth edition) of the type of workbook, combining scholarly writing and related cases, which has become a commonplace in management education.

This was followed, in 1965, by a similar work in the same field: *Business Policy – Text and Cases* (*BP–TC*). Over the years its authors have changed; but its intention, to provide 'the materials for a complete course in Business Policy', has not. Cases have come and gone – with a few exceptions; and some of the terms used have given way to the impetus of fashion. But, leaving aside a number of readily identifiable contributions made by M. E. Porter to its latest edition (1987), there is a remarkable ideological consistency evident in the text of all the editions – much of which can be explained by the signal role Kenneth Andrews has played in its writing throughout.

In a significant sense, Andrews could be said to personify a vastly important Harvard tradition. He not only speaks for his *BP–TC* co-authors, he also represents (with them) the current stage in the development of a corpus of general management thought and teaching created by probably the most distinguished grouping of scholars ever to come together in one business school.

In the work he is solely responsible for, *The Concept of*

Corporate Strategy, which is largely composed of the accompanying text to *BP–TC*, we quickly become aware of Andrews's empirical bent. Here is no Cartesian framework of axioms or principles from which will be derived a logically coherent corpus of management theorems. Instead, we are told that 'hundreds of case studies undertaken over the years, to understand how policy decisions are made in business, have made possible a practitioner-based theory of general management'. Moreover, when subjected to the analytical approach he later describes, his belief is that the cases reveal how the process of decision-making can be made more productive and accurate.

Andrews's empirical bent, however, is not of an orthodox scientific nature; that is, one where painstaking research leads to the promulgation of hypotheses, theories, or laws, upon which teaching, judgement, and decisions can be based. Indeed, he tells us that 'The literature of organization theory is by itself . . . of very little use in managing a live organization.' And we read (in *BP–TC*) that case studies 'present, not illustrations of principle, but data from which generalizations may to a limited degree be derived, and to which the idea of strategy may be applied'.

The phrase 'to a limited degree' is a key one; and is perfectly consonant with Andrews's view that strategic management, which he roughly equates with business policy, 'is, and will remain, more an art than science'. His view is not, however, a justification for *ad hoc* management practice. On the contrary, in the absence of logically established (i.e. necessarily true) principles, or scientifically grounded laws, there is an even greater need for intellectual effort because of the compulsion to understand – in order to manage – complex organizations striving to make their way in an increasingly complicated world. The equipment he and his Harvard colleagues offer, in their teaching and external consultancies, consists essentially of one over-arching concept (that of corporate strategy), and a related methodology which has been fine tuned by years of practical application.

The concept emerged, Andrews tells us, from business policy which is 'study of the knowledge, skills and attitudes constituting *general management'.*[1] What corporate strategy added to this elevated perspective was the capacity to conceive of the organization *as a whole.* And not just a whole when judged by some canons of structural and functioning coherence: but as an entirety purposefully relating to the world about it.[2]

General management, Andrews defines, in its simplest form, as 'the management of a total enterprise, or of an autonomous sub-unit'. However, there are many to whom the term may be applied. Among the obvious candidates are chief executive officers (CEOs), whether called chairman, president or managing director. Less obvious is the inclusion of every member of the general management hierarchy such as, for example, those who man the president's office. And there are yet others, both internal[3] and external,[4] all of whom should adopt the same stance.

The tasks of general managers, or at least of those who have to practise the role, together with the personal qualities they need, are so many and various that to 'multiply them . . . would put general management capability beyond that of reasonably well-endowed human beings', Andrews tells us. So he offers a simplification based upon viewing general management activities as distinguishable into three roles – **organization leader**, **personal leader**, and **the architect of organization purpose**.

The CEO as **organization leader**, has three principal functions:

1. To insist upon the achievement of planned results.
2. To maintain and develop the organized capability which makes achievement possible.

1. Harvard, perhaps earlier than any other business school, recognized the need to help the specialist department manager transform himself into the generalist CEO.
2. It was an idea whose time had come. General systems theory – which Andrews does not mention – with its central notion of open systems exchanging energy with the environment so as to hold off the forces of entropy, was already powerfully influencing both scientific and popular thought. Here, arguably for the first time, the company was viewed as an open system.
3. Such as 'senior functional officers whose concern is more for the contribution their subspecialists make to the operating organization, than for the technical complexity of their work'.
4. E.g. 'outside directors, financial analysts, consultants'.

3. To integrate the specialist functions which, as technology develops, proliferate and tend to lead the company this way and that.

Undoubtedly, the CEO is thought of, disagreeably and first of all, as a taskmaster. Now while he has to be this, he has also to be motivator and mediator – acting in the latter capacity with impartiality, when allocating resources among specialized functions.

In speaking of the CEO as a **personal leader**, Andrews seems to follow Henri Fayol, who saw the manager as someone whose personal qualities mark him out as uncommon. As an individual, the CEO contributes to the organization's quality of life, in addition to its performance. By example, he educates junior executives to emulate him. And, 'in areas of judgement where policy cannot be specified without becoming absurdly over-detailed', he establishes the level of ethical performance expected, by his own demeanour.

However, he is no despot. He invokes power 'as humanely and reasonably as possible in order to avoid the stultifying effects of dictatorship, dominance, or even markedly superior performance'. And currently, Andrews sees the representative type to be found in leading US companies as being more like a quarterback or team captain, than a hero or autocrat.

His most difficult task, in connection with his role as **the architect of organization purpose**, is to safeguard corporate objectives. He must be capable of detaching himself from day-to-day decisions and emergencies, and maintain the development of his company while preparing it for the long-term future, the most demanding of his functions being 'the installation of purpose, and the substitution of planned progress in place of drifting'.

Andrews sees the CEO, and the managers who work most closely with him, as well-rounded individuals. The CEO, for example, must possess such a high order of analytic intelligence that he can generate, or recognize, developments in the marketplace which realistically match the capability and re-sources of his company. And he should be able to combine the intellectual capacity 'most nearly unique to general management' of conceptualizing corporate purpose, with the dramatic skill to galvanize the energies of his people in support of that purpose.

Finally, he describes what he considers to be general management's most sophisticated function: continuous monitoring. What others view, at best, as mechanical and, at worst, as oppressive, Andrews sees constructively. He speaks of it as being informed by 'a kind of creative discontent' which is the enemy of complacency, and promotes the capacity as well as the performance of both the individual and his company.

At the end of what he acknowledges to be but a sketchy record of a CEO's duties – considering the enormity of the task the latter faces – Andrews attaches, by way of summary, four responsibilities to the three principal roles he has listed. They are:

1. Securing the attainment of planned results in the present.
2. Developing an organization capable of producing both technical achievement and human satisfaction.
3. Making a distinctive personal contribution.
4. Planning and executing policy decisions affecting future results.

Having set the general management perspective for corporate strategy, Andrews turns to the concept itself.

Corporate strategy he defines as 'the pattern of decisions in a company that determines and reveals its objectives, purposes, or goals, produces the principal policies and plans for achieving those goals, and defines the range of business the company is to pursue, the kind of economic and human organization it is or intends to be, and the nature of the economic and non-economic contribution it intends to make to its shareholders, employees, customers, and communities.'

Business strategy is distinguished from corporate strategy by being a subset of it. While the latter defines the businesses in which a company competes, business strategy determines 'how a company will compete in a given business, and position itself among its competitors'. And, he adds significantly: 'Both are outcomes of a continuous process of strategic management . . .'

The essence of this definition of corporate strategy Andrews identifies as *pattern*. He explains: 'It is the unity, coherence, and internal consistency of a company's strategic decisions that position a company in its environment and give the firm its identity, its power to mobilize its strengths, and its likelihood of success in the marketplace.' It is important therefore, he asserts, that goals should not be seen as separate from those policies designed to attain them.[5]

Andrews's insistence upon strategic consistency enables him to avoid taking part in the continuing academic debate on conflicting objectives – which he contends 'leads to mechanical conceptions of strategic management, and to endless logic chopping'. While, from a corporate standpoint, that same coherent pattern of goal and policy decisions makes it possible for the company to stand out, as ideally it should, uniquely among its competitors.

Corporate strategy is to be seen as 'an organization process, in many ways inseparable from the structure, behaviour and culture of the company...' It has two aspects (formulation and implementation) which, while intellectually separable, are actually interrelated in practice.

In formulation (that is, in deciding what to do), there is what he terms a logical subactivity, calling for a certain objectivity on the part of the analysts, which results in the matching of external opportunity (what a company *might* do) and corporate capability (what it *can* do), and attaches to the options thus revealed estimates of risk. This, Andrews calls an *economic strategy*. Two other types of consideration properly should influence the final choice of purposes. These are: individual value systems, ideals and aspirations (what people in a company *want* to do), and ethics (what a company *should* do).

Andrews identifies these considerations as the *four components of strategy*, and summarizes them as:

1. Market opportunity.
2. Corporate competence and resources.

---

5. For a contrary view see, especially, **H. Igor Ansoff**, pages 15–33 and **Charles W. Hofer and Dan Schendel**, pages 216–229.

3. Personal values and aspirations.
4. Acknowledged obligations to people in society other than shareholders.

And he adds, not unexpectedly, that identifying them is easier than 'the art of reconciling them in a final pattern of purpose'.

Turning to the implementation of strategy (that is, achieving results), Andrews says that it 'is comprised of a series of subactivities that are primarily administrative'. There must be:

1. An appropriate **organization structure** 'made effective by information systems and relationships permitting co-ordination of subdivided activities'.
2. **Organizational processes** which are 'directed toward the kind of behaviour required by organizational purpose'.
3. Top management **leadership**.

And each of these will be different in character according to the strategy chosen (e.g. no change, vertical integration, geographical expansion, diversification, etc.), and the type of company electing to follow that strategy (e.g. single product, related business, conglomerate, etc.). There is, however, a tension between what, curiously, he considers to be a logical proposition, 'that structure should follow strategy', and 'the organizational reality that strategy also follows structure'. But, Andrews argues, in examining these contrary tendencies we will come to understand how interdependent formulation and implementation are.

Turning to evaluation, he ponders how one can judge a strategy; or prefer one to another. By way of answer, he proposes that one should regularly ask ten important questions. There are no infallible indicators; but, given enough practice with the questions, one should arrive at some 'reliable intuitive discriminations'.

The questions are:

1. Is the strategy identifiable, and has it been made clear either in words or in practice?
2. Is the strategy in some way unique?

3. Does the strategy fully exploit domestic and international environmental opportunity?
4. Is the strategy consistent with corporate competence and resources, both present and projected?
5. Are the major provisions of the strategy and the programme of major policies of which it is comprised internally consistent?
6. Is the chosen level of risk feasible in economic and personal terms?
7. Is the strategy appropriate to the personal values and aspirations of the key managers?
8. Is the strategy appropriate to the desired level of contribution to society?
9. Does the strategy constitute a clear stimulus to organizational effort and commitment?
10. Are there early indications of the responsiveness of markets and market segments to the strategy?

After each has been discussed at some length, Andrews says that simple tests of soundness cannot be expected to deliver a complete evaluation. But judging a strategy against the 'several criteria here suggested will give anyone concerned with the quality of corporate planning more than enough to think about'. Indeed, strategy assessment is as much a matter of judgement as its original conception, and as subject to error – the commonest cause of which is wrongly evaluating current results.

However, his most severe strictures are directed at the mis-evaluation of strategy 'which stems from a pervasive conflict between the academic interests of financial economists and the practitioner orientation of the concept of corporate stategy'. He warns against the use of simple financial ratios (e.g. debt:equity ROI, EPS) 'as the determinants of decision', on the ground that they not infrequently lead, short-sightedly, to moves which meet the requirements of those ratios at the expense of strategic investment. Similarly, he inveighs against the misuse of portfolio analysis which 'leads to mechanical appraisal of separate businesses, rather than relating [them] to the future of the company as a whole'. People who overuse financial formulae in evaluating and shaping strategy do not appear to be aware that financial policy is the servant and not the master of corporate strategy.

In the final chapter of *The Concept of Corporate Strategy*, Andrews draws together a series of ideas that he has introduced earlier on the notion of strategy as a process.

Strategy formulation, he argues, is not the singular product of one man's mind, but a continuing organizational activity. As such, it is necessary to ensure that first senior, and then, later, intermediate and junior managers are engaged in it. Being an administrative process, we can make the distinction between *managing* it, and *performing* it. In complex organizations, senior strategists manage the process rather than 'make' the decisions. This is because, essentially, they ratify decisions put to them for approval by managers, junior to them, who have played an indispensable part in shaping those decisions. 'In this sense', Andrews contends, 'formulation is an activity widely shared in the hierarchy of management, rather than being concentrated in its highest levels.'

But whatever the size of the organization, the essential elements of the strategic management process are the same. Namely:

1. Participation by key individuals in the identification of problems and strategic opportunities.
2. Inclusion of personal preferences, organization values, and corporate capability in the analysis.
3. The marshalling of accurate and relevant data on further market growth.
4. The recognition of financial constraints with respect to capital sources and projected return.

So, as Andrews points out, the redirection of strategy (the object of the process), like its original conceptualization, brings into play, once more, his four components of strategy.

Bibliography

Kenneth R. Andrews, *The Concept of Corporate Strategy*, Richard D. Irwin, Inc., 3rd edn, 1987.

C. Roland Christensen, Kenneth R. Andrews, Joseph L. Bower and Michael E. Porter, *Business Policy – Text and Cases*, Richard D. Irwin, Inc., 6th edn, 1987.

2

H. Igor Ansoff

—

Igor Ansoff is one of the most influential figures to have appeared in business education in the last quarter of a century. His career has been characterized by a variety of academic posts on both sides of the Atlantic, a stream of papers and books – many written in co-operation with others, and a steady widening of the range of issues he has addressed, to the point where it might be thought he was attempting to develop a general theory of management. As this extension of his interests has taken place, he has not hesitated to press into service techniques, concepts and terminologies from a gallimaufry of disciplines – sometimes to curious effect. And his prolific output is unusual not just for the originality of some of his ideas, but also because of an engaging candour about those which have proved to be either flawed or impractical.

More than most of his fellows, Ansoff has an acute historical sense which he frequently reveals when giving perspective to his work. In looking at the US business scene, for example, he has divided the period from 1820 to the present day into three eras: mass-production, mass-marketing, and post-industrial – a term he adopts, after Daniel Bell, and prefers to P. F. Drucker's 'Age of Discontinuity'. This type of classification has enabled him to explain the changing, though largely internalized, preoccupations of business managers and their academic contemporaries up until the mid 1950s, when he believes the last era began. And it has additionally served to justify, almost as a matter of historical inevitability, the existence of our fascination with 'strategy' and everything 'strategic' – for which, to no small degree, he is responsible.

Fig. 2.1

Condition	Alternatives	Probabilities
Risk	Known	Known
Uncertainty	Known	Not known
Partial ignorance	Not known	Not known

But what do these terms denote, in Ansoff's scheme of things?

In what is still his most popular book, *Corporate Strategy* – published in 1965 – he distinguishes four basic types of decision: **strategy**, **policy**, **programme** and **standard operating procedure**. All but the first address recurring contingencies, such as the needs to organize overtime working, or prepare for bad weather. Once formulated, they obviate the requirement for an original decision every time additional work is called for, or it snows – for example. They thus assure consistency of action, realize what Ansoff calls 'economies of management', and, because of their characteristics, can be safely delegated to subordinate managers for execution.

Since these three types of decision deal with events which recur, much is known about the latter. It is, therefore, possible to identify all the alternatives and assign probabilities to the occurrence of each one. This approach, which Ansoff derives from the 'mathematical decision theorists', furnishes him with the typology given in Fig. 2.1.

It also enables him to rank his decision-types in the order of an increasing level of ignorance. At the bottom is the **standard operating procedure**, which addresses the most often occurring – and therefore the best known – events. This is closely followed by the **programme**, which is 'a time-phased action sequence . . . to guide and co-ordinate operations'. Ansoff associates both with 'conditions of certainty or partial risk'. Next are **policy** decisions. These are made in conditions of risk or uncertainty. And finally we have **strategies**, which are 'forced under conditions of partial ignorance'.

As can now be seen, a strategy is quite different to the other three types of decision. Because it is subject to the conditions of partial ignorance (where 'alternatives cannot be arranged and examined in advance'), it is not a contingent decision. Indeed, it is **a decision rule**: that is, it is 'a rule for making decisions'. And as such its implementation cannot be delegated downward, since last-minute executive judgement will be required'.

Having defined the noun (strategy), there should – one would think – be no trouble over its related adjective (strategic). But unfortunately, as Ansoff acknowledges, there is. One of Ansoff's most singular contributions to the subject has been his notion of **decision classes** – which we shall come to in a moment. The first of these he has called 'strategic': where this means 'relating to [the] firm's match to its environment'. Since strategies (along with standard operating procedures, programmes and policies) find a place in each of the decision classes – after all, partial ignorance can prevail anywhere – he cannot use 'strategic' in the other two decision classes where there is a condition of partial ignorance *but no firm/environment match issue*.

He resolves his linguistic dilemma by telling us that, since conditions of partial ignorance are dominant in the strategic decision class area (though not in the other two), 'the use of similar terminology is not entirely inappropriate'. But it is a resolution he, himself, is not entirely satisfied with: because, in a footnote to the same page, he adds, 'Perhaps a better term [for strategic] would have been *entrepreneurial*.' It is a thought which has a profound effect on his later work – as we shall see.

In describing how Ansoff initially construed 'strategy' and 'strategic', we have introduced – in passing – his decision class concept, and some of his ideas about what is conventionally covered by the umbrella term, risk.

Unlike financial theorists, who think of risk as being related to the variability of return on investment,[1] Ansoff – as we have observed – sees risk as being related to the quantity and quality of knowledge at the disposal of the manager; and, specifically,

---

1. See **Malcolm S. Salter and Wolf A. Weinhold**, pages 155–172.

that means knowledge of the factors bearing on any decision, and the causal connections among those factors. This general position has been adopted by many, if not most, of those who followed after. But his particular typology has had few intellectual consequences. By contrast, that of decision classes has proved highly influential: demonstrating his abilities at their best – eclectic,[2] yet original. Derived from A. D. Chandler Jr's[3] distinction between strategy and structure – like so much in this field – Ansoff's model redefined both concepts and added a third.

His starting point is that 'from a decision viewpoint' the firm can be conceived of as a 'resource-conversion process'. (Resources being its human, physical and monetary components.) His key question is, then: how can one configure and direct this process so 'as to optimize the attainment of the firm's objectives'? To which question Ansoff begins his answer by dividing what he terms 'the total decision space' into three 'classes': (the now-familiar) **strategic**; **administrative**, encompassing Chandler's 'structure'; and his own contribution, **operating**.

Strategic decisions address the selection of product-market opportunities. Operating decisions have to do with the budgeting, scheduling, supervision and control of resources: and, as such, realize the potential of strategic decisions. While administrative decisions, being concerned with the 'organization, acquisition and development of resources', are triggered and modified by the nature and outcomes, respectively, of decisions in the other two classes.

Fig. 2.2 is a reduced version of Ansoff's 'principal decision class' diagram.

Ansoff's precise definitions of each kind of decision class have largely been ignored. But his broad distinctions have been accepted, becoming familiar as *strategy*, *structure* and *process*.

By contrast, his detailed work on what he called 'growth vectors' has found much favour. His basic matrix, showing their components, is shown in Fig. 2.3. In interpreting it, the reader

2. As he says in the preface to *Corporate Strategy*, his purpose is 'to synthesize and unify' others' '*partial* analytical insights into strategic business problems'.
3. See **Alfred D. Chandler Jr**, pages 34–41.

Fig. 2.2

	Strategic	Administrative	Operating
Problem	To select product-market mix which optimizes firm's ROI* potential.	To structure firm's resources for optimum performance.	To optimize realization of ROI potential.
Nature of problem	Allocation of total resources among product-market opportunities.	Organization, acquisition and development of resources.	Budgeting of resources among principal functional areas. Scheduling resource application and conversion. Supervision and control.
Key characteristics	Partial ignorance. Decisions: centralized; non-repetitive; not self-regenerative.	Decisions triggered by strategic and/or operating problems.	Risk and uncertainty. Decisions: decentralized; repetitive; self-regenerative.

Key *ROI = Return on investment

Fig. 2.3

Mission	Product	
	Present	*New*
Present	Market penetration	Product development
New	Market development	Diversification

should know that Ansoff uses 'mission' in an idiosyncratic manner. He wishes it to mean 'an existing product need' – so that he can distinguish between that need and the customer (whether firm or individual) who possesses it.

Fig. 2.4

Customers	Products	
New missions	New products	
	Related technology	*Unrelated technology*
Same type	Horizontal diversification	Horizontal diversification
Firm its own customer	Vertical integration	Vertical integration
Similar type	Marketing and technology related*	Marketing related*
New type	Technology related*	Conglomerate diversification

* types of concentric diversification

Since strategy difficulties are at their most extreme when a firm diversifies (that is – employing his definition – when it moves into new product-missions), Ansoff has devoted considerable attention to it. The matrix shown in Fig. 2.4 (which is an expansion of the bottom right quadrant of Fig. 2.3) constitutes a landmark in strategic scholarship, and has proved invaluable to practitioners as well. Arguably, it was the first construct to demonstrate coherently how horizontal, concentric, conglomerate, and vertical integration moves can be distinguished from one another.

Before passing on to his later work, two of Ansoff's other insights should be commented upon: his distinction between objectives and strategy, and what he termed 'the components of strategy'.

His approach to strategy formulation in *Corporate Strategy* is avowedly normative.[4] In one of the best essays on objectives to be found in the literature of the period, he disagrees with R. M. Cyert and J. G. March's famous dictum by asserting that the

4. Nevertheless, he contends that it is practical in two senses: its 'framework is an outgrowth of several concrete problems' he has helped solve; and it has 'proved useful' in teaching business policy on graduate and executive courses.

firm can be said to have objectives which are distinct and different from those of its participants. He pronounces the firm's central purpose to be the maximization of 'the long-term return on [the] resources employed within the firm'. Once this has been precisely formulated as an objective, it will help guide the firm into the future, while it should be used retrospectively to measure what progress the firm has made along its chosen path. As such, an objective is seen as an end, while strategy is seen as a means to that end.

By separating objectives from strategy in this way Ansoff distanced himself from the position adopted by Chandler and his Harvard contemporaries, E. P. Learned, C. P. Christensen and K. R. Andrews.[5] He also began a debate, which is undecided to this day, as to the 'correct' relationship between objectives and strategy.[6]

For Ansoff, the separation is not a matter of convention. He perceives objectives and strategy as acting upon each other so that, together, they constitute a screening device when evaluating options. For example: having fixed upon a target ROI for some new product-market venture, the firm might discover that, regardless of what strategy it adopted, the target could not be reached; consequently, it could either lower its sights or reject the proposal entirely. Conversely, having calculated that a strategy promised more than the target return, the firm could raise its sights (with interesting effects on the way that it viewed its existing businesses) or, once again, reject the proposal. This means-ends concept of the relationship meant that the process of strategic decision-making became an iterative one, in which each cycle of the debate added refinement and realism to what had gone before.

Ansoff's 'components of strategy' approach was innovational at the time, and has been much imitated since. He devised it in an attempt to provide the firm with a rigorously definable 'common thread'. The notion of common thread (that is, a

---

5. See **Kenneth R. Andrews**, pages 5–14.
6. See **Charles W. Hofer and Dan Schendel**, pages 216–229.

recognizable coherence of activities which identifies the firm to
the outsider, and guides its management when thinking of the
future deployment of its greatest strengths), exercised academics
considerably in the 1960s. It was held to be important that
strategists, especially, should have the correct 'concept of the
firm's business'. Was the firm, for example, in the energy business, the transportation business, or the 'growth' business? If the
answer was 'yes' to any of these, then the firm could – and
perhaps should – tackle anything which, respectively, had to do
with energy, transportation, or looked like growing.

Now, useful as this type of concept may be for managers who
have become too restricted in their capacity to speculate, Ansoff
argued that it was so broad that it might, arguably, seduce
undoubted 'energy business' firms, such as oil producers, into
thinking they could – out of their own resources – successfully
diversify into, say, electricity generation.

To overcome this particular difficulty, and provide a practicable method of establishing a common thread between past and
future activities, Ansoff proposed four strategy components:

1. **Product-market scope** – an industrial listing so delimited as
   to confine strategic search to the similar and familiar.
2. **Growth vector** – describing how the firm could expand
   within and beyond its present field.
3. **Competitive advantage** – specifying what the firm had, or
   needed, to compete effectively.
4. **Synergy** – a desirable condition of complementarity between
   new and existing product-market activities.

Ansoff's next major work, *From Strategic Planning to Strategic
Management* (1976), which was essentially a symposium of contributions from sympathetically-minded colleagues, celebrated a
failure. Though he confirms his confidence in the salient points
of his earlier scholarship, he has to confess that, while strategic
planning[7] has been well known for some fifteen years, it has
hardly been widely adopted. This is partly because translating

---

7. It will be noted that 'corporate strategy' has become 'strategic planning'.

its precepts into practice has proved difficult. But it is also because 'attempts to install rigorous strategic discipline typically run into ... an organizational inertia which reject[s] planning efforts as a "foreign antibody"'.

But the way ahead is clear: external change, determined in conformity with the ideas laid down in *Corporate Strategy*, calls for major adjustments within the organization. Indeed, the 'entire pattern of internal capability[8] must ... be changed'.

Returning to his earlier categorization of decision-classes, Ansoff identifies what he now terms 'modes'. Strategic decisions equate with the 'entrepreneurial mode', and operating decisions approximate to the 'competitive mode'. In the entrepreneurial mode, the firm 'seeks effectiveness (profitability potential) through new [product-market] linkages'; while 'the competitive mode is focused on efficient (profitable) exploitation of existing linkages'. It is a formulation that owes much to C. Barnard and P. F. Drucker.[9]

So distinct are these two modes that 'when a firm transforms itself from a focus on competitive behaviour to an emphasis on the entrepreneurial, a fundamental transformation takes place in each of its major characteristics: its objectives, its value systems, its managers, its processes, its structures'. In other words, when a firm diversifies nothing less than a revolution occurs!

At this point, Ansoff sees strategic planning as merely 'a rational approach to assessing and redefining the linkages of the firm with both its business and societal environments,'[10] while 'strategic management' (which includes strategic planning) is seen as the activity that will *both* discern the external possibilities, *and* bring about the appropriate capability changes.

If the distinction between the entrepreneurial and competitive modes is conceptually clear, in practice it may be blurred by differing 'intensities of behaviour' in either mode. Each type of trading environment will call for a certain intensity. However,

8. By capability Ansoff means 'values, systems, structure, skills, power and technology'. 'Capability-pattern' *appears* to be synonymous with 'culture'.
9. See also **Charles W. Hofer and Dan Schendel**, pages 216–229.
10. Here we have a major development in Ansoff's thinking.

firms will vary in their responses to the demands made upon them; and that responsiveness will be a function of, among other things, each firm's internal capability. For example, success relative to competitive (i.e. existing) linkages may be inhibited where, say, aggressive marketing is necessary, but where complacent management refuses to innovate, invest sufficiently in promotion, or develop a strong selling operation. Equally, entrepreneurial (i.e. novel) linkages will require an appropriate, but perhaps quite different, intensity of behaviour which should be matched by an equivalent, internal intensity. And, remembering that each mode has a different focus (efficiency in the competitive, and effectiveness in the entrepreneurial), any attempt to create a homogeneous culture within the firm may introduce the conditions for conflict.

Ansoff's resolution of this dilemma is to suggest that, increasingly, firms will have to learn to live with a number of cultures – each of which is attuned to its own trading environment; and that 'integrative management', a new kind of activity directed at ensuring peaceful co-existence, will have to evolve.

In examining how cultural transformation could be managed, he contrasts what he calls 'adaptive learning' (that is, incremental change brought about by trial and error) with 'planned change': by which he means the process of imposing a clinical rationality on the shaping of an organization. Both types of change have defects: the first because it can be unrealistically protracted, and may culminate in a structure which is incoherent, and the second because it only seems to succeed when it yields an organizational form which is essentially an extension of what existed beforehand.

In his latest (and perhaps last) *major* work, *Implanting Strategic Management* (1984), Ansoff brings together many of the strands of thought which had preoccupied him for the previous thirty years – modifying, refining and developing them.

More than ever convinced that the world is changing faster and becoming less easy to predict, he is also more sensitive to the increasing complexity of organizations and of the people who inhabit them. His redefinition of 'strategic management' reflects this sensitivity, for it has now become: 'a systematic approach for managing strategic change which consists of:

1. positioning of the firm through strategy and capability planning;
2. real time strategic response through issue management;
3. systematic management of resistance during strategic implementation.'

The first is, of course, where he began when he invented the term. The second was added, principally, as a consequence of his experiences in the mid 1970s when he concluded that the ordinary strategic planning cycle was too slow and cumbersome to accommodate what he called 'mid-year surprises', emanating from government, foreign competitors, or R & D developments. To deal with these sudden challenges, he describes and proposes 'strategic issue management': a system which responds on a 'real time' (i.e. a near-immediate) basis. This is buttressed by two other proposals: a mechanism to detect 'weak signals' – and thus be in a better state of preparedness; and a 'strategic surprise system' which brings into play a 'strategic task force network', created in advance and rehearsed in readiness.

With the third element of his redefinition, Ansoff deals constructively with a phenomenon that has dogged him in the past (1976): the human and organizational inertias which have to be overcome when strategic change becomes necessary. His proposal is based upon a comparison of Western and Japanese methods of problem-solving. The former, he argues, are serial in character – largely because of our intellectual traditions, and most notably those originating with Descartes. The Japanese, by contrast, engage in what Ansoff calls 'a parallel planning-implementation process'. This not only leads to optimal decisions, but also – through the involvement of everyone concerned – ensures their 'cultural and political acceptance'. He then goes on to design a method which will, he believes, enable the process to be adopted in the West.

In 1987, Ansoff published a revised version of *Corporate Strategy*.[11] Not having re-read the original in some twenty years

---

11. With the assistance of E. J. McDonnell.

– in the belief that it was obsolete – he was surprised to find tha
a substantial part remained relevant. The new version 'is in
tended as an introduction to strategic management'. So, no
unnaturally, that is the perspective from which he judges, and
modifies, his earlier insights – in the first, and greater, part o
the book. The manager-student is thus presented with an un
usual, if not a unique, experience: a legitimate rewriting of the
past which renders a complete body of work internally coherent
Our interest, at this point, is therefore to see what major modifica
tions he has seen fit to make to his first book.

In comparing the two, one is immediately struck by how
much of the first five chapters has been retained. Predictably
the examples he gave have, for the most part, been brought up
to date. But on page after page, the original words have been
reproduced. His excellent essay on objectives, referred to above
and the subsequent one modelling 'a practical system' for
them, are barely changed. The same appears to be true for the
chapter on synergy – until one notices two detailed alterations in
a table showing functional synergy relationships among indus
tries; and then reads that, 'the past twenty years of experienc
have shown that management synergy quickly becomes negativ
[instead of being "moderate"] when a firm diversifies into an
industry whose ... turbulence is significantly different' from
what it has been used to.

This degree of textual fidelity means, of course, that th
content remains essentially the same. The firm is still viewed
as a resource-converter; the decision class concept is retained
in every detail; synergy is what synergy was; and strategi
decisions persist in being 'not self-regenerative'. (See Fig. 2.2
page 19.)

But why has so little changed in these early chapters?

In 1965, Ansoff was concerned to repair an intellectual omis
sion. Cyert and March had produced (in 1963) a behavioura
theory of the firm, and thus had 'made an important contribu
tion to the study' of the operating class of decisions. In 1962
Chandler had shed 'important light' on the administrative class
Ansoff's purpose was 'to construct a practical framework' for
the remaining class: strategic decisions. In the absence o

'adequate theory', he begins by 'constructing our own model of the firm': that is, in a typically normative or prescriptive fashion. A pertinent question about such modelling is: what is its basis? If it were systematically factual, then the approach would surely be descriptive – and not prescriptive at all. Does it stem from first principles? In which case it would be reasonable to ask where these came from. Or does it proceed from what might be called 'defensible assumptions' – defensible, perhaps, on the grounds of commonsense argument, or generally accepted propositions? Ansoff's model appears to be based on this last approach. (See page 20, note 4.)

The 1987 version, however, clears away all doubts. It is founded on 'practical prescriptions, invented largely within business firms'. 'Ideally,' as he tells us, 'theory is developed ahead of practical prescriptions.' But in the world of management, 'it has worked the other way round'. Problems beget solutions, which give rise to theories. And so it has proved to be in the case of the 1965 original – most of the material for which was based on prescriptions which have been validated by later theorizing and experience!

So, what in these early chapters has changed?

There is an addition – characteristic of the later Ansoff, as we have noted – of some seven pages of US business history. This concludes with the assertion that 'in the second half of the twentieth century, strategic and operating decisions require equal attention'; and that, consequently, the administrative decision class is brought into play by the need to provide a separate structure for each: that is, two structures which 'are not only different but inimical' to one another. We have, therefore, a timely connection – and not the only one – between the 1965 preoccupation with strategic decision-making and 1987 strategic management.

The main differences between the two versions become apparent with Chapter 6, in the middle of which we read: 'In summary, strategy is an elusive and somewhat abstract concept.' It is a view Ansoff compels us towards; for most of what seemed so straightforward then has now become highly sophisticated.

Certainly, there are familiar terms, usages and arguments. For example, risk, uncertainty, and partial ignorance continue as before. Objectives are still to strategy, as ends are to means; and, when employed together, 'filter projects'. But now *both* are decision rules – with primacy being given to the former; and they are interchangeable – according to timing, and organizational level.

Three of the original strategy components survive: growth vector (now known as **geographical growth vector**); competitive advantage; and synergy. Bringing the number, once again, to four is **strategic flexibility**. The first and the last of these are expressed in terms of three 'dimensions': **market need**, e.g. personal transportation; **product/service technology**, e.g. integrated circuitry; and **market geography** – which specifies the country, or some part of it, where the firm intends to do business.

These three replace Ansoff's original two, product and mission, which were used to describe his four basic growth directions. The matrix representing them – see Fig. 2.3, page 19 – has, therefore, been replaced by the one shown in Fig. 2.5. (In interpreting it, the reader will want to know that the most extreme move possible is from A to B. That is, from the present market need–geographical market–product/service technology combination, to a strategic position where each dimensional requirement is different. Plainly, there are many combinations of the three between A and B).

The four components form part of **strategic portfolio strategy**, which is one of two related types of strategy that 'in modern practice . . . are used to characterize the thrust of the firm's strategic development'; the other being **competitive strategy**. Portfolio strategy sets out to deal with the questions of what business(es)[12] the company is, and could be, in and establishes, coincidentally, how these will relate to each other.

Competitive strategy, on the other hand, 'specifies the distinct-

---

12. Ansoff calls these strategic business areas (SBAs).

Fig. 2.5

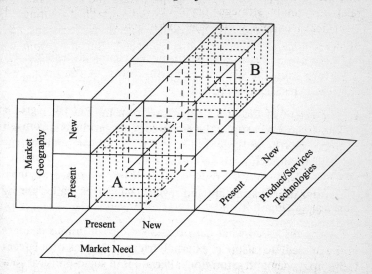

ive approach which the firm intends to use in order to succeed in each of the strategic business areas'. During the last twenty years – because markets could not be relied on to grow automatically, as they had in the past – new strategies have emerged to complement the familiar ones of 'market share maximization' (or 'cost/price minimization') and growth. Ansoff identifies these as: (1) market differentiation (market niche) – 'creating a distinctive image in the minds of potential customers for the firm's products/services'; and (2) product/service differentiation (product niche) – 'which differentiates the performance of the product/service' from those of the firm's competitors.

Whether talking of portfolio or competitive strategy, Ansoff distinguishes between **incremental**[13] and **discontinuous**

---

13. He associates this distinction with J. B. Quinn's 'logical incrementalism', apparently believing that the latter's theorizing advocated the *implementation* of small strategic steps; though, in fact, he was arguing for the *formulation* of strategy incrementally. See **James Brian Quinn**, pages 255–262.

changes. The first occurs when the firm 'makes a logical[14] and relatively small' strategic departure: e.g. an improvement in 'historical technology', or sales expansion to some part of another country.

By contrast, a discontinuous (or novel) change 'is a significant departure from the historical growth vector' of the firm. Two identifying tests can be applied:

1. The extent of the firm's departure from the market needs it knows how to satisfy, the technology its products are based upon, or 'the geographical, cultural, social, or political settings' it knows how to do business in.
2. The revisions in the firm's 'culture, power structure, systems, organizational structure and reward/incentives' called for by the change.

Having discussed what has occasioned discontinuous changes in the immediate past (e.g. external 'triggers' such as obsolescent technology, demand saturation, alterations in socio-political conditions; and internal drives such as entrepreneurship), Ansoff tells us that 'the path to new horizons took two distinctive forms': **internationalization** and **diversification**.

In 1965, internationalization hardly merited a mention – being subsumed under diversification. Its separate treatment – if nothing else does – calls for the additional illustration set out below. Replacing his original matrix (see Fig. 2.4, page 20), it marks a substantial break with the past.

As Ansoff explains, this diagram divides the cube of Fig. 2.5 'into two major types of growth vector, illustrated by the upper and lower slices of the cube'.

A **needs-related** departure occurs when a technology new to the firm is acquired so as to go on serving historical markets. When a historical technology is applied to new needs (e.g. 'the current flood of solid state electronics into the automotive industry'), the type of diversification is called **technology-**

---

14. He seems to be using 'logical' as though it meant 'coherent with past practice'.

a world scale, will be characterized more by co-operation between industrial giants (in order to attain 'critical mass') than it will be by the currently fashionable free trade ideology which ostensibly owes so much to Adam Smith. The world waits.

Bibliography

H. Igor Ansoff, *Corporate Strategy*, McGraw-Hill Inc., 1965, revised 1987.

H. Igor Ansoff, Roger P. Declerck and Robert L. Hayes, *From Strategic Planning to Strategic Management*, John Wiley, 1976.

H. Igor Ansoff, *Implanting Strategic Management*, Prentice-Hall International Inc., 1984.

3

Alfred D. Chandler Jr

—

Alfred Chandler is probably the most influential of all the post-war Harvard Business School luminaries. The word 'seminal' has been devalued by too much use of late, but it can be truly applied to his first major work, *Strategy and Structure* – published in 1962 and reprinted frequently since. Its subtitle, *Chapters in the History of the American Industrial Enterprise*, gives us an indication of his scholarly perspective: economic history. What it does not give us, however, is any idea of how fruitful an analytical recapitulation of events can be in providing us with enduring definitions and concepts.

Chandler began with the thought of writing a comparative history of administration in US business. Well aware of the enormous expansion which had occurred in the American economy after 1945, Chandler noted the concomitant increase in the complexity of problems being faced by managers in the, by now, much greater number of large companies benefiting from, and driving along, this expansion. The question arose: what developments in business administration had there been to cope with this new level of complexity? An answering study of the types of change which had happened then suggested that the area of organizational structure offered, as he put it, 'the widest possibilities' for his work; while it seemed that the study of innovation in that area furnished its proper focus.

A preliminary survey of fifty of the largest US industrial companies showed that there had been a general movement towards what was then called decentralization. This 'multi-divisional structure', as Chandler termed it, had its origins in the

1920s when the managers of a small group of large enterprises began gropingly to innovate their ways out of some newly discovered administrative difficulties.

The innovators were nine in number. For the purposes of his research, Chandler rejected four[1] on the ground that their 'administrative reorganizations proved to be less creative' than those of the four he finally selected to study – Du Pont, General Motors, Standard Oil (New Jersey), and Sears, Roebuck. And he eliminated the remaining company[2] since Sears – another merchandiser – was more complex, and information about it easier to obtain. The selected four qualified not only because they were among the very first to reorganize, but also because their structural developments owed nothing to what was happening in the rest of the four, or in any other company.

As his investigation proceeded, Chandler came to realize that:

1. Nothing less than an accurate record of each firm's administrative history was called for.
2. Any changes in organizational structure this revealed were related to its methods of growth.
3. These methods, in their turn, reflected changes in the US economy – and particularly those to do with demand for the firm's products.
4. Any reorganizations which had occurred were influenced by ideas and attitudes current at the time.

His acceptance of points 3 and 4 enlarged the study and, consequently, broadened its objectives. By comparing the growth and organizational records of the selected four with those for many other large companies, Chandler considered that he could make the process by which the four innovated more comprehensible, while gathering information on which might be based generalizations about 'the history of the industrial enterprise as an institution'. So what had started as 'an experiment in comparative business history' became an 'institutional history' entailing

1. US Rubber, B. F. Goodrich, Union Carbide & Carbon, and Westinghouse Electric.
2. The Great Atlantic & Pacific Tea Co.

the examination of nearly 100 of the largest industrial enterprises in the US.

Before, however, permitting the reader to approach the heart of his book – which comprises a general US historical setting, an immensely detailed case history of each of the selected four, a comparative analysis of organizational innovation, a study of the varied industrial acceptance of the multidivisional form, and a summarizing conclusion – Chandler engages in some intellectual ground clearing.

For the work to be meaningful when comparisons are made and analyses attempted – among the four, and more widely than that – he argues that he must precisely define the terms and the concepts to be employed. Accordingly, he proposes a 'set of general or theoretical propositions [which] *without reference to historical reality* ... try to explain in fairly clear-cut, over-simplified terms how the modern, "decentralized" structure came into being'. (The emphasis has been added.)

Chandler begins with a definition of the type of firm he is studying. An *Industrial Enterprise* is,

> in a broad sense ... a large private, profit-oriented business firm involved in the handling of goods in some or all of the successive industrial processes from the procurement of raw materials to the sale to the ultimate customer.

He then points out that, because this definition excludes purely transport and financial organizations as well as the utilities (such as gas, electricity and telephone companies), an industrial enterprise is but a 'subspecies of what Werner Stombart has described as the capitalistic enterprise': which, as an independent economic entity, is distinct from, and often lives longer than, those human beings who own or are employed by it.

An independent entity it may be, but its fortunes depend upon those individuals who guide it – now, and for the future – and whose responsibilities are 'to co-ordinate, appraise, and plan'. These individuals may also act as salesmen, accountants, buyers, engineers, and so on; but modern practice is for the execution of such functions to be left to subordinates whose work they supervise. Or, it could be that these same individuals administer the duties of other executives who, in their turn, supervise the work of subordinate functionaries. Whichever of these it is, Chandler encompasses it in his second definition. *Administration*

includes executive action and orders as well as the decisions taken in co-ordinating, appraising, and planning the work of the enterprise and in allocating its resources.

And this, in turn, leads him on to his first proposition:

That administration is an identifiable activity, that it differs from the actual buying, selling, processing, or transporting of the goods, and that in the large industrial enterprise the concern of the executives is more with administration than with the performance of functional work.

Which is followed, almost immediately, by his next:

That the administrator must handle two types of administrative tasks when he is co-ordinating, appraising, and planning the activities of the enterprise. At times he must be concerned with the long-run health of his company, at other times with its smooth and efficient operation.

The long-run health of the company is the object of *strategic* decisions. His description of their characteristics, by way of his third definition, has proved to be one of Chandler's most enduring – yet controversial – contributions to the literature. It is this: *Strategy*

is the determination of the basic long-term goals and objectives of an enterprise, and the adoption of courses of action and the allocation of resources necessary for carrying out these goals.

The formulation of policies and procedures, he tells us, can be either strategic or tactical (that is, dealing with those day-to-day activities which make for smooth and efficient operation). Whether strategic or tactical, both types of decision 'usually require implementation by an allocation or reallocation of resources'. Strategic plans may be formulated lower down in the hierarchy; but their implementation 'normally ... requires the resources which only the general office [see below] can provide'.

The executives who allocate these company-wide resources, 'because of their critical role in the modern economy', Chandler describes as *entrepreneurs*; and that type of decision as *entrepreneurial*. While those who 'co-ordinate, appraise, and plan within the means allocated to them' he terms *managers*; and that type of decision, *operational*.

Chandler's definition of structure has been as formative of later thinking as the one he gave to strategy.

Structure can be defined as the design of organization through which the enterprise is administered. This design . . . has two aspects. It includes, first, the lines of authority and communication between the different administrative offices and officers; and, second, the information and data that flow through these lines of authority and communication.

Both lines and data are necessary if managers are to carry out the company's policies and attain its goals. But, equally, they are needed to knit together the capital, physical equipment (including the sources of raw materials), and, most importantly, the various skills of its personnel, which he sees as comprising the total resources of the enterprise.

In a series of propositions dealing with the structure of the large decentralized company, Chandler identifies four different levels. From the top down they are: *the general office, the divisional central office, the departmental headquarters, and the field unit*. They are to be distinguished from each other not geographically – since they may all be housed in the same building – but in terms of the range of administrative activities they engage in, and the degree of authority they can exercise.

Typically, the general office allocates resources to, and administers the plans and policies of, a number of 'quasi-autonomous, relatively self-contained' divisions, each of which is responsible for a product line, or a sales region.

The divisional central office administers a group of departments responsible for manufacturing, purchasing, selling, engineering and other major functions.

Departmental headquarters manages field units – which may be manufacturing plants, purchasing offices, branch sales offices, engineering laboratories, and so on.

Only at the lowest level, that of the field unit, are there managers who carry on day-to-day activities; and even here the sheer volume of work may be such that they too are administrators – though operational ones.

At each of the four levels the executives have 'different business horizons'. Those in the general office concern themselves with several industries, or broad geographical regions of just one. Divisional officers focus on an industry – as opposed to a function. Executives at departmental headquarters manage a function – but on a regional or national scale, rather than locally. Conversely, those at field unit level manage a function in a local area – not nationally.

Now, why have these administrative levels, with their different responsibilities, degrees of authority, and horizons come about? Chandler's answer – and a crucial one for his main thesis – is that 'each *must* have resulted from a different type of growth'. (Once again, the emphasis has been added.)

For example: geographical growth, involving the creation of new facilities at a distance from the company's original base, required an office at that base to administer them. Or again: when an integrated enterprise diversified (that is, entered new businesses), it set up an integrated divisional unit administered by a general office.

At this point Chandler sharpens his 'naturalistic' account of administrative development by introducing to the argument his definitions of strategy and structure. Responding long-term to shifts in demand, or changing economic conditions, or technological developments, or alterations in supply, or competitive activity may call for 'the adoption of courses of action and the allocation of resources' which will facilitate that response. Such a new strategy may 'alter the business horizons of the men responsible for the enterprise [and] . . . have a profound effect on the form of the organization'. (And by 'form', Chandler clearly means 'structure'.)

He continues:

The thesis deduced from these several propositions is then that structure follows strategy and that the most complex type of structure is the result of the concatenation of several basic strategies.

The stimulus for strategic change, in Chandler's view, is always external. Simply stated, it comes down to the prospect of a new market, or the threatened loss of an existing one. Either may result in one or more of the three types of growth he identifies: *geographical expansion*, *vertical integration*, and *diversification*. And each calls for modifications to the structure – if the strategy is to be successful.

Geographical expansion (which is self-explanatory) calls for the setting up of departments and a headquarters to administer the requisite field units.

Vertical integration, which occurs when the enterprise adds functions previously performed for it by other companies (e.g. wholesaling, raw material supply, transport, and so on), needs a central office and multidepartmental structure.

And diversification (that is, when entirely new products are introduced) requires the multidivisional form, and a general office to administer the resulting divisions.

Towards the end of the promulgation of his 'set of general or theoretical propositions which attempts to provide some sort of conceptual precision', Chandler tells us that 'the actual historical patterns of growth and organization building ... were not, of course, as clear-cut as they have been theoretically defined here'. He repeats his intention that the propositions, and what he has derived from them, be used so as to make it easier to understand the complex realities of the enterprises he reports on later in the work. But so persuasively commonsensical is the development of his 'thesis', and so dependent is he upon it as a critical tool, that one wonders, first, what reliance we can place upon his early disclaimer that the propositions are 'without reference to historical reality', and second, whether he set out merely to validate the tool, rather than test it scientifically.

But perhaps it would be wrong to judge his thesis on the basis he apparently invites us to: that is, as a construct derived logically from a set of self-evident propositions – in the manner of Descartes.

Just as it would be wrong to argue that structure *must always* follow strategy. For, by Chandler's own definition, strategy includes means ('new types of personnel and facilities') as well as ends ('basic long-term goals'), and no one in his right mind is going to add either people or their equipment without making some provision in advance to administer them – and that implies structure. To which Chandler would no doubt retort, 'Agreed. My point is that, historically, it can be shown that there has tended to be a delay between setting strategy and installing *the correct type* of structure for that strategy.'

And that is what his book is about: how four large enterprises got the relationship between strategy and structure wrong – in quite different ways; how their paths twisted and turned, until they got it right; how their resolutions came to have so much in common; and, how – thanks to Chandler's thesis – we can now understand why.

Bibliography

Alfred D. Chandler Jr, *Strategy and Structure*, MIT Press, 1962.

4

Michael E. Porter

—

Michael Porter came to the attention of the world at large when his first major work, *Competitive Strategy*, was published in 1980. For some seven years before that he had been steadily making a name for himself teaching business administration at Harvard, and publishing articles which, as the 1970s drew to a close, explored in piecemeal fashion a number of the ideas and constructs he was to bring together in that explosive publication. And 'explosive' is not an exaggerated way to describe its effect. Tens of thousands of students now deploy his five-box schema as automatically as ever Pavlov's dogs salivated; while their mentors have been shown how to replace that vague concept, 'the firm's environment', with something substantial.

An indication of Porter's intellectual outlook is perhaps to be gained from his university education: his first degree was in aerospace and mechanical engineering, and his doctorate was in industrial economics. It may be thought unsurprising, therefore, that he deals in aggregates, structures and forces, and that his work is characterized by law-like pronouncements of a kind usually avoided by management scholars, but remarkably like those to be found in what used to be called 'the exact sciences'.

Adopting as a working definition of an industry 'the group of firms producing products that are close substitutes for each other', Porter lays his ideological foundations early in the first chapter. 'The intensity of competition in an industry,' he tells us, 'is neither a matter of coincidence nor luck. Rather, competition in an industry is rooted in its underlying economic structure and goes well beyond the behaviour of current competitors.' That intensity can vary greatly, from one industry to another; but

Fig. 4.1

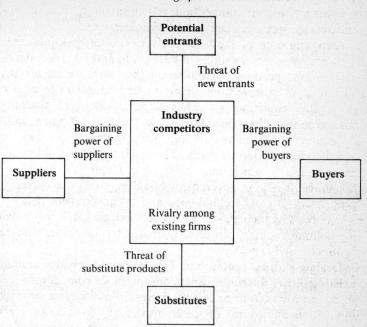

essentially: 'Competition ... continually works to drive down the rate of return on invested capital toward ... [what] would be earned by the economist's "perfectly competitive" industry.' And while the battle may be fought out within the industry, Porter argues that its intensity (and consequently the industry's profitability) depends upon the collective effect of five forces – which he illustrates using his now famous schema (Fig. 4.1).

This wider view of what constitutes industrial competition Porter terms *extended rivalry*. The object in formulating competitive strategy, therefore, 'is to find a position ... where the company can best defend itself against these ... forces, or can influence them in its favour'. However, it is important to distinguish between these *structural determinants* (the five forces) which have long-term effects, and short-term factors (e.g. raw material shortages, strikes or spurts in demand) which have but a passing effect on competition and profitability, and, consequently, are only significant in a *tactical* sense.

Analysing each of the forces in turn, Porter concludes that there are seven major sources of **barriers to entry**: (1) economies of scale; (2) product differentiation (by which he means the advantage to existing firms stemming from customer loyalties); (3) capital requirements – when large or risky; (4) switching costs occasioned by a once-for-all investment in equipment and/or training to accommodate any new products; (5) a lack of access to distribution channels; (6) cost disadvantages independent of scale – which may arise from factors as diverse as favourable locations, government subsidies, experience curves or proprietary product technologies; and (7) government policy – when licensing, regulation, or such requirements as those covering pollution control can directly limit entry, or render it more protracted and expensive.

Dealing with his central box, Porter says that **rivalry among existing firms** intensifies when one or more competitors feel under pressure (from price cuts, increased advertising, product innovation, and so on), or see an opportunity to make progress in the marketplace. In most industries, he considers existing firms to be *mutually dependent* – since moves by one of them may incite retaliation, or efforts to counter those moves, on the part of the others. Rivalry may be characterized variously as, say, 'cut-throat' or 'gentlemanly'. But when it is intense it is caused by interacting structural factors. He lists these as: 'numerous, or equally balanced, competitors; slow industry growth; high fixed or storage costs; lack of product differentiation or switching costs; capacity augmented in large increments; diverse competitors [that is, diverse in terms of strategies, personalities, origins or relationships with parent companies]; high strategic stakes; and high exit barriers'.

Substitute products he defines as those which 'can perform the same *function* as the product of the industry'. Their presence constrains the freedom of existing firms to set prices, and thus limits the potential for profit-making in the industry. Indeed, the threat they pose may well be a matter for action by the industry as a whole. Two kinds of substitutes deserve most attention: (1) those whose perceived value – relative to that of the industry's product – is tending to improve; and (2) those produced by highly profitable industries – especially if some development threatens to reduce returns there.

Buyers, Porter tells us, 'compete with the industry by forcing down prices, bargaining for higher quality or more services, and playing competitors against each other – all at the expense of industry profitability'. A buyer group can be said to be powerful, he tells us, when:

1. It is concentrated, or purchases large volumes relative to seller sales.
2. The products it purchases from the industry represent a significant fraction of the buyer's costs or purchases.
3. The products it purchases from the industry are standard or undifferentiated.
4. It faces few switching costs.
5. It earns low profits.
6. Buyers pose a credible threat of backward integration.
7. The industry's product is unimportant to the quality of the buyer's product or services.
8. The buyer has full information.

Moreover, these eight rules hold good whether the buyer is an industrial or commercial purchaser, or a consumer. Equally, they apply to distribution channel members – with one important addition: buyers can obtain power when they can influence purchasing decisions made downstream of them. (That is, wholesaler to retailer, and retailer to consumer.)

Porter similarly lists what he now calls the 'conditions' which make suppliers powerful. There are six of these; and, not unnaturally, they tend to resemble the converse of the rules/circumstances applicable to buyers. A **supplier group** is powerful if, as he says:

1. It is dominated by a few companies, and is more concentrated than the industry it sells to.
2. The industry is not an important customer of the supplier group.

3. The supplier group's products are differentiated, or it has built up switching costs.
4. The supplier group poses a credible threat of forward integration.
5. The supplier's product is an important input to the buyer's business.
6. It is not obliged to contend with other substitute products for sale to the company.

Reminding us that 'labour must be recognized as a supplier' Porter says that the principles which apply to it are the ones he has already enumerated. However, in assessing its power, one should take into account whether it is unionized, together with the character of the union(s); and if there are any skill shortages – especially when these are difficult to overcome.

After his detailed anatomy of the five competitive forces, we are treated to a short discussion on the role of government as a force in industrial competition.

Recalling that government was mentioned in connection with entry barriers, Porter goes on to say that since the start of the 1970s government must be acknowledged as having the potential to influence an industry's structure, directly and indirectly, in many, if not all of its aspects. It buys and supplies – these roles being shaped more by politics than by economics, on many occasions; its regulations can modify the behaviour of firms as suppliers or buyers; and through regulations and subsidies – as well as by other means – it can affect industries with competing substitutes. Porter concludes from this that any industrial analysis would be incomplete without taking account of how current or planned government policy will affect structure. However, in case it could be suggested that another box should be added to his five-box schema to accommodate the pervasive influence of government, Porter tells us that 'it is usually more illuminating to consider government effects *through* the five forces, rather than separately.

Relating structural analysis to competitive strategy, Porter says that identifying the forces (and their underlying causes) which affect competition in an industry will enable a firm to determine what its comparative strengths and weaknesses are. Strategically crucial are those strengths and weaknesses which emerge from establishing what the firm's posture is relative to those underlying causes. Where does it stand *vis-à-vis* substitutes, or the sources of entry barriers? How does it cope with rivalry from existing competitors? An effective strategy then 'takes offensive or defensive action in order to create a *defendable* [*sic*] position against the five competitive forces'. Possible approaches are:

positioning the firm so that its capabilities provide the best defence against the existing array of competitive forces;

influencing the balance of forces through strategic moves, thereby improving the firm's relative position; or,

anticipating shifts in the factors underlying the forces and responding to them, thereby exploiting change by choosing a strategy appropriate to the new competitive balance before rivals recognize it.

Finally, in his review of the structural analysis of industries, Porter returns to his starting point: the definition of what constitutes an industry. His hope is that structural analysis will virtually end the need for this debate, since it rests upon where lines should be drawn between his central box, on the one hand, and each of his surrounding boxes in turn, on the other. And drawing lines is 'inherently a matter of degree that has little to do with the choice of strategy'. The important definition is not that of what industry a firm is in, but where it wants to compete: which, for Porter, is the same thing as defining its business.

Porter's second major contribution to strategic thought is his more controversial notion of *generic competitive strategies*. These are three in number: **overall cost leadership**, **differentiation** and **focus**. They are *the* ways of coping with the five competitive forces, and outperforming one's industrial rivals. They are not mutually exclusive. But, since each 'requires total commitment and organizational arrangements', Porter – ignoring the logical consequence of what he has said – considers it rare for a firm to succeed by pursuing more than one at a time.

Overall cost leadership, which, Porter observes, has become increasingly common with the popularization of the (Boston Consulting Group's) experience curve concept, is the planned result of policies aimed at managing away expense. It provides a defence against each of the five competitive forces, respectively, by:

1. Enabling the firm to remain profitable when its rivals have eliminated their margins through price competition.
2. Exploiting buyers' capacity to drive down prices *only* to the level of the next most efficient competitor.
3. Providing more flexibility to cope with input cost increases from suppliers.
4. Raising entry barriers of an economy of scale or cost advantage nature.
5. Placing the firm in a favourable position, relative to its competitors, *vis-à-vis* substitutes.

It is not without its risks, however. Some of these are:

- Changes in technology which render past investments or experience obsolete.
- Experience inexpensively gained by industry entrants or me-too competitors through imitation or investment in state-of-the-art facilities.
- Emphasizing cost reduction to the point where product or marketing changes are not attended to.
- Cost increases which reduce price advantages necessary to combat a competitor's differentiation strategy.

Differentiation consists of offering a product or service 'that is perceived *industrywide* as being unique'. It can take many forms (design or brand image, technology, product features, customer service, dealer network, and so on); and, ideally, it is comprised of more than one form. It also enables the firm to cope with the five forces, but in different ways to cost leadership. For example:

1. It insulates the firm from rivalry by using brand loyalty to lower customer's price sensitivity.
2. The existence of brand loyalty, 'and the need for competitors to overcome uniqueness, provide entry barriers'.

Fig. 4.2

trategic target	Strategic advantage	
	Uniqueness perceived by the customer	*Low cost position*
dustrywide	Differentiation	Overall cost leadership
articular segment nly	Focus	Focus

. It yields higher margins with which to offset supplier power.
. Buyers are less price sensitive because they have no comparable alternatives.
. Having achieved customer loyalty, a firm is better positioned than its competitors *vis-à-vis* substitutes.

t also is not without risks. Porter lists three:

ie cost differential [relative to low-cost competitors] becomes too great for differentiation to hold brand loyalty;
ie buyer's need for the differentiating factor falls;
nitation narrows perceived differentiation: a common occurrence as industries mature.

'orter's third generic strategy, **focus**, is unlike the first two overall cost leadership and differentiation), in that it is *not* an idustrywide strategy. It is directed precisely at serving a particular buyer goup, a segment of the product line, or a geographic iarket 'more effectively or efficiently than competitors who ompete more broadly'. And, in so doing, it deploys one or both f the other two generic strategies (low cost and differentiation) its approach to that narrow target.

Fig. 4.2 shows how Porter illustrates the differences among ie three strategies.

The risks associated with the focus strategy are:

the cost differential between broad-range competitors and the focuse
firm widens to eliminate the cost advantages of serving a narro
target, or to offset the differentiation achieved by focus;

the differences in desired products or services between the strateg
target and the market as a whole narrows [*sic*];

competitors find submarkets *within* the strategic market, and outfoc
the focuser.

Aside from the individual risks which attach to each gener
strategy, there is what we might call (though Porter does not)
generic strategy error: *stuck in the middle*. This occurs when
firm does not elect realistically for just one of the three gener
strategies. (Equally, one supposes, it might occur if the firm do
not realize what are the 'true' options available to it.) For th
poor stuck-in-the-middle firm, Porter promises the direst co
sequences. Almost inevitably, its profitability will be low. Th
is because it will either lose low price/high volume customers t
low cost competitors, or retain them at the expense of reduce
margins. Moreover, to compound its difficulties, high marg
customers will move to its differentiated competitors, or to tho
who have focused on that type of customer. And if this was n
disastrous enough, the firm's culture may well become 'blurred
while its 'motivation system' and 'organizational arrangement
are beset with conflict.

A measure of the influence of Porter's second major wor
published in 1985, is that its title, *Competitive Advantage*, ha
passed into the language of the street and the sports ground. A
he acknowledges, it is hardly a new subject. Yet he has manage
to give it an impetus which causes it to come up in the mo
unstrategic of conversations.

The first chapter of the book (which aims to link formulatio
and implementation by analysing how the generic strategies a
put into practice) largely summarizes the essentials of *Compe
itive Strategy*. His recapitulation of the five competitive forc
reveals few changes. However, there are some differences
emphasis and language in his treatment of the three gener
strategies – as a comparison of Figs 4.2 and 4.3 will show.

He also introduces the idea of *sustainability*. Glimpsing wh
may appear to be obvious, he tells us, tautologically, that: 'Th

Fig. 4.3

Competitive scope	Competitive advantage	
	Lower cost	Differentiation
Broad target	1. Cost leadership	2. Differentiation
Narrow target	3A. Cost focus	3B. Differentiation focus

fundamental basis of above-average performance in the long run is *sustainable competitive advantage*' – a condition which is proof against 'erosion by competitor behaviour or industry evolution'. To achieve this, a firm should have some barriers that make its strategy difficult to imitate. However, since no barriers are insurmountable, the usual recourse is for the firm to present a moving target to its competitors by continually improving its position.

Competitive advantage, Porter asserts, arises out of a firm creating value for its buyers. And understanding competitive advantage requires a holistic view of the firm which, while cutting across the many disciplines and activities within the firm (e.g. marketing, production, control, finance), combines them by examining all of its sources in an integrated manner.

For this task he introduces his third important contribution to strategic thought: **the value chain**. This 'tool', as he calls it, identifies those of the firm's activities which are *strategically relevant* – so as to know how costs behave, and to find the current and potential sources of differentiation; the ultimate aim of the exercise being to perform these activities more cheaply, or better, than the competition.

A firm's value chain may well be peculiar to it – reflecting its history, past strategy and relative success with that strategy. It is adjoined by value chains upstream of it (in suppliers' companies) and downstream (in channel value chains and buyer values chains). Taken together, these value chains constitute what Porter terms **the value system**. Understanding how the firm fits

Fig. 4.4

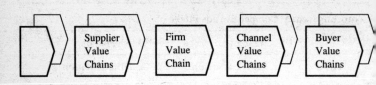

into this system is as important – in terms of competitive advantage – as understanding its own value chain. Fig. 4.4 illustrates the value system for a single-industry firm.

He distances himself from analysts such as McKinsey, Gluck and Bauron – who also developed 'business systems concepts' – by basing the value chain on *activities* rather than *functions*. The latter are the familiar departments, or divisions, of companies: e.g. R & D, marketing, manufacturing, finance. Activities, or more precisely **value activities**, are the means by which a firm creates value in its products. They are physically and technologically distinct, and of two types: **primary** and **support**.

Primary activities are divided into five *generic categories*:

1. Inbound logistics	The reception, storage and internal transport of inputs to the product.
2. Operations	The transformation of those inputs into the final product form.
3. Outbound logistics	The collection, storage and distribution of the product to buyers.
4. Marketing and sales	Persuading buyers to purchase the product, and making it possible for them to do so.
5. Service	The provision of service to enhance or maintain the value of the product.

Support activities are divided into four *generic categories*:

1. Procurement	The act of purchasing inputs, not the inputs themselves. Tending to

	occur throughout the firm, its wide dispersion often obscures its magnitude.
2. **Technology development**	All value activities embody technology – whether it is in know-how, or that to be found in process equipment.
3. **Human resourse management**	Those activities to do with the recruitment, hiring, training, development and pay of all types of personnel.
4. **Firm infrastructure**	Usually supporting the whole chain, it includes functions such as planning, finance, accounting, legal, and government relations, as well as general and quality management.

Porter next describes three *activity types* that play a different role in competitive advantage:

1. **Direct**	Those activities which are directly concerned with creating value: e.g. machining, assembly, sales operations, advertising, product design, recruitment.
2. **Indirect**	Those activities which enable direct activities to be performed on a continuing basis: e.g. maintenance, scheduling, sales force administration, buyer records.
3. **Quality assurance**	This is to be found nearly everywhere in the firm – though seldom recognized for what it is. Its activities ensure the quality of other activities: e.g. monitoring, inspecting, testing, reviewing, adjusting, reworking. *Quality assurance is not to be confused with quality management.*

Fig. 4.5

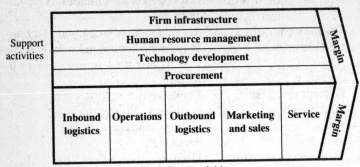

Primary activities

To complete his anatomy of the value chain, Porter adds the concept of **margin**.

'In competitive terms', he is careful to say, value is what buyers are prepared to pay for the firm's products. It is measured by 'total revenue, a reflection of the price a firm's product commands and the units it can sell'. The goal of any generic strategy is to create value which is greater than the cost of its creation; the difference between the two being margin. The function of the value chain, therefore, is to *display* 'total value' – which consists of value activities and margin.

Fig. 4.5 illustrates Porter's overall concept: the generic value chain.

Even though 'value activities are the building blocks of competitive advantage, the value chain is . . . a system of *interdependent* activities' – the relationships within which Porter terms *linkages*. These linkages 'can lead to competitive advantage in two ways: optimization and co-ordination'. An instance of the first would be where better design of a car's engine compartment, by making it easier to work on, leads to lower service charges for the owner. (Differentiation.) While superior co-ordination – throughout the firm – can bring about a smaller, overall investment in stocks. (Lower cost.)

Porter's detailed exposition of the value chain concept, which he supports with well-chosen examples, may deceive the too-casual reader into believing that its application is a straight-forward, even a mechanical task. Let us hope that these last two quotations act as a corrective (the emphases have been added):

Value activity labels are arbitrary, and should be chosen to provide the best *insight* into the business.

Often firms perform parallel activities, whose order should be chosen to enhance *the intuitive clarity* of the value chain to managers.

Bibliography

Michael E. Porter, *Competitive Strategy: Techniques for Analyzing Industries and Competitors*, The Free Press, 1980.

Michael E. Porter, *Competitive Advantage: Creating and Sustaining Superior Performance*, The Free Press, 1985.

PART TWO

The Consultants

Preface

There is, of course, a host of consultants on both sides of the
Atlantic. And it can be safely assumed that those who survive
do so because the companies they serve benefit from, or believe
they benefit from, their advice. For the most part, they devise
for their customers individual variations of the latest piece of
conventional wisdom which has found favour with the opinion-
makers of the business world. They are, in other words, the
suppliers of a derived demand. Only a handful can be said to
have something original to offer – though all claim to. Even
fewer publish their ideas in such a manner as to subject them to
public debate. All three represented here fall into this smallest of
minorities.

The Boston Consulting Group (BCG) – for which its founder,
Bruce D. Henderson, speaks here – has been, arguably, the most
influential of all consultants. Seized, in the 1960s, with a single
powerful idea ('cash in and out is all that counts'), it has been
principally responsible for three strategic innovations: the experience curve, the growth/share matrix, and the product portfolio.
Yet, while all of them have proved to be controversial, it is
difficult to find a textbook on strategy which does not – at the
very least – nod in their direction.

The Profit Impact of Market Strategy (PIMS) programme –
described by Robert D. Buzzell and Bradley T. Gale – has the
largest privately-owned corporate data base in the world. It
seems improbable that there cannot be found, within its recesses,
some instance of company health or pathology to guide a Chief

Executive Officer who is dubious about what to do next. More significant, for our purposes, is the capacity of the programme to elicit general statements about strategy from its store of information, *and* to act as a test bed for others' theories.

By comparison with these two, Kepner-Tregoe (represented by Benjamin B. Tregoe and John W. Zimmerman) has achieved less prominence in our field. Best known for teaching a system of problem-solving and decision-making to thousands of managers, this consultancy has pioneered the concept of 'the driving force' as a way of establishing the key to practical strategic change. It is a concept which, though valued by some scholars,[1] has yet to be properly appreciated by the world at large.

---

1. Notably by **Jay R. Galbraith and Robert K. Kazanjian**, see pages 206–215.

5

Robert D. Buzzell and Bradley T. Gale

—

The PIMS (Profit Impact of Market Strategy) programme, which started in 1972, was developed from some fundamental ideas originating with Sidney Schoeffler and put into practice, in the form of strategic planning models, by the US General Electric Company. Launched as an exploratory project with backing from an affiliate of the Harvard Business School, it was so well received that in 1975 Schoeffler founded the non-profit-making Strategic Planning Institute (SPI) to provide a permanent base for PIMS research, and, thereafter, educational support and advice for companies involved in the programme.

Robert Buzzell has a chair in marketing at Harvard, is a trustee of the SPI, and serves on the boards of a number of US corporations. Bradley Gale is Managing Director and CEO of the SPI, and PIMS Associates – its consulting subsidiary. Considering their contributions to the programme, it is not to be wondered at that their joint work, *The PIMS Principles*, has been described as 'definitive'.

Built into the PIMS approach, as in similar scholarly research – though there it is usually unstated – is a sizeable assumption. It is the belief that the future will resemble the past. More precisely, in the words of Buzzell and Gale, it is that they 'can relate business strategies to performance, by studying past experience'. The hope is that, by discovering whatever linkages there are between strategy and performance, some general principles may be established which 'can contribute to greater effectiveness for individual firms and for the economy as a whole'. They tell us, however, that such principles should not be thought of as providing 'formulas for resolving specific business issues'.

Rather, 'they can provide a foundation for the situation-specific analysis that is always needed to arrive at good decisions'.

There are two main components to the PIMS programme: an immense data base of company figures; and statistical modelling of considerable elaboration. The former comprises information, of a highly detailed nature, from over 2,600 business units; while the most complete form of the latter is so sophisticated, it is claimed that it can explain 70 per cent of the variations to be found among those business units relative to the two principal measures of profitability used in the programme (the returns on sales and investment).

The term 'business unit' is one of two concepts which are central to PIMS analysis; the other being the business unit's 'served market'.

A business unit (which occasionally Buzzell and Gale call an SBU, or strategic business unit), is defined as a 'division, product line, or other profit centre of a company' which common sense suggests needs 'a distinct, separate strategy'.[1] A business unit can thus be a single-product firm, or a division of a much larger company. If it falls into the second category then, they argue, its strategy should not be entirely independent of other divisions' strategies – for that could amount to 'corporate anarchy'. Better it should have a 'distinct but *partial* strategy within a broader framework'.

The second concept, that of the served market, is equally important to PIMS analysis because market share, growth rates, the identity of leading competitors, and assessments of relative quality are all determined in relationship to it. Essentially, it is the answer to the question, 'Where do you actually compete?' – since few business units serve the whole of a market.

PIMS modelling is based upon the contention that there are three major kinds of factor on which a business unit's performance depends: its strategy; its competitive position; and the market/industry characteristics of the field in which it competes.

---

1. That is: the business unit makes and markets 'well-defined' and related products/services to a 'clearly defined set of customers' within a 'reasonably self-contained geographic area', in the face of 'well-defined' competition.

Fig. 5.1 Some major dimensions of business strategy[2]

- Product/service policies
  : Quality of products/services
  : Relative rate of new product introduction
- Pricing policies
- Marketing programmes
  : Sales force
  : Advertising
  : Sales promotion

- Investment strategy
  : Mechanization/automation of operations
  : Capacity additions
  : Inventory levels
- Work force productivity
- Vertical integration
- Research & development

Strategy is a word Buzzell and Gale are unhappy with, and would have preferred to do without. They avoid any debate as to its 'proper definition', and only prescribe the way they employ it, which is:

The policies and key decisions adopted by management that have *major* impacts on financial performance. These policies and decisions usually involve significant resource commitments, and are not easily reversible.

They distinguish between business unit strategy and corporate strategy in the currently orthodox manner – but add to the latter a qualification of their own. It is not just concerned with resource-allocation among businesses; it is to do with 'the design of a portfolio of SBUs *that reinforce each other*'. (The emphasis has been added.) But whichever level is under discussion, the PIMS programme addresses only those aspects of strategy which: (1) are of general industrial relevance; and (2) are measurable. This means, on the one hand, that strategic matters peculiar

---

. It will be noted that market share, which Buzzell and Gale term 'a key dimension of competitive position', is not to be found in the list. This is because they see it as an objective – which should also be used, after the event, to measure results. They contrast their standpoint with that of many popular views in strategic management circles, where achieving a certain level of share, or striving constantly to increase it, is considered to be a strategy.

to any one industry are not explored; and, on the other, that i
ignores whatever cannot be measured in reasonably clear terms
Excluded by the second, therefore, are such considerations a
corporate culture, and the effects (which Buzzell and Gale d
not deny exist) it can have on success and failure. But include
are the 'major strategy dimensions' set out in Fig. 5.1.

When a new business is being started the choices availabl
among these dimensions is wide: constrained in practice only b
policy decisions, the limitations of capital and staff expertise
and what technologies the firm can command. An existing
business unit, however, is faced with the need constantly to bea
in mind its current 'competitive position' (which reflects th
consequences of past strategy) when formulating strategies fo
the future. So, management must assess how the company rates
relative to competition, using all of the interacting dimension
listed above.

In general terms, Buzzell and Gale argue, economists have fo
long accepted that there are certain 'market/industry factors
which affect firms' profitability. But, until the work of the US
Federal Trade Commission's "Line of Business" programm
(FTC–LB) began to be published, researchers had to be conten
with average industry, rather than individual competitors'
figures. These new data show beyond doubt that profitability i
systematically affected by variations in market conditions. PIM
researchers have confirmed this conclusion. In addition, the
have established that market/industry factors directly affec
growth as well as profit – just as competitive position does, bu
also interact with it (competitive position) and current strategy.

The factors which they have found to have most influence o
business performance are shown in Fig. 5.2.

But what do Buzzell and Gale mean by 'performance'? Fo
most current (four-year) performance measurement purpose
the PIMS programme uses ROI[3] and ROS;[4] though in som

---

3. Return on investment = net profit, before interest charges and tax, express
   as a percentage of an SBU's assets less current liabilities, or of pare
   company's equity plus long-term debt.
4. Return on sales = net, pre-tax operating profit as a percentage of sales.

Fig. 5.2 Market/industry factors that influence performance

- Stage of market evolution and growth rate
- Selling price inflation
- Degree of product/service standardization
- Supplier concentration
- Typical customer purchase amount and importance
- Degree of employee unionization
- Extent of industry exports and imports

circumstances cash flow[5] relative to investment will be included. For long-term measurement, 'value enhancement'[6] is employed.

Value enhancement was introduced in recognition of the extended period required to evaluate the effects of strategic change. Profitability can fluctuate widely, taking one year with another. So annual results are frequently misleading as performance indicators. Even ROI and ROS results averaged over a number of years do not constitute a complete measure of business performance, according to Buzzell and Gale. Cross-industry comparisons of value (which are essential to the PIMS programme) always need to take into account alterations in the cost of capital; and especially so when considering 'shareholder value'.

This concept, which has gained currency in response to criticisms of 'short-termism' practised by US (and other) business leaders, is equated with the sum of a company's dividends over a period, plus or minus any simultaneous changes in the price of its shares. As Buzzell and Gale then argue: 'When a firm makes investments that yield returns below the cost of capital, the result is a *reduction* in shareholder value. Value is reduced via a

5. Cash flow = post-tax profit plus depreciation less any change in total investment, as a percentage of investment.
6. Value enhancement is the sum of an SBU's cash flows over a five-year period added to its then estimated market value, all discounted to their present (start of period) values, and expressed as a percentage of present market value.

Fig. 5.3

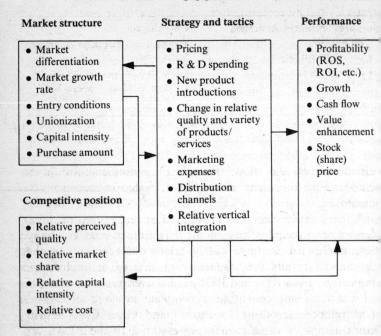

Market structure	Strategy and tactics	Performance
• Market differentiation • Market growth rate • Entry conditions • Unionization • Capital intensity • Purchase amount	• Pricing • R & D spending • New product introductions • Change in relative quality and variety of products/ services • Marketing expenses • Distribution channels • Relative vertical integration	• Profitability (ROS, ROI, etc.) • Growth • Cash flow • Value enhancement • Stock (share) price

Competitive position

- Relative perceived quality
- Relative market share
- Relative capital intensity
- Relative cost

decline in the market value of a company's stock [shares], relative to its book value.' Forecasts using this type of approach are, of course, difficult. But after-the-event calculations (as made in PIMS research) are straightforward; though imputing market values to unquoted SBUs does attract certain theoretical objections.

The components of PIMS' three major kinds of factor, together with those for 'performance', are illustrated in Fig. 5.3 in what Buzzell and Gale call, curiously, 'The PIMS Competitive Strategy Paradigm'.

'The arrows in the diagram *are meant to* indicate that each of the three classes of performance influences has a direct impact on results, and each interacts with the others.' (Emphasis added.) Buzzell and Gale continue: 'Thus, in the short term, strategy is constrained by competitive position and by market structure conditions. Over time, competitive position is shaped by past strategies and by performances, and each of these contributes to changes in market structure.'

No claim is made that the 'paradigm' includes all the things which can influence performance. Stock valuation methods (e.g. FIFO, LIFO), currency fluctuations, labour troubles, regulatory controls, for example, all affect one or more of its dimensions – but are omitted. Even so, it is contended that – once yearly fluctuations have been averaged out – 'the general, measurable factors' to be found there explain 'most of the variations' in business unit performance.

By mid 1986 the PIMS data base contained information, which covered a span of at least four years, for each of 2,600 businesses. The period to which its data relate extends from the early 1970s, and includes times of recession and expansion. Over 90 per cent of these business units are in manufacturing. And of these, about one-third are in consumer products; a fifth make capital goods; while the rest furnish raw (or semi-finished) materials, components, or 'industrial/commercial supplies'. Service and distribution businesses account for less than 10 per cent of the data base. But, at around 200, they still constitute, Buzzell and Gale contend, a reasonably large sample of those types of activity. Some two-thirds of all the business units are to be found in North America. The remainder lie outside – with about 200 each in the United Kingdom and certain other countries of western Europe.

One of the uses that has been made of this store of information is to study the variations that exist in the relationship between strategy and profitability among business units categorized in different ways. For example, Fig. 5.4 shows the broad effects on ROI of just a few 'key profit influences' according to the type of business (industrial product, consumer product, and service/distribution) and the location of the served market (North America v. other parts of the world).

But perhaps of greatest interest to the strategist are the 'general principles' which the PIMS programme was, in part, set up to discover. Buzzell and Gale list six 'of the most important linkages between strategy and performance'. They are:

Fig. 5.4 Differences in impacts of key profit influences by types of business (1); location of served market (2)

Profit influences	Differences in impact on ROI
Rate of price inflation	1. Not related to ROI for service and distribution businesses. 2. No relationship with ROI outside North America.
Typical customer purchase amount and importance	1. Impact on ROI greatest for industrial product manufacturers. 2. Effect on ROI significant in North America, not elsewhere.
Exports v. imports	1. Effect on ROI significant only for industrial product manufacturers. 2. Effect on ROI outside North America is reversed.
Plant newness	1. Effect is significant only for consumer products. 2. Impact is greater outside North America.

1. In the long run, the most important single factor affecting a business unit's performance is the quality of its products and services, relative to those of its competitors.
2. Market share and profitability are strongly related.
3. High-investment intensity acts as a powerful drag on profitability.
4. Many so-called 'dog' and 'question mark' businesses generate cash, while many 'cash cows' are dry.
5. Vertical integration is a profitable strategy for some kinds of businesses, but not for others.
6. Most of the strategic factors that boost ROI also contribute to long-term (shareholder) value.

Justice cannot be done here to the carefully constructed arguments Buzzell and Gale employ to support all six of these

Fig. 5.5

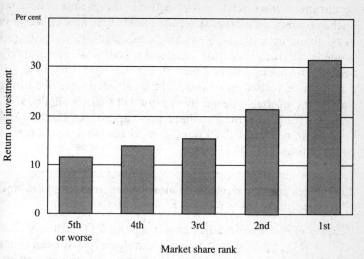

conclusions. The subject of the second, however, has been the cause of much controversy for nearly twenty years, and has involved such prominent figures as M. E. Porter, B. D. Henderson of the Boston Consulting Group (BCG), R. G. Hamermesh, as well as PIMS. If nothing else did, this alone would merit its inclusion.

PIMS uses a number of measures to establish a business unit's 'market position'. **Absolute market share** is the proportion of its sales to the total sales of the served market. **Market-share rank** places the business unit in the order determined by the size of its absolute market share, when compared to those of its competitors. **Relative market share** refines the concept of share rank by contrasting the business unit's absolute share with the structure of its market. (The BCG, for example, compares the unit's share with that of its largest competitor when arguing the 'experience curve' case.)

Buzzell and Gale employed the second of these measures (and the PIMS data base) to create Fig. 5.5.

This, together with an FTC–LB analysis in 1975 showing 'a significant positive relationship' between the pre-tax return on sales and absolute market share for some 3,000 lines of business in 258 manufacturing industry categories, constitute the principal grounds for their assertion that share and ROI are strongly related. Having established their theoretical base, they then ask a number of related questions – the most interesting, from our standpoint, probably being: 'Why is market share profitable?'

Again using the market-share rank approach, Buzzell and Gale examined the PIMS data base to see what relationships could be found:

1. Between market share and operating and financial ratios.
2. Between market share and 'measures of relative prices and relative quality'.[7]

Because of the mathematics governing the ROI equation (i.e ROI = ROS* [Sales/Investment]), variations in ROI can occur only if there are changes to the return on sales, the investment to sales ratio, or both. What they found, in their analysis of (1) above, was that, while the investment/sales ratio fell only slightly with increases in absolute share, there was a smooth upward trend in average ROS from fifth, or worse, ranked company (at 4.5 per cent), to market leader (at 12.7 per cent). Their conclusion, therefore, was that 'the major reason for the share/profitability relationship was the dramatic difference' in ROS. But how was this to be accounted for?

The BCG 'experience curve' theory, Buzzell and Gale contend, explains (what we might call) the extra profitability which accrues to the market leader as resulting solely from its lowest cost

7. Relative quality is a PIMS technique for determining the quality of a business unit's product/service offerings – looked at from the perspective of the customer, and relative to equivalent offerings from the unit's principal competitors. Management is 'led through' a process during which it identifies and weights all the non-price attributes 'that count in the purchase decision'. then rates the business unit's, and its competitors', performances on a scale of 1–10 for each attribute – expressing the overall results in percentiles. So, a business with a rating between 0 and 20 falls into the bottom fifth of the PIMS data base.

position – since it is further down the curve than its competitors. And it infers, from its data 'on how unit costs and cumulative volume have moved together *over time*, what the cost ratios are among competitors' at any particular time – the cost ratios being treated as differences in profit.

Now this should lead one to expect that it is possible to calculate the effects on profitability of any drive to secure share; and, indeed, BCG say it is the case. In 1978, they stated that a 2 to 1 share ratio should produce a 10 per cent, or greater, advantage in the 'cost of value-added' – cutting in half their 1973 estimate, incidentally. Making certain assumptions, based upon PIMS data, about the relationships of price to purchases and internal costs, Buzzell and Gale tested the BCG estimate on their data base companies. They found extremely wide variations between BCG expectations and their PIMS-based empirical results. Moreover, they claim, had they added procurement economies to those stemming purely from economies of scale, the variations would have been even wider.

Based upon this study and related arguments, they conclude that 'the competitive effects of cumulative volume [have been] misunderstood and overstated' – important as market share is, and has been.

Their analysis of (2) above (share *v*. relative price and relative quality), revealed the results in Fig. 5.6.

There seem to be, Buzzell and Gale observe, two distinct

Fig. 5.6 Market leaders have higher perceived quality and command higher prices

	Market share rank				
	5th or worse	4th	3rd	2nd	1st
Relative quality (percentile)	43	45	47	51	69
Relative price (per cent)	103.0	103.2	103.4	103.8	105.7
Number of businesses	301	240	347	549	877

Fig. 5.7

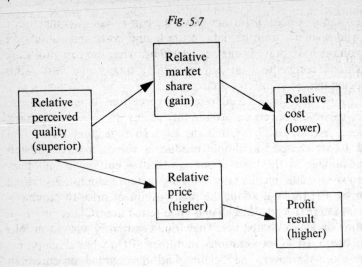

patterns operating here. One is a smooth, continuous relationship between market share and both relative price and relative
quality, as the ranking moves from fifth, or worse, to second;
while the other applies only to the leader. (Similar patterns are
to be found relative to cost and investment.) And in case it
should be objected that we are looking at some leadership bonus
effect, or mere statistical association, they quote from a special
study by Buzzell (with Dae Chang and L. W. Phillips) which
not only verifies the indicative worth of the concept of relative
quality, but concludes that it plays 'a causal role in influencing
business performance'.

They summarize their findings by telling us that: 'Market
leaders not only command higher prices but also maintain their
leadership position by offering products and services that are
superior relative to those offered by their competitors.' And
they append an even more informative diagram (Fig. 5.7).

We are back, of course, to the first of their 'most important
linkages between strategy and performance', listed above. Not
for nothing do they entitle one of their most closely reasoned
chapters 'Quality is King'. Nor has quality merely displaced

market share. If it has, Buzzell and Gale would argue, then a usurper has been removed from the throne. For their work with the PIMS data base has shown that market share is not a cause, but a measurement. A measurement which 'reflects two kinds of forces . . . that *do* cause high or low profits': quality and scale. The interplay between which – in answer to the question of why market share is profitable – they summarize in the 'key steps', below.

- By combining the skilful design of products/services with the 'proper' selection of market(s), a business can achieve superior relative quality.
- Superior quality enables a 'successful business to charge premium prices', *and* gain market share.
- Through increasing share, it attains scale 'and/or experience-based cost advantages over its competitors'.
- The combination of premium prices, equivalent or lower costs, together with advantages in procurement and capital utilization, results in higher profitability.

Bibliography

Robert D. Buzzell and Bradley T. Gale, *The PIMS Principles – Linking Strategy to Performance*, The Free Press, 1987.

6

Bruce D. Henderson

—

Bruce Henderson has the curious distinction of being less well known than an organization he founded (the Boston Consulting Group), and a theory he propounded (the experience curve). A graduate of Vanderbilt and Harvard Business School, his early career straddled both industry and consultancy, with vice-presidential responsibilities, respectively, at Westinghouse and Arthur D. Little.

In *The Logic of Business Strategy* (1984), he lays before us a complete ideology of business. The book starts with some quasi-historical speculations about his central concern: competition. 'It began,' he tells us, 'with life itself.' For centuries all that existed was 'natural competition'. This occurred because life burgeoned so abundantly that there was always a shortage of natural resources. Survival depended upon uniqueness: a matching of organism to environment which gave a particular species an advantage over its rivals for similar resources. He then contrasts this natural competition with what he calls 'strategic competition'. Once again speculating historically, he suggests that 'true strategy' was probably first practised when one tribe attempted to take over another tribe's hunting grounds. A necessary, but not sufficient, condition for strategic competition to occur is when someone has the ability to imagine and evaluate 'the possible consequences of alternate courses of action'. (It is thus an activity peculiar to mankind.)

Noting that many analogies have been drawn between business and military strategy, he offers what seems to be a business

management version of Von Clausewitz's famous dictum[1] with
the statement: 'Visible conflict is only a periodic symptom of a
continuing effort to manage a dynamic equilibrium between
adversaries.' However, unlike the great Prussian, who saw war
as a rational alternative to peace when contemplating how
a nation could secure its ends, Henderson considers it an
aberration: the result of some instability in relations between
competitors. His conclusion is that the study of geopolitical
relationships teaches us far more about business strategy then
battles can, because: 'For business, as for nations, continued
coexistence is the ultimate objective, not the elimination of the
competitor.'

In Henderson's eyes, therefore, competition (for scarce resources) has always existed; has always existed; and by implication, it always will. Indeed, trying to eliminate it – as did
Standard Oil, under Rockefeller, at the turn of the nineteenth
century – is a gross error, which can lead to very damaging
second-order effects.[2]

What is required – apart from the acceptance that, like the
poor, competition is always with us – is 'a general theory' which
would enable us to perceive it 'as a dynamic system in equilibrium'. But, in this quest, just as military strategy disappoints
him with its limited conceptual insights, so does economics –
which he considers to be the natural field of study.

Henderson regards the generally accepted models of competitive behaviour which economics has developed as highly theoretical and simplistic – being based upon assumptions both untested
and dogmatic. The notion of perfect competition, for instance,
describes a market condition which is inherently unstable; and has,
consequently, only ever existed for brief intervals. Yet it has
acquired the status of a goal – with other models of competition
being labelled imperfect.

Again, 'the traditional core of compartmentalized economics'
rests upon assumptions about the rational, self-interested

1. 'War is but a continuation of politics by other means.'
2. In the case of Standard Oil, these were the US anti-trust laws!

behaviour of individuals who interact 'through the form o market exchanges under a fixed legal system of property and free contract'. But, he argues: 'Only a limited portion of huma behaviour can be adequately represented by such self-impose constraints.'

Henderson believes that the emerging science of sociobiolog can succeed where military studies and economics have failed This is because, by encompassing population biology, zoology genetics, and the behavioural sciences, it provides a conceptua framework arising out of the study of species which were success ful because of their social behaviour. (Success being associate with access to, and control of, required resources: which, fo Henderson, tend to be the ultimate objectives of all strategy.)

Man may be the only animal capable of strategic competitio but he is nevertheless a social animal: and subject, therefore, t sociobiological laws. His economic activities are but a subset o the overall behaviour of his species; so business competitio while specialized, is governed by the same sociobiological prir ciples, and part of the same conceptual framework.

In a business setting, natural competition is seen by Hender son as evolutionary, incremental, low-risk and heuristic. Stra tegic competition, on the other hand, is revolutionary: that i where there 'may well be radical change in a relatively sho time'. (This he terms 'time compression'.) Taking some of th findings of sociobiology, and assuming that 'species' can b safely equated with a business, or firm, he postulates a grou of hypotheses. From these he derives what he considers to b strategic competition's basic elements, which he states as:

- Ability to understand competitive interaction as a complet dynamic system that includes interaction of competitor customers, money, people, and resources.
- Ability to use this understanding to predict consequences of given intervention in that system, and how that interventio will result in new patterns of stable dynamic equilibrium;
- Availability of uncommitted resources that can be dedicate to different uses and purposes in the present, even though th dedication is permanent and the benefits will be deferred.

- Ability to predict risk and return with sufficient accuracy and confidence to justify the commitment of such resources.
- Willingness to deliberately act to make the commitment.

It is Henderson's view that most business today (1984) is the consequence of selection brought about by natural competition. What has been accomplished may be awesome, but it owes more to intuition, expediency and chance than it does to 'an integrated strategy', the 'prerequisites' for which are:

- A critical mass of knowledge.
- An understanding of the system of competition.
- An assessment of alternatives over a substantial time span.
- Focus on specific objectives.
- A plan.
- Co-ordinated investment.
- Competitive intelligence.

Turning to the Boston Consulting Group (BCG), Henderson tells us that in its earlier work it attempted to develop a general theory of competition which he asserts was based upon:

- Observable patterns of cost behaviour.
- Considerations of the dynamics of sustainable growth and capital use.
- The role of capital markets in permitting these effects to be leveraged or discounted.
- The relationship between these in a system of competition.

Concluding that orthodox accounting theories could not provide an appropriate model of economic behaviour, the Group developed one which Henderson summarizes as 'cash in and out is all that counts'. And from this came the concepts of the experience curve, the growth share tradeoff, and the product portfolio.

BCG introduced the experience curve concept in 1966. In the more than a quarter of a century since then 'it has become commonly accepted as a real and important phenomenon', Henderson contends. Yet its application and its limitations have been misunderstood; and it has been oversimplified. Describing it as 'a rule of thumb', he expresses it in these words: 'Costs of *value added* net of inflation will characteristically decline 25 to 30 per cent each time the total accumulated experience has doubled.'

Although the curve is a cost relationship, accounting costs are not used to calculate it. It is 'derived by dividing the accumulated cash input by the accumulated end product output', the cost decline being the rate of change in that ratio. Moreover, the controlling factor is not experience. The role is played by volume – growth rates of which closely approximate to growth rates in accumulated experience. And it is a mistake to assume, taking industry experience as a whole, that differences in market share fully reflect cost differences. (Usually, the latter run at about half the figure share differences imply.)

Definition of the product is critical to any use of this relationship, Henderson tells us. Unless it is defined in terms of perceived value to the customer, it is useless. Products change. But so long as those developments satisfy the same needs and the same customers, existing experience cost curves can be continued with. Similarly, cost elements in the product change – and not uniformly. Each will have an effect on end-product characteristics, and therefore perceived value; which, in turn, will shift and readjust the size, potential and segmentation of a market. He then adds, significantly: 'The experience curve cannot be a strategy, or even the foundation for a strategy. It is merely a way to understand why and how competitive costs may shift.'

Assuming that an experience curve convinces you that one competitor 'can and should have a lower cost than another', then it enables you to predict that the former will displace the latter if their products, customers, perceived values, and margins are identical. 'That,' Henderson asserts, 'is the implication of the relationship between market share and the experience curve.'

It is, interestingly, also in conformity with what he calls at this point 'an ironclad law of competition', which he states as 'No two competitors can coexist for very long who make their living in the same way.'[3]

3. Here Henderson draws directly from biology by modifying Gause's Competitive Exclusion Principle, which earlier he has stated as: 'No two *species* can coexist who make their living in the same way.' (The emphasis has been added.)

Reminding us, in the manner of Pareto, that most firms make most of their profit from a limited portion of their business, Henderson argues that this is where a firm enjoys its greatest competitive advantage. His term for this is 'a competitively defined segment'. The interaction between that and experience curves enables us to gain a penetrating insight into a competitor's behaviour: the major unknown variable, and most critical strategic factor. The basis for that insight – the one which Henderson considers probably the most valuable application of the experience curve – is the prediction of how costs will vary among one's competitors. However, he warns us that in this and other applications there is a significant risk of error in the employment of the experience curve if its characteristics and limitations are misunderstood.

Shortly after it became generally known, Henderson tells us, the curve was 'applied as the basis for the horizontal axis of a two-by-two matrix, known as the growth/share matrix'. (The vertical axis being 'the rate of physical growth in the volume of a product'.) The commonsense foundation for the matrix was two axioms that he expresses in a variety of ways – the simplest of which is:

1. Products which grow need more capital.
2. Products which have a competitive advantage generate more capital than those that do not.

Based on experience curve relationships, market share was 'used as a surrogate for cost advantage': a substitution that was later justified, he adds, by the research work 'of the Strategic Planning Institute with PIMS by Buzzell and Schoeffler'.[4] Rather more informative than the now familiar star, cash cow, dog and question mark quadrant name formulation, is the alternative he gives us – to be found at Fig. 6.1.

Henderson's claims for the experience curve, and the growth/share matrix based upon it, are far less ambitious than many

---

4. See **Robert D. Buzzell and Bradley T. Gale**, pages 59–71, for their views on the experience curve.

Fig. 6.1 Use of cash proportional to the rate of growth

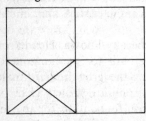

Many businesses require far more cash input than they can ever generate.

Question marks

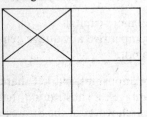

A few businesses generate far more cash than they can profitably reinvest.

Cash cows

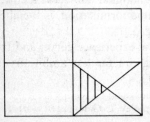

Some businesses are self-sufficient in cash flow. Over time they will become much larger and also large net generators of cash.

Stars

Most businesses, however, generate very little cash even though they use little. The reported earnings must be reinvested, and probably always will. These businesses are 'cash traps'.

Dogs

that others have made. For example: 'As a *schematic* for focusing attention and providing a conceptual framework, both ... can be *quite* useful.' (Emphases have been added.) The qualitative relationships they express are 'very important'; but 'as a basis for policy determination there are serious risks'.

The experience curve 'is not suitable for cost control, or forecasting over short time spans'. And great difficulty arises over market definitions. Where these are 'amorphous', only 'qualitative judgements' can be made. Again, 'definition of the products that make up the market is often equally ambiguous'. This is because 'Such products are often only parts of families of products ... [and] frequently ... only partially share their cost elements and their characteristics.' So, in these circumstances – when market and product definitions are imprecise – imputing probable cost differences based on share of the market' is hazardous.

These careful warnings, however, do not disqualify the experience curve from employment when applied to policy decisions.[5] They apply principally to quantitative judgements, where precision can prove to be specious unless definitions of cost components, products, and markets are well grounded in careful analysis; and where it is vital one examines 'effects that will be common to competitors'. As Henderson says: 'All competitors tend to come down some form of experience curve. The critical question is, "Who is coming down in cost the fastest?"'

Looking forward, but also locating the experience curve within his general ideological position, Henderson summarizes thus:

Future research should focus more on a conceptual framework for describing the system effects in business competition. When that has been accomplished, then the experience curve will become a far more useful concept. It is itself an example of a complex system of interactions.

5. Many management judgements are based on amorphous evidence, we should remind ourselves – even if Henderson does not. And we need conceptual frameworks then, more than ever.

Bibliography

Bruce D. Henderson, *The Logic of Business Strategy*, Ballinger Publishing Company, 1984.

7

Benjamin B. Tregoe and John W. Zimmerman

—

Benjamin Tregoe and John Zimmerman are respectively Chief Executive Officer and Senior Vice-President of Kepner-Tregoe Inc., as well as being members of its board – the former in the capacity of chairman.

Tregoe is probably best known as the co-author (with Charles H. Kepner) of *The Rational Manager*: a work which promulgated the system of problem-solving and decision-making they devised, and introduced world-wide through their eponymous corporation. His Harvard PhD was in sociology.

Zimmerman joined Kepner-Tregoe in 1961 after acquiring experience in industrial engineering, production management and corporate training. His particular fortes are conceptual research and corporate business development. He has a long-standing teaching relationship with the Centre d'Études Industrielles in Geneva.

Their book *Top Management Strategy* is the outcome of more than ten years of joint practical work in strategy formulation with senior managements – notably throughout the US.

Tregoe and Zimmerman begin by distinguishing between two questions: *what* the organization wants to be, and, *how* it should get there. Where others[1] see strategy as a 'means' by which objectives are realized, they contend that strategy attempts to answer the first question. It is concerned with the organization's *basic purpose*; and they define it as 'the framework which guides

1. See in particular, **H. Igor Ansoff**, pages 15–33 and **Charles W. Hofer and Dan Schendel**, pages 216–229.

Fig. 7.1

How	What	
Operations	Strategy	
	Clear	*Unclear*
Effective	I Clear strategy and effective operations have equalled success in the past, and will in the future.	II Unclear strategy but effective operations have equalled success in the past, but success is doubtful in the future.
Ineffective	III Clear strategy but ineffective operations have sometimes worked in the past in the short run, but increasing competition makes success doubtful in the future.	IV Unclear stategy and ineffective operations have equalled failure in the past, and will in the future.

those choices that determine [its] nature and direction'. The choices 'relate to the scope of an organization's products or services, markets, key capabilities, growth, return, and allocation of resources'. And once they are converted into operational decisions, the 'how' question is answered.

A failure to ask and answer the what/how questions – in other words, a failure to determine the nature and direction of the organization *and then* relate operational decisions to them – does not automatically bring disaster. Companies have been able to adapt, and therefore survive, by concentrating upon the efficiency of their operations. But as Tregoe and Zimmerman put it: 'If an organization is headed in the wrong direction, the last thing it needs is to get there more efficiently.' Equally, when heading in the right direction, it does not want to be thrown off course by operational actions unguided by strategy.

They illustrate the relationship between strategy and operations with Fig. 7.1.

Crucial also to their fundamental thinking is the distinction
they make between strategy and long-range planning (LRP).
They regard LRP as a useful tool when it is subordinated to
strategy. But when substituted for strategy, its shortcomings are
manifold. For instance:

1. It tends to be based on future projections about current
   operations. Consequently, managers are not occasioned to
   think strategically – that is, they are not required to think
   about what the organization wants to be.

2. Despite warnings in the literature which urge managers to
   start by setting objectives for the future, many do not –
   largely because they are not sure how to. A consequence is
   that the plans they produce determine their company's direction; instead of a prior sense of direction determining the
   plans.

3. LRP tends to be a bottom-up process – starting from where the
   basic data are to be found. Plans come from all the relevant parts
   of the company, to be aggregated into a corporate whole. By
   the time this has happened senior management's capacity to
   modify the component parts in any fundamental way has
   been greatly reduced. And, without a strategy to assess the
   results, senior management is under a compulsion to allocate
   resources only in the ways indicated by the plans.

4. LRP is more short-range than its advocates tend to admit. Its
   theory suggests a five-year forecast which is then related to
   the present day. But, Tregoe and Zimmerman ask, how is this
   possible when there is no structured framework for looking
   ahead five years? So sheer necessity causes managers to reverse
   the theory, and extrapolate from the current year's data. Such
   data are, of course, more reliable; subsequent years' projections can always be changed, while those for the coming year
   cannot; and performance rewards are set relative to that first
   year of the plan. Everything, therefore, conspires to make the
   coming year *the* budget.

Implicit in item 3 above is the idea that strategy is the responsibility

Fig. 7.2

Category	Strategic area
Products/markets	Products offered
	Market needs
Capabilities	Technology
	Production capability
	Method of sale
	Method of distribution
	Natural resources
Results	Size/growth
	Return/profit

of top management. Tregoe and Zimmerman are emphatic
that this should be the case; and that the strategy should be
made explicit. Any abdication at the top will leave the organiza
tion vulnerable to being pulled this way and that by middle
managers with a clear view as to how the functions they control
should progress. And leaving the strategy implicit risks it being
modified haphazardly by external, as well as internal, events and
people.

Their research, we are told, suggests that there are nine basic
strategic areas – which can be grouped into three **categories**, as
shown in Fig. 7.2.

While all nine strategic areas are 'critically important', at any
particular time only one can be considered to be what Tregoe
and Zimmerman define as 'the primary determiner [*sic*] of the
scope of future products and markets'. This they term the
Driving Force.[2] It and 'the product and market scope it suggests
provide the basis for defining the other choices in the strategic
profile'. They illustrate the dominance of the driving force
within the **Strategic Framework** by Fig. 7.3.

2. For further thoughts related to this concept, see **Jay R. Galbraith and
   Robert K. Kazanjian**, pages 206–215.

Fig. 7.3

Strategic Framework

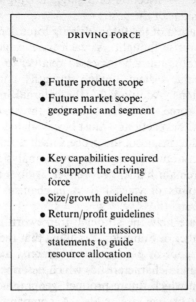

DRIVING FORCE

- Future product scope
- Future market scope: geographic and segment

- Key capabilities required to support the driving force
- Size/growth guidelines
- Return/profit guidelines
- Business unit mission statements to guide resource allocation

The strategic framework is timetabled using such criteria as: product development lead times; market trends; product life-cycles; the degree of flexibility in capital intensity; and rates of change in technology, customer preferences/needs, social, economic, and political conditions.

Identifying the present driving force of the organization and then determining whether it should be changed is, according to Tregoe and Zimmerman, the most difficult aspect of strategy formulation. The principal reason for this is that the approach does not permit the use of abstraction. For example, when identifying the present driving force, questions must be asked about what determined past choices over product entries; why certain market opportunities were pursued, or rejected; and the justification for acquisitions made or refused. Out of this analysis may come the realization that the organization has been committed to more than one driving force at a time, a consequence of which should be the selection of a single driving force so as to avoid the confusions of the past.

The determination of the future driving force demands equivalent hard and precise thought. As each practicable candidate is examined, its status must be assessed relative to the organization's current value system, unique strengths, and growth and return expectations. Additionally, the external implications of the new driving force – in terms of market threats or opportunities, and competitor reactions – must be calculated.

In managerial terms, also, the process itself is salutary, Tregoe and Zimmerman argue. So rigorous is the analysis that nothing can ultimately remain hidden. Moreover, it does not just bring out differing points of view: it is a mechanism for resolving those differences.

To demonstrate how the strategic framework is applied, we are given a number of examples. Recalling that the driving force determines the scope of products and markets, scope is defined as 'a set of common characteristics which describe the extent or boundary within which future product, geographic market, and market segment choices are made'. A company is then cited which had grown indiscriminately – after starting in the health care field, with a chemistry-based series of products used for testing purposes. Its top management determined its past and future driving force to be technology. This led, we are told, 'to a tight set of product and market characteristics which provided much better guidance and control for future product and market choices'. In addition, world-wide geographic markets 'where significant health care insurance was available' were indicated, and customer group targets were extended to include physicians and clinics, along with existing laboratories.

Given the joint effect of the driving force and its related scope decision, a new priority among capabilities may be necessary. This is illustrated with the description of a company which, under pressure from competition that was rapidly overhauling its technical lead, saw that it had to replace its current driving force (technology) with another (products offered). The latter does not call for innovative products typical of technology driving force firms, but concentrates on improving the present range-expanding via market penetration and entry into new segments and markets. So, as a consequence of the move to products offered, the key capabilities of the company became production and sales; and the research capability was subordinated by being modified to product development.

Dealing with the Results Category's Strategic Area components (size/growth and return/profit), Tregoe and Zimmerman carefully distinguish between their operational and strategic aspects. Acknowledging their importance for operational monitoring, they deplore their all-too-common use as strategic surrogates: that is, when extrapolations from historic financial data are employed to identify winners and losers for the purpose of allocating future resources. Their strategic role, relative to the driving force/product and market scope/key capabilities analytical process, is to help answer questions about likely growth and profitability performances, and their trends, for the period of the strategy. In particular, it is to guard against results too low for the firm's survival, or lower than the current strategy promises, or not large enough to stave off competitors' counter moves.

Return/profit as a company's driving force is most easily thought of in connection with the corporate level of a diversified organization. In this instance, each of the separate business units making up the corporation may well have different driving forces. The link between corporate and business level strategies is created and maintained by Business Unit Mission Statements which lay down the rationale for the unit being part of the corporation, its expected contribution to the corporation, and therefore the emphasis it receives from the corporation relative to other units. This being Tregoe and Zimmerman's position, it comes as no surprise to be told that acquisition programmes, the application of portfolio theory, forward/backward integration, and so on – moves which most consider to be strategic – are classified as operational, since 'they are put at the service of a particular driving force'.

They see strategic management as a continuing process

consisting of a sequence of activities: strategy formulation; implementation; review; and updating. As we have noted, the first is the sole responsibility of top management. By implication, so are review and updating. Implementation, however, involves people dispersed throughout the organization. Here the difficulties are not the largely conceptual ones of formulation; they come down to what Tregoe and Zimmerman describe as the 'identification, management and resolution of . . . Critical Issues'.

Critical issues (CI) are defined as 'those major changes, modifications, additions to the organization's structure and systems, to its capabilities and resources, to its information needs and management that result from setting strategy'. Of two kinds (strategic and operational), they are a function of two factors: (1) differences between a current and a future driving force; and (2) the general health and strength of the organization.

Understandably, they vary from one company to another. But they are usually to be found in areas such as:

- **The alignment of business unit:**
  A CI can occur when the determination of a driving force reveals that existing business units, or certain products and markets, 'do not fit within the intent' of the strategy.
- **Communications:**
  Typically, CIs arise in the mechanics of communicating a strategy so that it is well enough understood to be carried out properly. But, for competitive reasons or because of the risk of internal disruption (should, say, a divestment be in prospect), the extent of disclosure, to whom, and when, may constitute a CI.
- **Resource capabilities:**
  Changes to the driving force may call into question the future adequacy of staff and management. Middle managers can find their responsibilities unacceptably reduced in importance. Or top managers may not be able to go along with the new driving force. CIs like this abound in the human aspects of organizations.
- **The external environment:**
  This is a similar CI minefield. Being responsible for strategy,

top managers must make themselves sensitive to changes in the world about them – especially with the advent of a new driving force. They must ensure that information is gathered, analysed, and presented to them in a form useful for strategic decision-making.

Tregoe and Zimmerman advocate the systematic agenda-management of CIs, starting with their identification, and followed by ranking them in importance – to enable top management to 'concentrate its efforts where it [*sic*] really counts'.

After this discussion of the specifics of implementation, they mention a number of wider issues which call for greater thought. Despite much study of them, they are unresolved as yet. And they will remain so 'until top management takes them personally and firmly in hand'. From among them they itemize, and debate, such matters as: defining the role of the board of directors in the strategic process; developing and rewarding strategic thinking and accomplishment; determining the place of LRP in strategy formulation; and setting up to influence the environment.

Bibliography

Benjamin B. Tregoe and John W. Zimmerman, *Top Management Strategy*, John Martin Publishing, 1980.

PART THREE

The Scholars and Researchers

Preface

Corporate strategy has proved to be such a powerful conceptual tool, and is of such wide application, that no one can be surprised at the quantity of scholarship and research which has been devoted to it. It is also not surprising, therefore, that this is the largest section of the present book.

It could have been much larger. For it seems impossible to escape the tens of thousands of words published during the average year – whether in the serious or the popular journals of management – which set out to verify, negate, or merely apply in a foreign context some minute part of its enduring canon. Most of this outpouring has to do with either the ever-burgeoning PhD industry, or the publications race upon which so many academic promotions seem to depend. And, while one can – indeed should – be dismissive of the excess of casuistry these give rise to, there can be no doubt that some of the most valuable work has come about as a result of them. But how to find it? ·

The tests applied here are two in number: (a) is the work quoted widely by other writers? or (b) does its apparent neglect stem not from a lack of quality, but because its full impact has yet to be felt? Into the first category fall Richard P. Rumelt, Henry Mintzberg, Oliver E. Williamson, Joseph L. Bower, and Derek F. Abell, while Richard G. Hamermesh, and the joint works of Malcolm S. Salter and Wolf A. Weinhold, and Robert A. Burgelman and Leonard R. Sayles, come into the second.

Both the books by Rumelt and Bower which are dealt with

here have acquired what amounts to reference status. That is, their findings are far more likely to be quoted than questioned. While Rumelt's is of wider application, since it is essentially taxonomic, Bower's study of resource allocation is not as esoteric as its title may suggest. Burgelman and Sayles, for example, found it invaluable when exploring internal corporate venturing.

Mintzberg and Williamson are what might be termed originals – but in quite different ways. It has been said that the former is merely eclectic. But that is to ignore his talent for analysing familiar concepts in such a manner as to give us entirely new insights into them. Williamson is similarly creative. But, in his case, one is aware of an immense scholarship drawing upon many, sometimes unexpected, disciplines. Each writer gives the reader a sense of movement: that of an unending intellectual quest.

It is impossible to pretend that Abell's book is undemanding. But part of its difficulty can be explained by what it asks the reader to abandon. Abell sweeps away many of the assumptions the latter may have laboured long and hard to grasp. He considers the concept of a product-market to be inadequate for the purpose of business definition which, he argues, is the pivotal act in the setting of business strategy. So out it goes: to be replaced by a concept with three 'dimensions' which he names, and then renames. The notion of distinctive competences does not fit the new three-dimensional framework, and is also set aside. Again, we are told, market boundaries do not define businesses, but are defined by them. Thus, the reader is repeatedly required to re-examine the conventions of strategic discussion. If he can readily do this, the book is a mine rich with stimulating insights. If not, he will find it a minefield.

By contrast, Hamermesh's work is straightforward in the extreme. Much has been written about the theoretical virtues and shortcomings of portfolio planning. Refreshingly, Hamermesh goes out into the field to study how it is actually applied, and with what consequences.

Marrying theory and practice is what Burgelman and Sayles are also partly engaged in. Their starting point, as we have noted, is Bower's framework. But they augment and modify it in

heir description of the process (sometimes called intrapreneur-
hip) by which large companies may innovate technologically
rom within.

Salter and Weinhold's work is not only interesting to the
pecialist who is concerned with diversification through acquisi-
ion (their central theme), it is also valuable to the general
eader who is looking for a map of the strategic area as a whole.
This is because they have attempted to integrate three models
nto a working unity. These models – which they term 'the
strategy model', 'the product-market/portfolio model', and 'the
isk/return model' – while not in theory mutually exclusive, have
ften been treated as such: especially by proponents of the first.
t is, therefore, salutary – in an intellectual sense – to see the
rthodox methodology of strategy challenged by being consid-
red as merely one of a number of models, and one which could
enefit from supplementation.

8

Derek F. Abell

—

Derek Abell is a member of the professorial staff of Harvard's Graduate School of Business Administration. He is probably best known for his work in connection with business definition, which he comprehensively expressed in *Defining the Business*, published in 1980.

Arguably, Abell's essential position is a reaction against the then-fashionable nostrum that, as he puts it, 'the starting point of [strategic] planning is the decision to hold, harvest, or build market share'; for he was writing at a time when the experience curve and its offspring, portfolio planning, were especially influential. Not that he denies the linkage between market share and profitability. The mistake is to believe that share is '*the* primary strategic lever'. Formulating strategy, he asserts, is altogether a more creative act than that. Market share results from strategy: 'it is not strategy itself'. Indeed, the pivotal act in setting business strategy is '*defining* the business in a way that leads to competitive superiority in the customer's eyes'. Any company, therefore, which concentrates on growth and market share without having first explicitly resolved 'the definition of the activity within which that share is to be measured', is putting the cart before the horse.

In taking this stance, Abell is aligning himself with a number of authorities[1] whose pronouncements pre-dated the revolution begun by the Boston Consulting Group. And having declared himself, he proposes not to debate the issue any further; but,

---

1. Such as P. F. Drucker, T. A. Levitt and S. Tilles.

instead, 'to provide a new way of looking ... [at] *how* to define a business'. Citing some analyses of examples where companies had engaged in redefinition, he notes that these 'seem to suggest that a business has to be defined in terms of its scope'; in particular, a broader concept of its market activities.[2] But, he contends, the matter is much more complex. Managers, these days, are well versed in asking what business they are in; but few know how to formulate the problem so as to argue in a satisfactory manner for, say, packaging in preference to cans, or market segmentation rather than a broad product offering. This, then, is his principal concern: 'how a business should be defined at the stage at which *it sells* its final product'. (Emphasis added.)

Existing literature on the subject, Abell tells us, suggests the possibility of two major ways of thinking about it: conceiving of the business in terms of (1) 'some key distinctive competence or skill' (that is, a *resource* capability); or (2) *programmes* of activity. In the first case, the definition might take the form of '*manufacturing* high value, low priced, electro-mechanical devices', and in the second, '*providing electrical motors for marine and pumping applications*'.

Now, while he does not wish to contest the importance of defining resource capabilities, he proposes to deal with business definition only in terms of programmes. (The reason for this is his belief that the two 'dimensions' of product/market strategy are inadequate to the task of programme definition; and that consequently, 'new ways are needed to think about this side of the problem'.) He also proposes to break with convention by asserting that three, not two, dimensions are required to define a business adequately.

In this departure he makes no claim to being original. Others have come to the same conclusion, and developed a typology using the concept of 'differentiation': that is, when a firm serves two or more segments of a market, having designed 'separate

2. Tilles, for instance, describes how some US can manufacturers, in the 1960s, began to see themselves as being in 'packaging' – and encountered a new group of competitors and trading conditions, as a consequence.

3. Notably W. R. Smith and P. Kotler.

roduct and/or marketing programmes for each'. Abell, however, points out – perhaps for the first time in the literature – hat differentiation can also be used in the case of a company vishing to distinguish its products from those of its competitors.[4] But whichever meaning differentiation is given, there has to be a basis for segmentation'. In the first case (which Abell terms differentiated marketing'), the implication is that segments have lready been identified; and in the second ('competitive differen-iation'), that a particular class of customer can be appealed to.

Following this discussion, and 'based on a synthesis of existing heory', Abell sets out his first group of working assumptions: **That one can define (or redefine) a business in terms of what e now calls three 'measures': (1) scope; (2) differentiated marketing; and (3) competitive differentiation.**

A further analysis of authorities[5] leads to his second group of vorking assumptions: **That scope and both types of differenti-tion 'should be viewed in *three* dimensions, in terms of: (a) ustomer groups served; (b) customer functions served; and c) technologies utilized'.**

And thirdly, after similar discussion and synthesis, he adds hese working assumptions: **That 'the success of a . . . business efinition is a function of certain factors, which may differ rom situation to situation'. And that 'these factors can be rouped under the following general headings:**

i. **customer buying behaviour;**
i. **differences in marketing, manufacturing, R & D require-ments, and so on, resulting from market segmentation;**
i. **cost behaviour;**
v. **company resources/skills.'**

Writers on business definition, Abell asserts, have rarely distin-uished satisfactorily among the various organizational levels of

---

He gives as an example General Motor's differentiation of its range into 'price-classes' (Cadillac, Buick, etc. to Chevrolet) which, in the 1920s, success-fully deprived Ford of the market leadership it had won with the standardized Model T.
Including H. I. Ansoff, T. A. Levitt, and M. Hanaan.

strategy: corporate, business, product line, and so on. One o
the reasons for this may be that these levels are not discrete
Much depends upon the type of organizational structure .
company adopts, and the way that it determines the scope of it
divisions, businesses, or product lines. To overcome thes
organization-related difficulties, he introduces the notion c
resource-relatedness as a basis for business definition.

If one conceives of an organization as being composed of
number of hierarchical levels which differ in the degree to whic
they use the same resources, then one can think – at the lowes
level – of definitional choices based on product or marke
segments where, say, the sharing of the same manufacturin
plants demonstrates high resource-relatedness. Similarly, abov
that level, definitions would concern products or markets whic
were only partly related through the common use of just sale
resources – for example. While at the business level, choices c
whether the units were unrelated, or slightly related, woul
depend upon how resource-specific their activities were.

This argument leads to Abell's fourth working assumptio
**That '"business" definition covers the definition of activitie
at any level at which some degree of relatedness in terms c
resources used exists'.**

Conventionally, he argues, businesses tend to be described i
part by their market scope; and because of this, 'serious semant
and conceptual problems' occur when market boundaries a
defined independently of them.

Terms such as market, product/market, competitive product
market, and industry, are often used as though they were sy
onymous. Also unfortunate is the popular tendency to identi
an industry by its technology: as in 'the steel industry', or 'the c
industry'. And this results in firms from different industri
competing in the same 'market'.

Generally, the outer boundaries of a market are defined
terms of a reasonable interchangeability in use of the produ
and its substitutes, or cross elasticities of demand between ther
But difficulties arise when these come to be measured, because
among other things – of an absence of identifiable, and agre
upon, 'natural discontinuities'.

'There is a conceptual notion, however, that . . . at least for antitrust purposes' submarkets can be defined within a defined product/market.[6] Called segments when considered as demand, they are to be distinguished from one another by the differing patterns of need of the buyers within them. And their suppliers may be divided into 'strategic groups', according to how similar are their approaches to the marketplace. Yet firms may differ *vis-à-vis* vertical integration and diversification (together with varying degrees of each), advertising magnitudes, branding, whether distribution is exclusive or not, national *v.* regional activity, or in a multitude of other ways.

Difficulties in defining product/markets or their subdivisions create further difficulties when it comes to measuring market share. Moreover, it is implicitly assumed that competitors define their activities in the same ways, and that their market shares 'can all be measured in the same space'. If, however, their product/market strategies are dissimilar, then this may not be the case. More categorically, Abell tells us that it is a fallacy to presume, in connection with 'measures of supply concentration or product differentiation', that 'all competitors in a market are similarly defined'.

This discussion leads on to his fifth working assumption: That **'individual business definition determines market boundary definition'.**

It is the converse of the orthodox view; but one which common sense suggests is perfectly tenable – Abell considers. It is also extremely important to his position, since it enables him to view a competitive market 'as a series of overlays of differently defined businesses intersecting with one another, but not necessarily congruent with one another'.

His sixth working assumption follows immediately: **That market boundaries can be defined in the same three dimensions as businesses, rather than in product/market terms.**[7]

6. Abell equates this term (after the manner of PIMS, see **Robert D. Buzzell and Bradley T. Gale**, pages 59–71) with 'served market': that part of the overall market the firm elects to do business in.

7. See his second group of working assumptions, page 97.

And after a critique of the product life cycle theory (which he finds wanting when applied to factual examples because it does not 'incorporate the dynamic aspects of business definition'), he subtly modifies his sixth assumption in proposing his seventh: **That market boundaries will be redefined in terms of the three dimensions as businesses are redefined in them.**

The status Abell gives these working assumptions is not that of hypotheses. Nor does he wish to test them rigorously in his next four chapters – which are dedicated to how companies[8] usually define their businesses. Instead, he sees them as 'clues that act as bridges connecting existing theory, practice, and new theory'.

There are, principally, two outcomes of the study: a theory of business definition, and a theory of market boundary definition. Important as the second is, the first is more germane to our purposes. We shall, therefore, deal with it and its strategic implications.

Abell's work confirms the value of his three-dimensional, as against the conventional two-dimensional (product/market), approach. Indeed, he argues, the danger of the latter is that business definition may be seen 'as a choice of products on the one hand, and of markets on the other'. What should happen is that the product 'be considered simply as a physical *manifestation* of the application of a particular technology to the satisfaction of a particular function for a particular customer group'. In other words, the product is not chosen and then applied to a market; rather, a combination of customers to serve, functions to satisfy, and technologies to be utilized, is chosen – from which the product results. He then adds: 'Along the three dimensions, *scope* and *differentiation* define the business.'

The *scope* of any business may be defined along these dimensions of customer groups, customer functions, and technologies; but the dimensions are primitive in the sense that other dimensions may be derived from them by subdivision.

---

8. IBM, Docutel Corporation, competitors in the computerized tomography business, and Timberjack Machines.

Customer groupings, for example, may be identified in terms of: geography, socio-economic class, demography, personality traits, and so on – for consumer goods; and user industry and company size – in the case of industrial goods.

Customer functions (that is, those functions performed for the customer by a product) have to be distinguished from the way the function is performed (technology), and, 'the attributes or *benefits* that a customer may perceive as important criteria for choice'.[9]

Functions are related to each other in different ways. Abell describes 'three broad possibilities': complementary, similar, and unrelated.

Of these, the last is easiest to deal with since it refers to a customer's range of needs, each one of which is separate from the others.

Functions are complementary if one implies another: as, for instance, when loading implies unloading; or writing, something to write upon. However, complementarity is not always so straightforward. Abell cites the clearing bank business where customer functions can be thought of as either cashier functions (e.g. cash dispensing, depositing and transference) and information systems functions (e.g. cheque clearing, account recording and analysis); or security functions (e.g. cash protection and burglary prevention). In this fashion, he argues, new and creative ways can often be found to combine functions.

Functions can be said to be similar when they are performed in a similar manner. In these cases, one product may perform 'two essentially separate but similar functions'.

Technologies are, in a sense, solutions to customers' problems. They, like customer groups and customer functions, can be subdivided,[10] but unlike them, they are dynamic – in that one technology may displace another.

---

9. Abell illustrates the distinctions by citing transportation as a function; transport by taxi as a way of performing the function; and, price, comfort, speed and safety as attributes or benefits.
10. In the example above, where transport is the function, the optional technologies might be thought of as road, rail and sea. The first might then be subdivided into taxi, private car, rented car, bicycle and public transport.

Differentiation was shown by Abell in his preliminary work (see above) to have two meanings: across segments (differentiated marketing); and across competitors (competitive differentiation). He now argues that these are connected through 'relative evaluation'. By differentiating his product offerings *across segments* a competitor will, in general, increase their appeal to those segments, Abell contends. A relative evaluation by customers of all their segment product offerings will then determine the success of that differentiation. 'Thus', he concludes, 'relative evaluation includes an assessment of product differentiation' *across competitors*.

To help us understand the complex relationship between scope and differentiation, Abell introduces a 'typology of business definitions' based on the classification of strategies as being focused, differentiated, or undifferentiated.

A **focused strategy** is one where a business concentrates its activities on a particular group, function, or technology segment.

A **differentiated strategy** is where 'a business combines broad scope with differentiation across any or all of the three dimensions'.

An **undifferentiated strategy** is where 'a company combines broad scope across any or all of the three dimensions with an undifferentiated approach to customer group, customer function, or technology segments'.

And since 'the choice of focused, differentiated, or undifferentiated strategy exists in customer group, customer function, and technology dimensions', strategy may be defined in any one of twenty-seven [3 × 3 × 3] distinct ways. For example, the nine strategies for customer group focus, when variously combined with Focused/Differentiated/Undifferentiated customer functions and technologies, are:

| Customer functions | F | F | F | D | D | D | U | U | U |
| Technologies | F | D | U | F | D | U | F | D | U |

Similarly, using this three-dimensional framework, *redefinition*

Fig. 8.1

Strategy	Scope (or differentiation) across:		
	Customer groups	Customer functions	Substitute technologies
1	Same	Same	Different
2	Same	Different	Same
3	Different	Same	Same
4	Same	Different	Different
5	Different	Different	Same
6	Different	Same	Different
7	Different	Different	Different

of a business can occur in seven[11] different ways – as in Fig. 8.1. Strategy 7, Abell terms 'outright diversification'.

Although Abell illustrates the table's components with examples from his researches of scope, it is important, he tells us, not to overlook redefinition in terms of differentiation. 'Finding a new way to segment a market and differentiate the offering . . . is a creative act'. An act he instances with Ford's introduction of the Mustang: which was calculated to appeal to customers who wanted a car that was sporty, yet inexpensive.

But what is the basis for preferring one business definition to another? Abell contends that there is a natural tendency for companies to gravitate towards attractive market segments. Necessary as it is to evaluate such attractiveness, defining (or

11. He compares this with two-dimensional (i.e. product/market) schemas which give rise to two basic options for conceiving redefinition: taking existing products to new markets, or developing new ones for existing markets. According to Abell, these moves are popularly thought of by managers and academics as 'diversification'; and he appears to associate Ansoff with this usage. Yet the latter explicitly reserves the term (in four forms) for the application of new products to new markets. See **H. Igor Ansoff**, pages 15–33.

redefining) the business on such a basis would be incomplete if the impact of the definition on performance was ignored. And to understand that we must understand *how* business definition 'may result in high financial and market performance'.

A strategy may bring about such performance, he suggests, either because it is more efficient than those of its competitors (where efficiency is measured by relative costs and prices); or because it is more effective (in the sense of meeting customers' needs in a superior way). Generalizing, he then argues that:

- A *focused strategy* emphasizes effectiveness – by fitting the product and its marketing strategy to the exact needs of one customer/function/technology segment.
- An *undifferentiated strategy* emphasizes efficiency – with a standardized product and/or marketing strategy covering numbers of customer groups, customer functions, or technologies: an approach which promises widespread economies of scale.
- A *differentiated strategy* 'seeks the best of both worlds' by gaining efficiency through broad scope, and effectiveness through differentiation.

After this exercise in discrimination, Abell applies the results to the question of definitional preference – utilizing his field studies to gain some insights into how the factors identified in his third group of assumptions (see above) 'can affect the desirability of different approaches'.

Customer buying behaviour, he asserts, may influence business definition in any of three ways:

1. *Price sensitivity* on the customer's part determines whether a broadly defined competitor enjoying cost economies can turn these into market advantages. Where, however, the customer group is more interested in non-price benefits (e.g. product quality, technical assistance, service support, etc.), such an approach – though yielding greater margins – may be at a disadvantage compared with a focused, differentiated (i.e. effective) approach.
2. The customer may want to purchase a *full line* of complementary products, or a complete *system* of products (for several

related functions), from one supplier. In such circumstances, a narrowly defined competitor serving only single functions may not survive – unless his products offer peculiar benefits to the customer. Where, therefore, broad scope relative to customer functions (or technologies) is a benefit, it is an effective, as well as a potentially efficient, approach.

3. The greater is the *differentiation of customer needs* across group, function, or technology segments, the more strategy will have to be differentiated in terms of product and/or marketing. Consequently, resources will have also to be differentiated – with commensurate reductions in potential efficiency.

Resource requirements (e.g. manufacturing, marketing and sales, distribution, R & D, service, and so on) have to be considered separately from one another where there is differentiation of customer needs, because the programmes of activity for each may be similar or vary considerably across the range of groups, functions, and technologies associated with the product. These resource requirement similarity/difference assessments do not lend themselves to easy quantification. They are thus matters of judgement: and judgement of a relative, not an absolute, kind.

Cost behaviour, considered from the standpoint of cost/volume measurement, is complicated in the extreme – a point Abell admirably demonstrates. The efficient use of resources depends upon:

(a) The relative similarity of resource requirements across customer groups, customer functions, or technology segments, which, as we have seen, is a 'function of customer need differentiation'; and

(b) High volume actually leading to low costs.

Efficiency superior to competition will be achieved with an overall volume advantage. But that may be due to a narrowly defined business with a large share, rather than a broadly defined one with a small share.

Company skills of sufficient range are often possessed by multidivisional companies to enable them 'to allow broad

Fig. 8.2

Factors	Focused strategy (narrow scope, high competitive differentiation)	Undifferentiated strategy (broad scope, low market differentiation)	Differentiated strategy (broad scope, high market differentiation)
Customer behaviour			
1. Price- or benefit-oriented	Benefit-oriented	Price-oriented	Mixed/segmented
2. Full-line interest (systems or technology options)	Low	High	High
3. Differentiation of needs by segment	High	Low	High
Resource requirements	Differentiated	Similar	Differentiated
Cost/volume sensitivity	Low	High	High
Company skills	Narrow	Narrow	Broad

definition . . . *even if resource requirements are differentiated'*. In contrast, the less well endowed, needing highly differentiated resource requirements, may have to concentrate on a single group, function, or technology. And this may lead to their incapacity – with its attendant risks – to offer 'system purchases or . . . full-line supply based on complementary or substitute products'.

Abell 'summarizes the general propositions that may be made about the determinants of the three broad classes of strategy', as in Fig. 8.2.[12]

'Business definition . . . takes on a somewhat different *meaning* at different levels,' Abell tells us. Adopting, for the purposes of illustration, the conventional hierarchy of corporate, business

12. The figure takes no account of 'the fact that scope and differentiation may be different across customer group, customer function, and technology dimensions'.

nd 'programme' strategies, he points out that – at the corporate
vel – business definition is usually talked about in terms of
diversification'. Since he has been employing the term in its
opular sense (see page 103, note 11), he introduces the more
nformative 'related diversification' to replace it.[13]

Related diversification obviously entails relatedness of some
ind. What Abell has in mind is resource-relatedness – which he
rst considered in formulating his fourth working assumption.
arises, as he stated then, out of any similarity of activity in
rms of customers, functions, or technologies, which permits
e sharing of one or more resources – such as manufacturing,
& D, sales, distribution, etc. Since, therefore, any changes in the
ree dimensions potentially bring with them changes in the use
f resources, he argues that he is enabled to use the dimensions
r definitional purposes at *both* corporate and business levels.

In dealing with 'individual programmes of activity' during his
searches, Abell consistently applied his three-dimensional
amework to them. However, following that experience, he
ecides to modify his terminology so as to make it more appropri-
te to the programme level, and to bring business definition into
ne with conventional marketing concepts. *At the programme
vel*, therefore, he proposes to use: 'customer segments' instead
f customer groups; 'customer needs' instead of customer func-
ons; and 'marketing mix' or 'marketing approach' instead of
chnologies – because customer needs in marketing include
formation, reassurance, service, and availability, as well as
ose needs met by the product itself.

The consequence, he contends, is that market segmentation
nd positioning can be seen far more realistically. We can now
lk of a market being segmented using the distinctive dimen-
ons of customer segments, customer needs, and marketing mix.
ositioning becomes 'the process of defining a programme of
ctivity, by making explicit choices along each of these three
imensions', while a marketing offering is the manifestation of
ose choices.

. The distinction to be made is with 'outright diversification', which is analysed
into its component characteristics in Strategy 7, page 103.

Fig. 8.3

Level of decisions	Decision of category		
	Definitional decisions	Decisions about objectives	Functional strategy decisions
Corporate	Related diversification strategy	Corporate portfolio decisions	Financial and control policies
Business	Product/market strategy	Product/portfolio decisions	Manufacturing, R & D, procurement policies
Programme	Segmentation and positioning strategy	Budget-allocation decisions	Marketing mix

Finally, Abell sets out how he sees the relationship between business definition and overall business strategy.

His field studies indicate that a business unit's strategic plan comprises three classes of decisions: those which affect the definition of the business;[14] those pertaining to the objectives specifying market and financial performance;[15] and those to do with its functional strategies.

Relating these classes of decisions to the levels at which they are made, Abell gives us Fig. 8.3. 'Business strategy is an elusive animal to describe,' he tells us. So what we have here is his 'personal view of what it is and how it should be conceptualized – and in particular the role of business definition in an overall business strategy'.

14 and 15. Abell says of these that they are made 'either explicitly or implicitly'. What the field studies do not show, however, is that they are made 'in any particular sequence'; and, he argues, this is probably because – especially the case of definition – they are implied by functional decisions and budgets.

Bibliography

erek F. Abell, *Defining the Business: the starting point of strategic planning*, Prentice-Hall Inc., 1980.

9

Joseph L. Bower

—

For nearly thirty years Joseph Bower has been a member of th
élite group of Harvard Business School professors which ha
laboured so mightily in the field of business policy. At the outse
an economist, his work in strategy has ranged widely – with
tendency to concentrate on large, diversified organizations. Argu
ably, his most influential book has been *Managing the Resourc*
Allocation Process, first published in 1971, and regarded as
classic.

At the beginning of the preface to its 1986 edition, Bowe
says:

> That economics has ignored social organization is now legendar
> That the study of human behaviour has sidestepped economics is les
> acknowledged, but also true. Yet the problems of business manageme
> clearly require research drawing from both disciplines.

And so, in three sentences, he sets the scene (in the manner o
R. H. Tawney at the start of *The Acquisitive Society*) for wha
he is about to tell us, by pithily stating a few home truths.

The book arose out of his conviction that adequate models o
the resource allocation process were not available. To be sure
there was capital budgeting, whereby discounted cash flow
from competing investment projects could be compared on th
same, that is net present value, basis. But this, while theoretical
sound, had little to do with what the general managers of larg
corporations were engaged in. They were exercised over strateg
moves which directed critical resources towards perceived oppo
tunities in a changing world. Exercises which called into play, a
Bower puts it:

1. Intellectual activities of perception, analysis, and choice which are often subsumed under the rubric 'decision making'.
2. The social process of implementing formulated policies by means of organizational structure, systems of measurement and allocation, and systems for reward and punishment.
3. The dynamic process of revising policy as changes in organizational resources and the environment change the context of the original policy problem.

Bower asks how the picture sketched above differs from the assumptions underlying traditional capital budgeting theory. His answer is directed at two of the theory's critical assumptions: first, that choice from among the options (selection) is the key step in the procedure; and, second, that a small number of quantitative measures can usefully summarize a capital project. Dealing with the first assumption, he argues that selection is, *in fact*, inseparably part of the strategic process carried out by the whole of general management; and that treating the project as a financial security, with only top management choosing from among a clear-cut set of options, makes 'for a descriptively inaccurate conceptual framework'. Today's large corporations are of such size and complexity that, perforce, the tasks of planning *and of choosing* have had to be separated. But, while the board may reserve to itself the ultimate selection, any number of critical decisions (e.g. the choice of sales forecasts, the definition of a facility's scope and design – even whether to submit a request for capital) have already been made before the directors exercise their prerogative. Indeed, evidence of the extent to which top management has delegated its capital appropriating powers – largely because it is 'convinced of the qualifications' of subordinates – is to be found in how few projects are rejected.

Bower's objection to the second assumption is that it is false in theory since it takes no account of uncertainty. Cash flow calculations for different projects, which are made by management, are rarely comparable. And this is because the degree of uncertainty characterizing such numerical projections varies with:

1. The kind of project – research showing that cost reduction forecasts are more accurate than those for sales expansion, and especially so relative to new product launches.
2. The kind of business – where risk classification is frequently called for, but only crudely approximates to the truth.
3. The kind of manager.

Of this third source of uncertainty, Bower says that most managers are not devious and narrowly self-interested. Rather, 'for reasons of temperament or design [the manager's] numerical estimates ... reflect his attitude as he tries to fulfil what he sees to be a key requirement of his job: convincing his superiors to fund whatever series of programmes he thinks is best for the company ...' Which, Bower contends, 'is precisely the job his "bankers" have given him'.

The proposition that decisions made by subordinates crucially affect the choices presented to their superiors is obviously true – once stated, he argues. It is equally obvious that these subordinate decisions are the real determinants of corporate commitment. Yet no new analytical concepts in the literature of capital budgeting have addressed this well-known phenomenon. Indeed, only in the field of business policy has a concept been formulated – that of corporate strategy – which contemplates decentralized resource allocation in a diversified company.

Following his analysis of the defects of traditional theory, Bower poses what he considers to be *the* question of real interest: 'How can we use our new understanding to help top management change the process by which resources are invested so that strategic objectives are more effectively achieved?'

Paradoxically, he acknowledges, having just argued for the recognition of complexity in terms of decision-making, Bower puts forward a 'very simple' conceptual scheme with which to view the firm. Taking its position, at any one time, to represent the culmination of past resource allocation acts and decisions, he suggests that the process of changing that position consists of two parts: (1) *routine* – the continual use of assets and the generation of profits, day-to-day; and (2) *critical*. Of routine change, he proposes to say nothing.

Critical change is conceived of as having two aspects: (1) *the business planning process* – problem solving leading to the choice of markets and broad product objectives; and (2) *the investment process* – by which discrete resource investment decisions are made in order to achieve strategic objectives. Both processes are defined as critical because they 'provide a direction and a framework within which other routine activities take place'.

Putting his simple scheme together with some current research conclusions, Bower then deduces a working hypothesis, for empirical testing and modification, during a two-year study of a large diversified company. His research goals were, he tells us:

1. To provide an accurate description of the system of forces that affect the investment process.
2. To seek patterns from the data that evidence from other studies, as well as existing theory, which may provide the basis for an improved model of the process.

Since he was concentrating on the investment process, Bower took the business planning process as a 'given': background for the development of a descriptive model of the former. His early analysis revealed that the investment process could be said to consist of two sub-processes: *definition* and *impetus*; and that both were influenced by the same set of forces, which he termed *context*.

Definition 'is the process by which the basic technical and economic characteristics of a proposed investment project are determined'. It is initiated by a facility-oriented manager in response to a stimulus from elsewhere in the organization. That stimulus Bower calls *discrepancy*, because it stems from the manager's realization that information from, say, marketing, accounting or general management indicates that, in order to achieve his work objectives, he will have to take certain steps involving a facility investment.

Impetus is 'the force that moves a project toward funding'. It involves the willingness of a general manager to commit himself to sponsoring a project, in the knowledge that, by so doing, he risks his reputation for good judgement. A record of successful project support gains him the future confidence of his superiors, judgemental deference from his peers, and the feeling among his subordinates that he is the man to back their creative work. He therefore, carefully calculates what such a commitment means to *him*, in terms of costs and benefits.

Context is 'the set of organizational forces that influence the processes of definition and impetus'. It has two subsets: *situational* and *structural*. Situational context is made up of personal and historical factors. At any one time it can be of great significance – even critical to the solution of the problem at hand. But each situational context is unique; logically, therefore, it cannot be generalized about, nor included in the model. In contrast, because it exhibits considerable regularity, structural context finds a place in the model. It comprises 'the elements of *corporate structure*: the formal organization [with associated definitions of managers' jobs], the system of information and control used to measure performance of the business, and the systems used to measure and reward performance of managers'.

However, Bower asserts that one cannot examine structure's role in influencing behaviour without making certain assumptions about that very behaviour, and its sources. And this means, in organizational life, choosing between 'maximizing' and 'satisficing'. Equating the former with the 'rational' man postulated by 'a mathematical model of behaviour that no one believes to be explanatory, [and] almost no one believes to be descriptive', Bower opts for satisficing – even though he concedes that is also flawed descriptively. Then, following one of H. A. Simon's later ideas, he finds merit in the term 'intendedly rational', which Simon uses to denote behaviour that is purposive, and rational in the sense that it adjusts means to ends in the light of existing – if not later – knowledge. But Bower cannot bring himself to accept the tainted 'rational', so he substitutes 'purposive' for both words. He now has the behavioural assumption he was seeking: the purposive (or intendedly rational) manager, who – it is also assumed – is 'pursuing corporate and personal goals guided by a structure that helps him relate the two'.

The purposive manager's assumed personal goals are: economic wealth, and the power to influence affairs. And these

Bower argues, he can pursue by meeting the objectives of his company.

Having now dealt with the issue of human behaviour, Bower reintroduces structural context, and says that 'it is the principal way in which the purposive manager learns about the goals of the corporation'. Moreover, because it is the principal way, structural context 'shapes the purposive manager's definition of business problems by directing, delimiting, and colouring his focus and perception; [and] . . . determines the priorities which the various demands on him are given'.

All of the elements of structural context can be controlled by top management. So the latter are in a position to influence the behaviour of managers further down the hierarchy – which can be done merely by letting it be known what the corporation regards as desirable behaviour on their part.

Finally, in the preparation of his working hypothesis, or descriptive model, Bower adds a number of refinements in the form of phases – *initiating*, *corporate*, and *integrating* – which are to be found in the two sub-processes, definition and impetus, as well as in the set of forces influencing both, context.

The initiating phase of definition, considered as an activity (as opposed to a location within the firm), is a 'product-market-oriented process' which is 'triggered by a discrepancy defined in product-market terms'.

Aggregate financial planning is necessary at the other extreme of the planning activity. Here there is concern not just for share performance, cash flows, dividend policy and the like; there is also concern over broader issues such as business/government relations, the corporation's overall labour policies, and its international growth patterns. Once again, concern is triggered by discrepancies – but now they are between the company and its environment. This is the corporate phase of definition.

The third phase, integrating, comes into play because of discrepancies between sub-unit plans and those of the corporate whole. It is a phase when there are upwards and downwards transmissions of information, needs, standards and pressures. As Bower puts it: 'Somehow or other, plans which are formulated in the strategic specifics of product-market sub-units get translated into terms which are sufficiently comparable to permit aggregation in financial terms.'

In the impetus sub-process, the same three phases are to be found. Initiating starts when a project gets under way. That is the moment when someone says, 'I've got a great idea'; and means it in the sense that he puts his judgement behind it. The corporate phase is where the ultimate 'yes' or 'no' decision is made. And between the two is the integrating phase, which manages the relationship between the part and the whole. Here managers 'evaluate projects against their understanding of corporate criteria for evaluating managers, and place their bets'.

Turning to structural context, Bower considers it in another light: not as the set of forces principally influencing definition and impetus, but as the process by which structure is developed. Then, basing his position on A. D. Chandler Jr's finding that structure follows strategy, he says:

the initiating phase ... is the perception of a discrepancy between strategy and results, that is attributed to structure. The corporate phase is the choice of a new structure; and the integrating phase is the process of analysing the strategy and competence of the corporation in order to determine which, from among the alternate modes of restructuring available to the company or its sub-units, ought to be selected.

Bower's model is now ready. It is shown at Fig. 9.1. While more detailed, it is 'not fundamentally different from the description on which it is based', we are informed. It does not purport to tell managers what they should do. It attempts to explain what happens.

Understandably, by the conclusion of the study, the model had been modified (see Fig. 9.2). Most notably, there was the addition of a fourth column: measurement of the strategic process. This came about because of discovered needs to relate corporate to product-market tasks, and then measure them since their performance proved critical to the development of an investment project. While measurement of the planning process could have been regarded as part of the structural context, for the purposes of analysis, Bower concluded that it was useful to separate strategic measures from those of operations.

Fig. 9.1 The resource allocation process

Phase	Process		
	Definition	*Impetus*	*Determination of context*
Corporate	Aggregate, financial company-environment	Yes or no	Design of corporate context
Integrating	Financial, aggregate · · · · Product market strategic	The company 'wants' · · · · The businesses 'want'	Corporate needs · · · · Sub-unit needs
Initiating	Strategic product-market	I've got a great idea	Product-market not served by structure

Summarizing his findings, Bower uses two medical analogies. 'The most important implication of this study for the general manager is that he must look at resource allocation ... [as] a doctor looks at circulation in a patient ...' Indeed, to toy with a seemingly malfunctioning part – without considering the effects elsewhere – is as dangerous to companies as it is to human beings. The general manager needs to be a diagnostician; and the model at Fig. 9.2 provides him with a convenient tool. An organization is like the body in other ways. It is constantly changing; and while usually healthy, it is prey to illness. (However, 'politics' is not a sickness. It is a fact of organizational life, which top management must influence and monitor.) Bower counsels the manager to act constantly as if he were a research scientist – testing his understanding of the system's operations against the evidence he receives, and being careful not to prejudge patterns of events he does not understand.

To aid diagnosis, Bower sets out three key questions:

Fig. 9.2 Revised model of the resource allocation process

Level of task	Definition	Impetus	Determination of structural context	Measurement of the strategic process
Corporate	Company-environment financial	Yes or no	Design of context	Return on equity, growth
Integrating	Does the company need it? / Should the company want it?	Will I be rewarded for it? / Should I not be rewarded for it?	Corporate organizational objective / New organizational needs of sub-units	Pricing strategies / Qualifying financial measures
Initiating	Product-market strategy	Here is a great proposal	The process isn't working	Strategic measures

1. **Location:**
   where each of the three phases of the two sub-processes, a
   well as those for context and measurement, are being carrie
   out. (The answers to these questions, additionally, provide a
   map of the parts of the process which is needed to deal wit
   Co-ordination.)
2. **Co-ordination:**
   of which three principal aspects need to be reviewed:
   (i) the linkages across functions and levels;
   (ii) the consistency of focus among those performing parts of
   the process;
   (iii) the timing of the different phases.
3. **Quality:**
   by far the most taxing of the key questions to deal with, sinc
   the requisite standards are often lacking.

In principle, the job of evaluating the definition process is feasible, because the data are there for scrutiny. But determining the quality of impetus is far more difficult. This is, firstly, because evaluating project selection depends upon knowing intimately those people who elicit, and those who provide, sponsorship. And, secondly, because the project alternatives – if any – should be known, along with the rules governing selection.

Finally, Bower argues that the manager evaluating structural context and the related process of strategic measurement faces yet one more extraordinary problem. He can rely on little other than his own judgement when he tests 'the elements of context to see if they are consistent with each other and with strategy'. Moreover, theory cannot tell him much about how structure may be modified to bring about particular changes in behaviour. Worse: consistency of means with ends is the sole test available; and if the ends are strategic, he will have to wait for years to see how things turn out.

Bower is not sanguine about the outcome of a diagnosis based on the questions he has itemized. The result 'is likely to be a long list of organizational ailments associated with the location, quality, and co-ordination of the resource allocation processes'. And, while this might have been anticipated, he reminds us of a remark he makes at the very beginning of the book about how little attention science has paid to the study of large organizations – and the consequently short 'list of remedies' available to the scientist-manager.

His conclusion, not unexpectedly, is that the 'process of diagnosis itself is likely to be the most *generally* useful and important activity recommended here. Managements ... must be ready to devise approaches *specific* to the needs of *their* own company's situation.'

Bibliography

Joseph L. Bower, *Managing the Resource Allocation Process*, Harvard Business School Press, 1986.

10

Richard G. Hamermesh

—

Richard Hamermesh is a Managing Partner of the Center for Executive Development, an educational consultancy he helped to found, with other highly experienced former Harvard Business School professors, in 1987. He is probably better known to the manager-student for the case study he co-authored[1] on Crown Cork and Seal.[2] This, with a complementary article in the *Harvard Business Review*,[3] subjected to critical examination the Boston Consulting Group (BCG) experience curve hypothesis as a universally applicable strategic imperative.

In 1986 he published *Making Strategy Work*, which had the twin objectives of examining how strategy is planned and carried out in large, diversified companies, and providing a critique of the uses of portfolio planning by their Chief Executive Officers (CEOs). It is the latter we shall concentrate on – as he does.

Hamermesh defines portfolio planning as:

those analytic techniques that aid in the classification of a firm's businesses for resource allocation purposes, and for selecting a competitive strategy on the basis of the growth potential of each business and of the financial resources that will be either consumed or produced by the business.

And he traces its conceptual origins to BCG's experience curve. The curve's derivative, the growth/share matrix ('the matrix')

---

1. With K. D. Gordon and J. P. Reed.
2. Crown Cork and Seal, Inc. – *ICCH*: 9-378-024.
3. 'Strategies for Low Market Share Businesses', *Harvard Business Review*, May-June, 1978; with M. J. Anderson and J. E. Harris.

Fig. 10.1

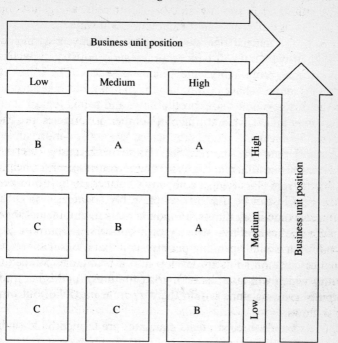

together with the analyses of the Strategic Planning Institute – through their PIMS programme – and 'the screen' developed by McKinsey and Company with General Electric (GE), furnished the intellectual, empirical, and practical bases for what was to come. (Since the first two are dealt with elsewhere,[4] we shall devote more attention here to the third.)

'The Company Position/Industry Attractiveness Screen' is depicted by Hamermesh in its usual nine-block form, as in Fig. 10.1.

Both matrix and screen 'seek to categorize a company's cash

For information on the growth/share matrix (and the experience curve), see **Bruce D. Henderson**, pages 72–80; similarly, see **Robert D. Buzzell and Bradley T. Gale**, pages 59–71.

flow position'. However, leaving aside the obvious classificator implications of possessing nine boxes, or cells, as against four the screen is different in subtle but important ways.

As in the matrix, one axis (industry attractiveness) include market growth; but it also incorporates such industry characteristics as size, profitability, and pricing practices. The other axis includes market share (again, like the matrix), but takes account of the business unit's size, profitability, and technological standing – *inter alia*. This factoring of a number of variables into each of the two measures renders the screen 'generally a more subjective tool' than the matrix; but, Hamermesh adds, this is ' feature that its adherents applaud and its critics deride'.

Aside from classifying a company's businesses, portfolio planning devices can be used for selecting what Hamermesh calls 'strategic mandate': that is, a fundamental, all-embracing object ive for the competitive strategy of a business. Its purpose is t establish a capital spending pattern such that a business receive finance early on so as to develop into a profitable, competitiv entity which will later, as its market matures, fund other, mor rapidly growing units within the corporate portfolio, out of it cash flows.

The screen's three strategic mandates are termed build (indic ated by A in the figure above), hold (B), and harvest (C).

Historically, as Hamermesh puts it, 'the portfolio approach t strategic planning' began in 1970, when a McKinsey report wa adopted by Fred Borch, the then CEO of GE. In the perio since, portfolio planning has come to form part of the stock-in trade of virtually all business consultants; and was found to b utilized by over half of some 300 'Fortune 1,000' firms surveye in the early 1980s.[5] However, its reputation has waned as well a waxed. In 1980, a celebrated article[6] contended that it was on of the causes of industrial decline in the US. Yet GE, which ca claim to be among the world's most successful companies, ha never faltered in its use.

5. By P. Haspelagh.
6. By R. H. Hayes and W. J. Abernathy, *Harvard Business Review*, July–Augu 1980.

Despite being surrounded by controversy, its widespread acceptance – as Hamermesh sees it – has much to do with the way that key parts of it apply to a perennial difficulty confronting the CEOs of all large, diversified companies: resource allocation. In such companies – where, typically, there are many levels of general manager and much industrial diversity – the CEO suffers under a tendency for the hierarchy to unite in support of every one of its divisional projects: while he is still struggling to comprehend the competitive natures of each of his company's numerous marketplaces. The consequence can be, as Borch discovered at GE, that the company launches more strongly-backed projects than it can afford to finance.

The *theory* underpinning portfolio planning came to be preferred to capital budgeting, because it links requests for capital 'to the competitive performance of divisions and to their strategic plans'. No longer, for example, would managers be able to carry the day by so arranging their profit projections that they virtually always cleared the company's hurdle rate. Instead, 'each business's performance [could] be measured within its market', and decisions then made relative to that performance. Individual projects would still require evaluation. But portfolio planning – as a first step – could determine whether the business proposing a project was worthy of funding at all. As Hamermesh puts it, when a business is classified as 'grow', using the screen (or 'star', using the matrix), 'not only is the explicit statement made that the . . . strategy should include growth as a central objective, but the implicit assumption is that the business will receive the investment funds it needs to grow'. And, by the same token, a 'hold' classification equates with an allocation decision to remove cash from that business, and invest it elsewhere.

But these are just broad indications as to the theoretically preferable allocation, or reallocation, of funding – usually originating from cash flows. As Hamermesh points out, the theory '*does not predict* its various uses . . . [and] . . . *offers no advice* on how it should be used and what impact the techniques are likely to have'. (Emphasis added.) To bridge the gap between theory and practice, he therefore determined on a phased programme of concentrated research which involved extensive interviews with CEOs and senior managers, the analysis of two portfolio planning data bases, the detailed study of nine companies, and a review of related case material.

In summarizing his findings, Hamermesh tells us that his research was guided by questions over why portfolio planning was adopted, the issues which were then faced, and the impact it had upon strategy. His main conclusions are set out below.

Why have CEOs adopted portfolio planning techniques?

● Portfolio planning is introduced by most companies after a fall in profitability and the onset of a cash crisis. These are circumstances for which it is 'uniquely well suited', since:
(a) It furnishes precise guidelines for capital allocations in ways that balance the needs for, and the uses of, cash.
(b) It usually results in the divestment of cash-hungry businesses with poor prospects of high returns.

Once profit-making has been resumed and cash flow improved, however, Hamermesh asks why companies should persist with it. From his research it appears that CEOs have found a number of different uses for it – those uses changing according to the company's needs and the intentions of the CEO – as we shall see.

● We have observed that portfolio planning's underlying theory suggests its employment as a discriminative device for allocating resources among businesses. And, in practice, this is indeed what occurs. But, additionally, Hamermesh discovered that it has been used 'to promote divestitures and corporate restructuring': far riskier applications – concentrating attention outside, rather than inside, the company.

● It has provided senior managers with a way of comprehending their complete portfolio, as well as each of the individual businesses which make it up. The screen, for example, by locating every component of the portfolio within its nine blocks, facilitates 'a rudimentary understanding of deficiencies and imbalances' in that portfolio's overall composition. While a similar grasp of each business can be obtained with the use of 'just a few variables, such as market growth and market share'.

● It has been employed by CEOs to improve the quality of business unit strategies – especially where these, in the past, have been flawed by a lack of specificity in connection with, say, goals for market share or cash flow.

What issues do companies face when using the portfolio approach?

Hamermesh tells us that numbers of rarely acknowledged but recurrent dilemmas arise out of its adoption – and require effective management.

● The first of these is the defining of business units. *The typical approach to this has been to regard it as matter determinable by technical analysis alone*: a preliminary to, and less important than, how units are categorized and what strategic mandates they are given.

But one of Hamermesh's major findings is that business unit definition is of paramount importance. This is because the definitions:

(a) Shape the market perceptions of both corporate and unit managers.

(b) Are themselves influenced by administrative and resource allocation considerations.

(c) Must be responsive to changes in markets, competition and technology.

He concludes that senior managers should, therefore, always be ready to redefine their units to accommodate alterations in their circumstances, whether internal or external.

● An unfortunate consequence of business unit definition which must be guarded against is what Hamermesh calls the self-fulfilling prophecy. It most commonly affects those mature units which are labelled as cash cows, which do not benefit from new investment and are subjected to stringent controls. Because of these constraints, morale and performance may drop disastrously: thus accelerating the unit's decline, and causing its disposal well ahead of schedule. But growth businesses are not immune. They also require careful management if their star status comes to mean 'unquestioned support and loose control', and leads to lower profitability.

● Portfolio planning *tends* to bring about a centralization of the strategic processes. Indeed Hamermesh argues that it is 'perhaps best suited for chief executives who wish to manage the outcomes of these processes', because it enables them to have control of both resource allocation and the assignment of strategic mandates. However, it can be made compatible with systems where lower levels in the organization are involved in the strategic process. And Hamermesh suggests that this can be done by such arrangements as: permitting corporate and unit managements to negotiate over cash flow and strategic objectives; not labelling unit strategies; a two-tier process of resource allocation; and making line management responsible for strategy.

What impact have portfolio planning techniques had on the strategies companies adopt?

● Portfolio planning's greatest impact has been on decisions about which businesses the company will compete in and the resources they will be given, Hamermesh tells us. However, within that field (which he defines as the responsibility of corporate strategy), it could be said that its impact has been greater relative to businesses the company *will not* compete in, rather than the reverse. This is because it has helped managers identify and dispose of irrecoverable units 'in a more timely, dispassionate, and analytic manner'.

● By contrast, its impact upon internal growth and business development has been small. But, as Hamermesh argues, these are types of activity which it does not address. Here is, therefore, a limitation in the approach which should be made good with the use of other planning techniques.

● The portfolio approach to strategic planning has a mixed effect when it is employed to formulate business strategy.[7] If

7. Hamermesh defines business strategy as 'the determination of how a company will compete in a given business, and position itself among its competitors'.

used alone – that is, if strategy is set simply by the location of the business unit on the screen (or the matrix) – it can be misleading. This is because, in general, portfolio techniques overemphasize growth and share compared with the issue of how the unit can secure competitive advantages. But used with caution, 'and in conjunction with other techniques for analysing the industry and the competition', they can help managers arrive at a realistic understanding of their markets and their positions in them. Hamermesh then adds, significantly:

The important point is that cash flow and market share objectives are not substitutes for sound business strategy analysis and development, and that they should be seen as the results, rather than the purposes, of strategic actions.

● Portfolio planning has the least relevance to 'the basic character and vision of the company' – which is how Hamermesh defines institutional strategy. But then, he contends, it was probably never meant to have. Even so, one should take steps to prevent its techniques damaging the current strategy, and inhibiting subsequent developments of it.

After summarizing the findings of his research, Hamermesh discusses their implications for managers at a number of levels.

Beginning with top managers, he argues that:

1. They should not make the mistake of equating portfolio planning with overall strategy; and they should see to it that all three types of strategy (institutional, corporate, and business) receive adequate attention.

2. Its particular applicability to corporate strategy can delude managers into believing that their sole purpose is to buy and sell businesses, instead of providing 'long-term commitment and integrity to the company's operations'.

3. They should be aware of the deficiencies of portfolio planning, and offset them with other 'techniques, processes, and approaches'.

   (At the least, this entails: (a) supplementing the 'general prescriptions' of the portfolio approach with detailed studies of the industry and competition; and (b) attending to opportunities presented by internal growth and business development.)

4. The CEO must lay down what purpose(s) portfolio planning serves in the company, and how it will be applied. Since its uses are manifold (e.g. as an aid to resource allocation, corporate restructuring, and senior management's understanding of the company's businesses), 'it cannot be viewed solely as a tool for developing strategy'. It is, however, a tool with which the CEO can *implement* his objectives and strategy.

Turning to Division Managers, Hamermesh contends that:

1. Despite the centralizing of strategic processes which portfolio planning tends to bring, division managers should not necessarily see its introduction as a means by which top management gains control over business strategy. Where it leads to corporate managers' greater understanding, or improvements in the quality of strategic thinking, 'the result is often a greater emphasis on high-quality business strategy development'.

2. The use of the approach does not remove the responsibility of these managers for formulating creative business strategies, which – to be successful – should be precise and specific. Strategic mandates do not meet these requirements, because they are only guidelines – of a general and abstract nature. Mandates do not constitute strategy, therefore.

Finally, in connection with Staff Planners, he says:

1. 'Portfolio planning, with its jargon and numerous nuances, is particularly susceptible to being run by ever-larger planning staffs.' The latter are best employed performing the analyses (e.g. to do with consumers, competitors, and changes in technology), which the operating/line organization might not otherwise engage in. Their work should stop short of strategy development – which Hamermesh considers to be the responsibility of operating/line managers. Indeed, he argues, should

staff planners *alone* develop strategy, not only will the quality of strategic thinking at the operating/line level stay unaffected, but also their plans are more likely to be rejected at that level.

2. At the introduction of portfolio planning – to ensure a common approach by all business units to information and its analysis – the documentation must be uniform. Thereafter, as experience with its techniques accumulates, time is better spent on each unit's 'key issues and decisions', rather than on form-filling. This may well reduce the visibility of the planners' role; but it is a consequence they must reconcile themselves to, as the company takes to thinking strategically.

3. Planners, more than most, should be aware of the limitations of the portfolio approach. (See above.) They should also work to overcome them. The most important weakness is its small contribution to internal growth and business development. The challenge for planners, in preference to corporate acquisitions, is to ensure that the organization has the necessary people and resources 'to identify and create' the opportunities each existing business can exploit.

Concluding the summary of his research findings, and their implications, Hamermesh argues that portfolio planning is 'a tool, not a solution'. It is no substitute for 'creativity, insight, or leadership'. Companies are not 'strategic abstractions of assets'; they are constituted of 'real businesses, competing against very [*sic*] real competitors, staffed by fallible human beings who need leadership to give purpose to their efforts'.

On the wider question of the effects of portfolio planning on US competitiveness, he offers a 'perspective' – since 'no conclusive evidence' emerged from his work.

In so far as it has led to underinvestment in, and the abandonment of, mature businesses, it has not helped competitiveness – and could have contributed to the decline of some industries. A similar judgement can be arrived at where it has inclined senior managers to concentrate on the acquisition and disposal of businesses, instead of the development of competitive strategies for them. However, the market realism 'it can help foster has led to timely rationalization of capacity in some industries'; and the reallocation of such resources in favour of 'high-potential businesses ... can contribute to economic growth, rather than to decline'.

Hamermesh's point is, it appears, that portfolio planning, *per se*, is neutral. Whether its effects on competitiveness are malign or benign depends upon what it is used for, and how.

Bibliography

Richard G. Hamermesh, *Making Strategy Work – How Senior Managers Produce Results*, John Wiley & Sons, 1986.

11

Henry Mintzberg

—

Henry Mintzberg is one of today's most prolific writers in the field of management. An academic (currently at McGill University, Montreal) who has covered a wide range of subjects, he is probably best known for his work on structures, cultures, and management styles. Naturally sceptical, he combines extensive scholarship with a no-nonsense practicality in ways which inform, provoke – even interrogate – his reader into realizing that much has yet to be thought, said and learnt about organizational life. Because of his exploring attitude, this survey – more than that for most of the authors dealt with here – should be seen as a progress report, rather than an ultimate distillation.

Where others either avoid the definition of 'strategy' (assuming that its meaning will become clear, later), or adopt some conventional form of words (their own, or more usually a modification of someone else's), Mintzberg, typically, plunges straight into the semantic minefield. He believes that it is in the nature of human beings, perhaps foolishly, to look for a single definition for each concept. Yet, in practice, we use the word strategy in many different ways – implicitly accepting any number of definitions, while tending to reserve just one for our own formal purposes. He, therefore, proposes we should look at five, and their interrelationships – playfully, one suspects, choosing words that begin with the same letter. They are: plan, ploy, pattern, position, and perspective.

To most people, '**strategy is a plan** – some sort of *consciously intended* course of action . . .' Used like this, strategy: (1) is created ahead of events; and (2) is cerebral and purposive. It can be formally documented, or just clearly thought through by someone. It can be general, or specific. If it is specific, however it may be used in the sense of it also being a ploy. That is, a manoeuvre to outwit an opponent: such as when a firm *threatens* to expand in order to deter a competitor from putting up a new factory. Here, what is consciously intended (strategy-as-plan) is the threat, not any actual expansion.

His third definition, **strategy is a pattern**, applies where we find – after the fact – '*consistency* in behaviour, *whether or not* intended'. In other words, we infer from, say, a competitor's actions (which we find consistent with one another), that he is following a certain strategy. We may well go beyond that and argue that the pattern must surely rest on a plan – that there is an intention which brings about such a consistency. But we should be cautious. Our assumption may prove false.

Since 'plans may go unrealized, while patterns may appear without preconceived plan', Mintzberg argues that his definition of plan and pattern can be quite independent of each other. Labelling strategy-as-a-plan an intended strategy, and strategy-as-a-pattern a realized strategy, Mintzberg distinguishes between *deliberate* strategies and *emergent* strategies. A deliberate strategy is one 'where intentions existed and were then realized'; and an emergent strategy is one 'where patterns developed in the absence of intentions, or despite them, which went unrealized'. (It will be noted that Mintzberg has moved from an inference [we observe consistency of behaviour, therefore a strategy exists] to a statement of fact [strategies do develop without intentions and I shall call them emergent].)

Continuing, he argues that a truly deliberate strategy is as unlikely to exist as a truly emergent one. The first would require 'a pattern to have been intended *exactly* as realized'; and the second: 'consistency in action without any hint of intention'. Instances of both forms may well exist; but the likelihood is that most strategies possess both deliberate and emergent characteristics.

In discussing **strategy is a position**, Mintzberg begins by asking what strategy is about. From the military we acquire the idea that it was about important things; while tactics was about detail. The difficulty with this distinction is that, after the event, details sometimes prove to have been strategic. He quotes R. P. Rumelt's observation that 'one person's strategy is another's tactics – that what is strategic depends on where you sit'. 'Where you sit', Mintzberg contends, refers to your location in an environment – which for a company usually means a market. By this definition, strategy is a way of identifying that location: it is 'the mediating force – or "match" – between organization and environment'. As for what strategy is about: it can be about anything, since labelling something as strategic – in advance – is dangerous to the extent that it may 'imply that some issues are *inevitably* more important than others'.

Military studies and game theory focus on what is known in business as head-on (that is, one-to-one) competition, he argues; whereas strategy-as-position permits the application of the concept to 'games' with many players. Head-on competition being rare in business, management theorists generally concentrate upon these n-person games; 'although they have tended to retain the notion of economic competition'. (Here, Mintzberg cites Porter's *Competitive Strategy* by way of example.) Strategy-as-position, however, can go beyond this notion. After all, market niches are sought in order to *avoid* competition. And, quoting Rumelt once again ('Strategy is seeking and maintaining a sustainable advantage'), Mintzberg concludes that this means finding a position where there is such an advantage – directly competitive or not.

Strategy is a perspective, Mintzberg's final definition, 'looks inside the organization, indeed inside the heads of the collective strategist'; and, relative to the organization, it is analogous to the personality of an individual. Demonstrably, strategy is a concept. By implication, all strategies are abstractions which exist in the minds of those people they make an impact upon. What is important is that people in the organization share the same perspective 'through their intentions and/or by their actions'. This is what Mintzberg calls the realm of the collective mind; and reading that mind is essential if we are 'to understand how intentions . . . become shared, and how action comes to be exercised on a collective yet consistent basis'.

Considering his definitions as a whole, Mintzberg argues that no one definition should be preferred to the others. In some ways they compete – as substitutes for one another. But perhaps in more important ways they are complementary, with each adding important elements to the discussion. For example:

Plan introduces the notion of intention, and emphasizes the role of conscious leadership; pattern focuses on action . . . and introduces the notion that strategies can emerge; position introduces context, rooting strategy in external situation and encouraging us to consider competition and co-operation; and perspective reminds us that strategy is nothing more than a concept, and focuses our attention on the collective aspect of strategy.

His belief is that, by explaining and deploying a number of definitions of strategy, we can avoid those confusions which stem from poorly defined, even contradictory, uses of the term – thus enriching our understanding of the process itself.

Perhaps Mintzberg's most influential work has to do with the structural configuration of organizations. On the basis of research findings made with some of his colleagues at McGill, he has proposed a typology of these configurations. There are, for the moment, five 'pure types': the Simple Structure, the Machine Bureaucracy, the Divisionalized Form, the Professional Bureaucracy, and the Adhocracy. He, of course, deals with each exhaustively. However, our preoccupation with strategy requires us to concentrate on his insights into that – with only an identifying outline of the other characteristics of each type.

The principal characteristic of the **Simple Structure**, Mintzberg tells us, is that it is not elaborated. It is organic; and, in a sense, is a non-structure. He describes it in this way:

Typically, it has little or no technostructure [i.e. staff analysts who design systems which form the basis for processes controlling the work of others], few support staffers, a loose division of labour, minimal differentiation among its units, and a small managerial hierarchy.

Power over important decisions tends to lie with the chief executive officer (CEO), who has a wide span of control – sometimes with everyone reporting to him. So, communications are informal and mostly between the CEO and everybody else.

Work flows tend to be flexible, with operating core tasks largely unspecialized and interchangeable. Decision-taking is similarly flexible – centralized power making for rapid responses.

Unsurprisingly, therefore, strategy is formulated solely by the CEO. It tends to be 'highly intuitive and nonanalytical, often thriving on uncertainty, and oriented to the aggressive search for opportunities'. (These findings accord well with some earlier conclusions Mintzberg came to after an extensive review of the literature on what he calls *the entrepreneurial mode*.)

The CEO rarely makes his strategy explicit. Indeed, it often amounts to a straightforward expression of his personal beliefs, and personality. However, when informed by an intimate and detailed knowledge of his company and its environment, the CEO carries in his brain 'a personal vision ... a concept of the business'. Given this, and his almost unhampered power to act, Mintzberg's research showed just how effective such knowledge can be in an individual with a strong commitment to his organization's future development. This notwithstanding, the business has to be capable of being comprehended by one brain, unaided. But when this is the case, 'the entrepreneurial mode is powerful, indeed unexcelled'.

Mintzberg's summarizing view is that, in the simple structure, entrepreneurship 'is very much tied up with the creation of vision, essentially with *concept attainment*'. That vision being personal, strategies are, for the most part, deliberate (as opposed to emergent). However, 'in the absence of specific plans, the details of these strategies are likely to emerge, so ... it is only the broad vision (strategy as perspective) that is really deliberate'.

Examples of the **Machine Bureaucracy** such as a steel company, a prison for long-term inmates, an airline, or a large car manufacturer are 'structures fine-tuned to run as integrated, regulated machines'. What they have in common are: 'highly specialized, routine operating tasks; very formalized procedures in the operating core; a proliferation of rules, regulations, and formalized communication throughout the organization; large-sized units at the operating level; reliance on the functional basis for grouping tasks; relatively centralized power for decision making; and an elaborate administrative structure with a sharp distinction between line and staff'.

Managers at what Mintzberg calls the strategic apex of these organizations are ceaselessly engaged in searching for more efficient production methods. But that is not all. Keeping the structure intact also absorbs much energy. For 'conflict is not *resolved* in the Machine Bureaucracy; rather it is *bottled up* so that work can get done'.

These managers are the organization's generalists – with everyone else a specialist. They possess not only *formal* power, established by hierarchy and the chain of authority; they have considerable *informal* power, since that is based upon the kind of knowledge which can only come together at the top of the hierarchy. Strategy-making is, therefore, a top-down process in which relevant information is ostensibly sent upwards and formulated into a strategy that is then sent down for implementation, by way of programmes and action plans.

Mintzberg observes that this strategy making system – as it should operate, that is – has two main characteristics:

1. All decisions are meant to cohere into a tightly integrated whole – with exceptions flowing up the chain of authority to be dealt with at the appropriate unit level, or at the apex if they involve more than one major function; and decisions flowing back down for implementation in specific contexts.
2. Uniquely in this structure, formulation and implementation are sharply separated: the apex formulates; 'the middle line and [the] operating core implement'.

However, as Mintzberg and his McGill colleagues discovered from their empirical studies, this (*the planning mode*) – which his previous literature searches had led him to believe would be the strategy-making process in the Machine Bureaucracy – served only to operationalize strategy; it did not create it. Moreover, he argues, the planning mode may actually inhibit the creativity necessary for strategy-making. This is because it emphasizes analysis at the expense of that synthesis of thought needed for concept attainment: the essential basis for the formulation of a new strategy. So planning appears to encourage extensions of, or marginal changes to, existing strategies; or else the copying of those adopted by other organizations.

Strategically speaking, all goes well with the Machine Bureaucracy as long as its environment remains stable. But environments change; and when these changes become frequent, and increasingly non-routine, managers at the apex become overloaded since there is an organizational propensity to pass whatever is non-routine up the hierarchy to them. The resulting bottleneck causes the requisite decisions to be made quickly, perhaps using incomplete information.

Theoretically, the quality of that information should be assured by the existence, within the Machine Bureaucracy, of a Management Information System (MIS). However, Mintzberg considers that the typical MIS tends to suffer from a number of defects. For instance:

- Information passes through many levels on the way up – so losses occur.
- Not all the losses happen naturally. There are intentional distortions. 'Good news gets highlighted and bad news blocked.'
- The MIS emphasizes hard (that is, quantitative), aggregated data. But, arguably, this is not as useful, for strategic decisions, as 'soft, specific information'.
- The sheer mechanics of the MIS (data gathering, report writing, report assimilation) cause delays which can be crucial at times of swift environmental change.

So, by the time the MIS delivers its messages to the strategic apex, they are often too bland to be relied on.

The real culprit, in Mintzberg's eyes, is the dichotomy between strategy formulation and implementation. The justification for it rests upon two assumptions: (1) the formulator's information is complete, or at least as good as that available to the implementor; and (2) the situation is sufficiently stable or predictable to obviate the need for strategy re-formulation during implementation. If either condition is not met, the dichotomy collapses, and formulation and implementation proceed concurrently – 'in an adaptive rather than a planning mode'.

Mintzberg draws two conclusions from this part of the discussion:

1. 'Strategies must be formulated outside the machine bureaucratic structure if they are to be realistic.'
2. 'The dichotomy ... ceases to have any relevance in times of unpredictable change.'

Given this inherent incapacity to develop radically new strategies, how does the Machine Bureaucracy change to meet a changing world? Mintzberg's answer, again based on his findings, is: revolution. He pictures a leader coming into office with a new 'vision': someone strong enough to suspend established procedures, ignore staff planners, and gather enough power to him/herself to enable that vision to be realized. In effect, the Machine Bureaucracy temporarily becomes a Simple Structure; and the mode alters from planning to entrepreneurial.

There is, however, a snag – for the new leader. The Machine Bureaucracy cannot tolerate such autocratic management for long. Once the necessary changes have been made, it 'is likely to spit out its entrepreneur'.

The **Divisionalized Form** is described by Mintzberg as 'not so much an integrated organization as a set of quasi-autonomous units coupled together by a central administrative structure' – with, generally speaking, the former being called divisions, and the latter, headquarters. It is widely used. The vast majority of the 'Fortune 500' have this form, or a variant of it; and it is to be found outside the US private sector in higher education (multiversities), and health care (groups of specialized hospitals), as well as in so-called planned economies – where the equivalents of divisions are state enterprises, and government ministries are the headquarters.

The divisions are created to serve particular markets, and then given control of the operating functions needed to serve them. Mintzberg's Typical Organigram for a Divisionalized Manufacturing Firm is set out in Fig. 11.1.

Since each division's powers are confined to decisions over its own operations, this seemingly pronounced decentralization 'is highly circumscribed – not necessarily more than ... delegation

Fig. 11.1

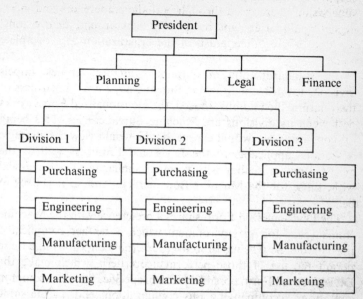

from the few managers at headquarters to the few more managers who run the divisions'. In the Divisionalized Form, therefore, decentralization is of the 'parallel, limited vertical variety'. And, sometimes, the divisions themselves can be 'rather centralized': when, that is, their managers have such a measure of power that further decentralization down the chain of authority (vertical), or to staff specialists and operators (horizontal), is precluded.

Headquarters generally monitors divisional performance, after the fact, in quantitative terms: e.g. measures of profit, sales growth, and return on investment. To this 'prime co-ordinating mechanism' (the standardization of outputs) is added those of 'the standardization of skills' and 'direct supervision' – though their role is more limited because divisional heads are mini-general managers. Training (to standardize management skills) and indoctrination are used to ensure that they give priority to corporate rather than their own divisional goals, while direct supervision is exercised through periodic conferences and meetings at headquarters, and by rotating them around the divisions, so as to develop their grasp of the organization as a complete whole.

The standardization of outputs, Mintzberg argues, impels divisions towards the Machine Bureaucracy form – regardless of their natural inclinations. Indeed, the Divisionalized Form works best when its divisions are Machine Bureaucracies. This being his conclusion, we would expect that he would view the strategic conditions applicable to the Divisional Form, as well as the mechanisms for dealing with them, as similar to, if not identical with, those for the Machine Bureaucracy. And so it proves to be.

The Divisionalized Form shares a preference with the Machine Bureaucracy for an environment which is neither complicated nor volatile, he tells us. Moreover, external conditions like these permit the use of those performance criteria which make the Divisionalized Form possible. He then specifies the most common conditions accompanying this configuration, and, at the same time, demonstrates the relationship between it and the Machine Bureaucracy with the statement: 'The Divisionalized Form is the structural response to a Machine Bureaucracy, operating in a simple, stable environment (typically without huge economies of scale), that has diversified its product or service lines horizontally.'

The principal co-ordinating mechanism of the **Professional Bureaucracy** is the standardization of skills – since it is the one which 'allows for standardization and decentralization at the same time'. Both of these are needed in organizations such as universities, general hospitals, accountancy firms, welfare agencies, and craft production companies, where 'the operating work is stable, leading to "predetermined or predictable" . . . behaviour'; but which is at the same time complex, 'and so must be controlled directly by the operators who do it'.

In these professional bureaucracies the operating core makes up by far the largest part of the organization. It consists of specialists whose control over their own tasks means that they work with a degree of independence from their colleagues, but closely with their clients.

Their training and indoctrination are complicated. Initially, they receive special training over a number of years in a university or special institution. Typically, this is followed by a long period of on-the-job training (e.g. as an articled pupil), during which they learn to apply their formal knowledge, perfect their skills – while being supervised by members of their profession, and finish their indoctrination. But even after they have qualified, they continue to add to their knowledge and skills by reading, attending conferences, and perhaps going once again to an institution for formal retraining. And all this, Mintzberg asserts, 'is geared to one goal – the internalization of standards that serve the client and co-ordinate the professional work'.

The 'source of standardization' distinguishes the machine from the professional bureaucracy. The former structure generates its own (output) standards; while the latter acquires them (skills) from outside. A consequence is that the Machine Bureaucracy relies upon the power of office, while the Professional Bureaucracy emphasizes the power of expertise.

The Professional Bureaucracy is, thus, highly decentralized. It is also, at least within its large operating core, democratic. The latter characteristic, together with the degree of operator autonomy it accords those same professional staff, makes it 'unique among the five configurations', Mintzberg believes, 'in answering two of the paramount needs of contemporary men and women'. However, these very characteristics of democracy and autonomy bring with them major problems. For, when the time comes to change, their combined effects constitute a formidable resistance to the process of innovation. (The consequences of this diffusion of power provide a stark contrast with the Machine Bureaucracy, where a minority – the managers at the apex – can impose what it considers to be unavoidable change upon the rest of the hierarchy.)

Being geared to stable environments, Mintzberg argues, all bureaucracies are performance structures, not 'problem-solving ones designed to create new programmes for needs that have never before been encountered'. Moreover, the habitual mode of thinking in the Professional Bureaucracy is *convergent*: 'the deductive reasoning of the professional who sees the specific situation in terms of the general concept'. Given instability in the environment, however, when innovative problem-solving is called for, there is a need for inductive reasoning: 'the inference of new general concepts ... from particular experiences' But since this type of thinking is *divergent* – breaking away from old routines or standards – it conflicts with everything the Professional Bureaucracy is organized to do. So when members campaign for some entrepreneurial innovation, they can inevitably expect political strife accompanied by intrigue and manoeuvring.

By way of summary, Mintzberg asserts that all the above configurations are incapable of what he terms sophisticated innovation: that is, the variety of innovation which occurs in difficult-to-understand environments. To be sure, the Simple Structure can innovate: but only simply. And, as we have just seen, the bureaucracies are performance, not problem-solving structures – 'although the Divisionalized Form resolves the problem of strategic inflexibility in the Machine Bureaucracy' When sophisticated innovation is necessary (in, for example, a avant-garde film company, a space agency, or an integrated petrochemicals company), that is, when experts with various kinds of expertise have to be fused into *ad hoc* project teams, fifth, and very different, configuration is required. This – borrowing from Alvin Toffler – Mintzberg calls the Adhocracy.

The **Adhocracy** is highly organic in structure. There is 'little formalization of behaviour; high horizontal job specialization based on formal training; a tendency ... to deploy [specialists in small, market-based teams to do their work; a reliance on the liaison devices to encourage mutual adjustment, the key coordinating mechanism, within and between these teams; and selective decentralization to and within these teams, which . involve various mixtures of line managers and staff and operating experts'. The configuration, therefore, runs counter to most of the 'principles of management' – and particularly that of 'unity of command'.

Mintzberg distinguishes between operating and administr

ive adhocracies. The first works on behalf of its clients – as in
the case of a creative advertising agency. The second serves
self. Their two *raisons d'être* determine different relationships
between the administrative and operating aspects of the organiza-
ion. But in neither, paradoxically, do the managers at the
strategic apex spend much of their time on strategy-making.
Rather, they spend it on conflicts over strategic options,
and other disturbances which occur throughout these fluid
structures.

Mintzberg's thoughts on how Adhocracy-like organizations
o about making their strategies turned first to his earlier
terature searches. These indicated that the term 'adaptive'
might be most appropriate for concerns with no clear goals, and
where power is divided among members of a complex coalition.
Such organizations 'were characterized as reacting to existing
problems rather than searching for new opportunities, and . . .
inclined to make decisions that are disjointed, taken in serial,
incremental steps'. His empirical work with his McGill colleagues
appears to confirm this description in general terms, though not
all of its particulars.

Many adhocracies, it was found, fight shy of decisions which
commit resources, or set patterns, for the long term. This is
largely because they have to respond *continuously* to complex
environments they cannot predict. Instead of general product-
market investments, 'they tend to make marginal decisions closer
o their actions – how to serve *this* customer, how to adapt *that*
product'. Mintzberg concludes that the strategy-making process
s, therefore, best thought of as strategy *formation* because
strategy is formed implicitly by a stream of discrete decisions,
instead of being formulated consciously by individuals. Action
planning, therefore, cannot be extensively depended on. Indeed,
any process that separates conception from action – planning
from execution, formalization from implementation – impedes
the flexibility of the organization to respond creatively to its
dynamic environment.'

But is the Adhocracy, with its continuous and decentralized
response to the environment, merely reacting to problems rather
than proactively seeking opportunities? The McGill studies

suggest that it does both: attempting to read the environment so as to find out where to go next; but doing so in order to offer new products and/or services to that environment. An approach to strategy-making which Mintzberg calls *opportunistic reaction*.

Reminding us that he has designated the strategists of the Simple Structure and the Machine Bureaucracy, respectively concept attainers and planners, Mintzberg describes their adhocratic equivalents as *pattern recognizers*. Accepting, as an umbrella, some broad general guidelines as to corporate intent, they look for a specific strategy (or pattern) emanating from the environment (their clients). Strategies deemed inappropriate may then be discouraged; but those which are considered emerging may be accommodated by changes to the umbrella. In which case, we have the organizational paradox of a leadership changing its intentions to accord with performance. But, as Mintzberg then says, that 'can be the key to successful strategy-making in the Adhocracy'.

Bibliography

H. Mintzberg, James Brian Quinn, and Robert M. James, *The Strategy Process – Concepts, Contexts and Cases*, Prentice Hall, 1988.

12

Richard P. Rumelt

—

is said that when Johannes Kepler, the outstanding Swedish
tronomer, was asked how it was that he had seen so far, he
plied – referring to Copernicus and Galileo – that he had
ood on the shoulders of giants. Something similar can be said
 Richard Rumelt. Taking his perspective (the relationship
tween strategy and structure) from A. D. Chandler Jr, he
ant on the work of B. R. Scott, L. Wrigley, and – to a lesser
tent – M. S. Salter, in a study which, by developing their
sights and adding clarity and precision, set the tone as well as
e standards for most of the later scholarship in this particular
ld.

This study, *Strategy, Structure and Economic Performance*, is
t just a model exercise in methodology. Published at a time
986) when the business world on both sides of the Atlantic
as hell-bent on conglomerate diversification, it was the first
search-based work to challenge the economic justification for
is particular strategic move. And it brought forth an epigram,
grettably less often quoted than Chandler's 'structure follows
rategy' but – in its own way – equally significant: 'structure
so follows fashion'.

The subject of the book, Rumelt tells us, is the 'interrelation-
ip of diversification, organizational structure, and economic
rformance in large American industrial corporations'. (Its
nitation to the US is important to keep in mind, since some of
e study's findings are not borne out elsewhere.) His initial task
 to define the terms he proposes to use. He follows Chandler
actly over 'strategy': 'the determination of the basic long-term
als and objectives of an enterprise, and the adoption of

courses of action and the allocation of resources necessary f
carrying out these goals'. But, interestingly, Chandler's definiti
of 'structure' is not mentioned. Incorporating some of the ide
in Harvard's recently formulated 'concept of corporate strateg
Rumelt defines a *diversification move* as 'any entry into a ne
product-market activity that requires or implies an appreciab
increase in the available managerial competence within the firm
It is a definition which, as Rumelt himself points out, 'identifi
diversification in terms of the degree to which a new produc
market activity taxes the ability of the firm's *management*
together with the administrative structure it has created'. B
since it only covers a single product-market addition, he needs
for the purpose of inter-firm comparisons – a definition of
diversification strategy. And this, combining Chandler a
Andrews, he specifies as: '1. the firm's commitment to diversi
per se; together with 2. the strengths, skills or purposes that sp
this diversity, demonstrated by the way new activities are relat
to old activities.'

To develop suitable categories of diversification, Rum
began by adopting Wrigley's system. This classifies firms in
four categories which, simply described, are:

1. Single Product – firms which had not diversified.
2. Dominant Product – primarily single product firms, b
   diversified to a minor degree (i.e. with more than 70 per ce
   of total sales coming from the single product area).
3. Related Product – firms which had diversified into ne
   product areas which shared some market or technologic
   features with existing ones.
4. Unrelated Product – firms which had diversified, usually
   acquisition, into areas sharing no such common features.

In (2) above, the 70 per cent figure (normally expressed in t
form 0.7) is an example of *the specialization ratio* (SR). It w
discovered by Wrigley when he was examining the usefulness
establishing the degree of a firm's diversification by calculati
the proportion of its overall sales stemming from its large
product area in any one year. As he has put it, firms 'tend
either to diversify by a small amount in relation to total outpu

or go the whole way'; and, of all the possible benchmarks, the 70 per cent point commended itself as being the most realistic. He employed it – as can be inferred from his classification – to discriminate between Dominant Product firms and those with an SR of less than 0.7 (i.e. both Related and Unrelated Product firms).

Rumelt attempted to verify Wrigley's 0.7 finding, using the data from his own study. He ran into difficulties of precise comparison, but could advance no cogent reason for preferring another SR. And though he modified the definition of the specialization ratio (as we shall see), he retained it to measure the first component of his diversification strategy concept: 'the firm's commitment to diversity *per se*'.

As Rumelt's investigations proceeded, it became apparent that Wrigley's definitions ought to be made more precise (if replication by other researchers was to be facilitated); and that subtler distinctions (notably by way of subcategories) would have to be introduced to accommodate firms otherwise falling into several of the original categories, or – by virtue of being vertically integrated – proving equally difficult to classify. Moreover, he came to realize that Wrigley had used the term 'product' more broadly than is usual. He, therefore, replaced it with 'business' – so that the category titles changed from Single Product to Single Business, Dominant Product to Dominant Business; and so on.

Underlying Wrigley's system, he considers, is the notion that it is conceptually possible to anatomize a multidivisional company into businesses which can be *managed* independently of one another, and, therefore, could be described as 'discrete'. What Rumelt found, however, is that one firm's discrete business could well be an inseparable part of a larger business in another's; so it was impossible to specify what made for discreteness generally, on that basis. His solution was to introduce the concept of *strategic independence* as the way of defining a discrete business. A business, or product-market activity, was discrete if you could make basic changes to its nature or scope without either running into constraints imposed upon it by other businesses within the firm, or materially affecting their operation or strategic direction.

The application of this new definition to Wrigley's original Unrelated and Related classifications recategorized a number of firms. And this revealed, in its turn, difficulties in defining the archetypal Unrelated Business firm. To deal with them, Rumelt added another ratio, *the related ratio* (RR), which measured the proportion of a firm's sales engendered by its largest group of related businesses. Here again the 0.7 figure was chosen: this time as the demarcation point between Related (70 per cent and more) and Unrelated firms. Rumelt tells us, 'it seemed to match fairly well the judgements expressed by informed observers'. And it had the additional justification – since it was identical with the SR – that no firm which had already qualified as a Dominant could also qualify as an Unrelated on the basis of its RR.

Rumelt's closer examination of the Related group showed that two other distinctions should be made. There were those firms which, as he puts it, 'had stayed relatively close to home'. These he termed *Related-Constrained*. And there were those which had steadily added businesses to the point when the newer activities 'considered by themselves, were virtually unrelated'. This type of firm he called *Related-Linked*.

He applied the same distinctions to the Dominant Business category, naming the resulting subdivisions *Dominant-Constrained* and *Dominant-Linked*. These distinctions, of course, apply to the 30 per cent or less of the firm's revenues un accounted for after the firm had qualified as a Dominant via the 0.7 SR. As does the one he created to accommodate firms where more of those revenues come from product-market activities unrelated to businesses which are themselves related, but not included in, the largest single (i.e. Dominant) business. This he termed: *Dominant-Unrelated*.

Vertically integrated firms posed special problems for Rumelt since they did not readily fit any of his existing definitions of Single, Dominant or Related businesses – yet he was reluctant to increase further the already expanded number of categories. Repeatedly, he found difficulty in answering two questions:

1. When is a by-product a separate business, or merely part of an existing one?

2. How do you determine whether a firm, which has integrated forward into a wide variety of manufacturing activities, is diversified or not?

Eventually, he concluded that he would have to adopt a compromise solution based upon a third ratio: *the vertical ratio* (VR). This he defined as 'the proportion of the firm's revenues that arise from all by-products, intermediate products, and end products of a vertically integrated sequence of processing activities', in any given year. By combining the VR with the other two ratios in various ways, he classified vertically integrated firms as:

Single Business:	if 95 per cent or more of their sales came from single end-product activities.
Dominant-Vertical:	if their SR was less than 0.95, and their VR equal to, or greater than, 0.7.
Related Business:	if their VR was less than 0.7, and their RR equal to, or greater than, 0.7.
Unrelated Business:	if both their VR and RR were less than 0.7.

Finally, Rumelt turns his attention to the conglomerate firm. By his definition, conglomerates are, of course, Unrelated Businesses. However, he argues, not all Unrelated Businesses are conglomerates since – and here he adopts the position of H. H. Lynch's 1971 study – the latter are essentially acquisitive. He, therefore, uses this characteristic to distinguish between two subclasses of the Unrelated Business category: the *Acquisitive Conglomerate*, which grows by deliberately adding unrelated businesses – financing its purchases by issuing new equity; and the rest, to which he gives the self-explanatory title *Unrelated-Passive*.

Rumelt's nine-fold categorization, therefore, comes to this:

1. Single Business
2. Dominant Business
   (a) Dominant-Vertical
   (b) Dominant-Constrained

    (c) Dominant-Linked
    (d) Dominant-Unrelated
3. Related Business
    (a) Related-Constrained
    (b) Related-Linked
4. Unrelated Business
    (a) Unrelated-Passive
    (b) Acquisitive Conglomerate

Turning to the issue of organizational structure, Rumelt begins
by observing that there is virtually no limit to the number of
possible structures. He therefore proposes to reduce that complexity by adopting a 'top-down' perspective so as to concentrate on
the *major* options open to top management, 'and their potential
impact on the general management task'. This is a task which,
in his eyes, consists of managing a complete economic unit – no
matter how described – that has the authority and resources to
act as an independent force in the market place. (He thus
deliberately excludes those managers who may be powerfully
enough placed to manage a firm's world-wide marketing or
manufacturing, on the ground that their responsibility is purely
functional.)

He then draws, principally, upon the work of Chandler, Scott
and Salter to describe and comment upon four structural types:
(1) the 'one-man show'; (2) the functional; (3) the multidivisional;
and (4) the geographic-division. Rejecting the first as lying
outside the scope of his research, he argues that the work of his
chosen authorities offers us an assurance that the remaining
three possess such different properties that they represent distinct
categories of organization. To these Rumelt adds two more: (5)
the holding company; and, (6) the functional-with-subsidiaries –
a hybrid, consisting of a functional structure with one or more
product divisions, but *without* the orthodox multidivisional
headquarters office – which he can claim to have discovered
in the course of his research. And, of this pair, he says that –
though there is no supporting evidence – 'it is expected that
these categories also represent organizational patterns that are
significantly different in kind'.

Rumelt's gross data base was the 'Fortune 500' for the years 1959 and 1969, supplemented by material from the 1949 US Federal Trade Commission report which was adjusted to cohere with the Fortune format. Wrigley's 1967 data, suitably corrected for changes between then and 1969, provided the foundation for the final year. Independent random samples of 100 firms for each of the designated years were then produced; three were dropped for lack of appropriate information, to leave sample sizes of 100, 100, and 97; and the total number of firms studied was 246.

The concluding chapter of the book is divided between Findings and Implications. Of these, probably the latter are more important to today's theorists and practitioners, since a number of Rumelt's discoveries about the 1949–69 period have become the historical bedrock upon which much of our current conventional wisdom is founded. Even so, some of his Findings are of abiding interest.

The creation of what may have seemed an over-elaborated categorization of diversification is vindicated on two grounds:

1. That simpler methods of classifying diversity would not have revealed the differences in financial results which enabled Rumelt to state and hypothesize why, for example: (i) the Dominant-Constrained and Related-Constrained groups outperformed all the others; (ii) Acquisitive Conglomerates only achieved above average returns on capital by using gearing (i.e. leverage), while outperforming Unrelated-Passive firms by every economic measure; (iii) Dominant-Verticals were among the worst performers of all.
2. That, in explaining performance differences, overall diversity was less important than the way firms related new businesses to current ones.

It became evident, during the research, that the adoption of the multidivisional form in the 1960s came about not because of strategy-structure stresses – similar to those documented by Chandler, but because it had become so well known. (Hence Rumelt's epigram, quoted at the beginning of this piece.)

In his Implications, Rumelt turns to the issue of general

management skills. With the sweeping change towards the product-division structure in large US corporations has come not only a greater need for general managers, but increasingly, he argues, the necessity for these generalists to be better trained and more effectively employed. Early on, the superiority of the organizational form itself conferred a competitive advantage on the restructuring firm. Its now almost universal adoption means that the form must be fully exploited; and he believes that two of the ways this might be done would be with 'improved systems of strategic review', and formal intervention systems for dealing with crises in divisional operations.

The superior financial performance of Dominant-Constrained (D-C) and Related-Constrained (R-C) firms might tempt us into believing that these strategies are to be preferred to all other types of diversification. This would be a mistake, Rumelt warns us. All he could show was a statistical association (i.e. not a true causal connection) between strategy and performance. *However*, it is the case that 'the intensive cultivation of a single field', on average, has proved to be more successful than 'bold moves into uncharted waters'.

These same categories had markedly the most favourable 'risk premium ratios'. (RPR is, of course, the ratio of variability in earnings to growth rates in earnings.) Rumelt employs this finding to mount an argument which 'should be of interest to managers who expect product-market diversification to protect their firms from financial instability'. Its essential components are:

1. There were no significant differences in earnings variability among the nine categories.
2. The differences in RPR must, therefore, relate to earning growth: the critical factor being 'the firm's *strategy of expansion*'.
3. The RPRs for the other seven categories were not only poorer than those for D-C and R-C, they were 'approximately equivalent' to each other.
4. 'The implication' of this is that the little or great diversity of the seven is inferior to the 'carefully controlled' form of

diversification characteristic of both D-C and R-C, in reducing earnings fluctuation.

5. Thus, any firm which 'seeks stability through diversification into tenuously related areas is merely *averaging* risks', which at most 'reduce[s] uncertainty to the level experienced by the economy as a whole'.

Rumelt's practical explanation for this phenomenon, while not having the logical force of the argument establishing it, is nevertheless persuasive. Constrained firms, he tells us, address themselves to satisfying *functional needs*, such as convenience foods or business-information processing. Products meeting those 'fairly constant' needs will lose their appeal as tastes change, or as the needs themselves become modified. By being sensitive to these developing mismatches between product and market, the firm can search its product line for weak points, and innovate accordingly.

Finally, Rumelt ventures overseas. He believes that his findings connected with the Dominant-Vertical firm should be of interest to European, and particularly French, planners. Their typical response to US competition is to assume that what is needed is larger, more financially powerful, organizations. Sheer size may be of help, he concedes. But if the result is the creation of Dominant-Vertical or Unrelated-Passive companies, with perhaps little by way of domestic competition, then their national economies will forgo the stimuli necessary for product-market innovation and the development of generalist skills essential for success in today's world.

And Afterwards . . .

In the sixteen years that have passed since Rumelt's work was published, much has changed in our world; so one could be forgiven for wondering how relevant are his findings today. In 1982 he extended his original study to include the period 1970–74. Yet later, in 1986, he reflected further – on both pieces of work – in the preface to the latest edition of the book. And, of course, other scholars have gone over the same ground.

To be sure, there have been adjustments. In his second study, for example, Rumelt merged the Dominant-Linked and Dominant-Unrelated into a new sub-group: the Dominant-Linked-Unrelated; and he ceased to distinguish between the two different types of Unrelated Business. He thus reduced his original nine categories to seven. Even so, he was able to report that his system of classification had endured surprisingly well.

The later work, as Rumelt puts it, 'corroborated the original associations'. In particular, 'the Dominant-Vertical and Unrelated Business categories show levels of profitability significantly below those of the other categories'. And: 'As before, the Related-Constrained group is the most profitable.' However, the high return-on-capital performance of the last group proved to be 'an industry effect': their results being on a par with other types of firm in the same industries.

Yet significant as these results are, it is one of his more general comments – arising almost incidentally out of his long acquaintance with the subject – which seems most compellingly informative. When he began his work, in 1972, he followed Chandler in seeing 'the decentralized product-division structure as the solution to the problem of managing diversity'. By 1986, however, he had become 'increasingly sensitive to the unanticipated side effects of this structure: the financial orientation it imposes on general management; the way planning systems in diversified firms drive out subtlety; and the lure of exciting large-scale acquisitions and mergers to managers suffering the ennui of a move from an operating job to a headquarters position'.

Bibliography

Richard P. Rumelt, *Strategy, Structure and Economic Performance*, Harvard Business School Press, 1986.

13

Malcolm S. Salter and
Wolf A. Weinhold

—

Malcolm Salter has for long been a distinguished member of faculty at Harvard. He is also on the faculty of the John F. Kennedy School of Government; and he presides over the activities of an international strategy consulting firm: Mars and Co. Wolf Weinhold now runs his own private investment company, with offices in Boston and Sarasota, and consults on the application of industry economics to the development of corporate strategy. This special competence arose from an extended period of research at Harvard, and complemented Salter's work in corporate strategy, organization, and governance. As a result, they jointly published a number of papers dealing with mergers and takeovers, and the more comprehensive work considered here: *Diversification Through Acquisition.*

What brought about this particular venture, they tell us, was the failure of many initiatives in diversification to live up to the expectations – in terms of shareholder benefits – of a growing number of informed individuals in the US. The returns on capital for many – though not all – multibusiness companies had fallen behind that of the economy as a whole. Yet diversification through acquisition remained popular. This increasing concern, and the apparent risks of the strategy, had therefore prompted them to review and synthesize 'the current state of thought about diversifying acquisitions'.

In the period since they wrote (1979), little has changed. Their study is, consequently, as relevant today as it was then – on both sides of the Atlantic.

Since 'diversification' is used almost indiscriminately, they early set about its semantics. Confining it to product-market applications, they note that there are difficulties associated with defining both products and markets – especially the former. Their way out of the inherent ambiguities is 'to accent the heterogeneity of markets as well as products in the definition'. They argue that two criteria can be employed to define market heterogeneity:

1. If demand for Product A, the price of which remains constant, rises more or less proportionately with increases in the price of Product B, then this high cross-elasticity of demand 'means that the two products are close substitutes [for each other] and therefore belong to the same market'. (Conversely, separate markets would be defined by low elasticity of demand, or low substitutability.)

2. If one can rapidly shift resources from the manufacture of one product to the manufacture of others, then 'the products *are most likely* very similar'. (The emphasis has been added.)

Two consequences flow from their argument. First: 'a company's degree of diversification increases as the heterogeneity of the markets served . . . increases'. And second: product heterogeneity 'is distinct from diversification if it involves only minor differences of essentially the same product'.

This discussion owes much to the work of M. Gort, which is consistent with the concept of relatedness devised by R. P. Rumelt,[1] and whose three basic categories (dominant business, related business, and unrelated business) Salter and Weinhold adopt. As our authors say of the two researchers, their focus on the technological properties and market characteristics of product or business. The more similar these are – and 'market characteristics' include the marketing system as well as the market itself – the more related businesses can be said to be.

However, in practice, Salter and Weinhold contend, 'relatedness has as much to do with required management skills as does with product market characteristics'. Assuming that these

kills and business experience are critical to success, then diversi-
cation strategies should be classified in accordance with them.
Business experience, they argue, can be best defined in product
market portfolio terms; while skills divide broadly into those of
general management, and functional activities (i.e. R & D,
production and manufacturing, marketing and distribution).

They then argue that, using these criteria, one can discriminate
among types of diversification with some ease.

An **unrelated diversifier** (whether an actively managed conglomerate or a more passively managed holding company) seeks
growth in product markets with dissimilar key success factors:
and, consequently, looks for few, if any, functional skill transfers
across its businesses.

Related diversifiers, on the other hand, diversify on the basis
of their functional activities or product market skills. There are
two subsets to this strategy:

. **Related-supplementary diversification** (R-SD) – which
  occurs when a company expands by entering product markets
  that call for functional skills identical to those it already
  possesses.
. **Related-complementary diversification** (R-CD) – which
  occurs when a company adds key functional activities and
  skills to those it already has, but does not substantially
  change its final product market.

The 'purest forms' of R-SD and R-CD are, respectively, horizontal diversification (e.g. when a company with blast furnaces
acquires another in a different region), and vertical integration (e.g. when a food processor moves downstream into food
wholesaling).

Salter and Weinhold illustrate the distinction with Fig. 13.1.
In using it, they caution us not to treat the scales of the axes
as absolute – 'they merely reflect the relative direction of a
diversification alternative'. And more generally, we are warned
not 'to overdraw distinctions between related and unrelated
diversification'.

The second caveat is entered because they have in mind the
possibility of a company acquiring a business dissimilar to an

Fig. 13.1

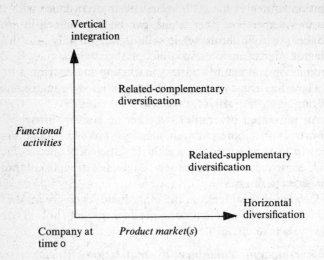

existing business in terms of marketing and technology (and therefore, strictly unrelated), but similar to it by virtue of it skills – strategic, organizational, and operating. In such a case the acquisition *may be viewed by management*[2] as related. The therefore accept that the distinction they want to make (betwee related and unrelated diversification) is not always perfectl clear-cut.

They emphasize the same point in discussing synergy,[3] whic 'related diversification often leads to'. Although, in theory, ther is a potential for synergy between businesses which are relate practising managers know how difficult it is to realize tha potential. Moreover, should they fail, administering a group o related businesses will resemble the management of a conglomer

2. Management perceptions as to what constitute related or unrelated acquis tions play an important part in Salter and Weinhold's conclusions.
3. Which is 'said to exist when the combined return on a company's resources greater than the sum of its parts'.

ate. Therefore, distinguishing between related and unrelated diversification is full of subtlety, and requires great care.

With these definitions, distinctions and warnings in place, Salter and Weinhold turn to establishing a framework for strategic and economic analysis.

The first difficult task which companies encounter when they become interested in diversification through acquisiton is to determine what precisely are their objectives. Typically, this task compels managers to consider how related or unrelated their businesses should be, and 'how economic values can be created by various kinds of diversifying acquisitions'.

Once the objectives have been formulated, three issues must be dealt with:

1. How to develop workable acquisition guidelines.
2. How to identify acquisition candidates with high potential, efficiently.
3. What kind of strategic and economic analysis should be engaged in to estimate the worth of such candidates to the acquirer.

The approach of each company to these issues will tend to be idiosyncratic. Even so, it is possible that many would benefit from using a framework 'based on recent extensions of capital market theory, planning models developed during the past decade, and more established strategic-planning practices': which is, of course, exactly what Salter and Weinhold intend to demonstrate.

The second and third of these framework components (which they term, respectively, **the product-market/portfolio model**, and **the strategy model**) are covered elsewhere in these pages.[4] As a consequence, only those of Salter and Weinhold's

4. Relative to the product-market/portfolio model, see especially **Bruce D. Henderson**, pages 72–80; **Robert D. Buzzell and Bradley T. Gale**, pages 59–71; and **Richard G. Hamermesh**, pages 120–130. Similarly, for the strategy model, see **Kenneth R. Andrews**, pages 5–14; **H. Igor Ansoff**, pages 15–33; and **Charles W. Hofer and Dan Schendel**, pages 216–229, in particular.

comments which are relevant to their own project will be touched upon here. The remaining component (**the risk/return model**), however, will be discussed in more detail.

They identify two important characteristics of the strategy model:

1. It is not descriptive of 'common policy-making behaviour': rather it is a 'normative approach to policy formulation that has been designed to fit the well-documented needs of general managers'.
2. In its basic form, it is most applicable to single-business firms or company divisions.

Being normative, it specifies the sequence to be followed in strategic decision-making; and it stresses consistency. Since its focus is on the relationship between the organization and the world about it, 'it maintains that consistency between a company's internal resources and its external opportunities is the primary determinant of success or failure'.

Yet, though it emphasizes strategy formulation, the model makes certain assumptions about what the objectives of a business should be; and that these ought to be multiple in number. A singular preoccupation with profit maximization,[5] for instance, is 'irrational' – perhaps endangering the survival of a business, by misdirecting its managers.

Even so, profitability is taken to be the ultimate test of a business's performance – measuring the soundness of its efforts, and constituting the 'risk premium' which covers the costs of its continued existence. While profit, itself, ensures future supplies of capital for growth and innovation.

With its stress on matching resources to opportunities (i.e. on strategic fit, and operating compatibility), the strategy model – at least the version promulgated by Andrews, according to

---

5. Salter and Weinhold contend that the concept of profit maximization – as used in the model – owes nothing to that of the economist. For here it 'suggests a minimum condition that must be met in order for managers to retain control over policy governing the use and allocation of corporate resources'.

Fig. 13.2

Industry attractiveness	Business position		
	High	Medium	Low
High	No diversification	R-CD	R-CD
Medium	R-SD	No diversification	R-CD
Low	R-SD	R-SD	No diversification

Key R-CD = Related-complementary diversification
R-SD = Related-supplementary diversification

alter and Weinhold – favours closely related diversification. This is because acquisition decisions are dealt with using 'essentially the same process as that by which general strategic options are evaluated and selected'. As they say, the model's 'underlying theory is both simple and intuitively appealing', in that it equates success with the development of distinctive competences or competitive advantages, together with an ability to anticipate market and technological trends. And since these conditions are better met where diversification is related rather than unrelated, the former is to be preferred.

It follows that, when a candidate for diversification by acquisition is being considered, the resource requirements of both the companies must be evaluated in the pursuit of strategic fit. However, in practice, it can be shown that identifying and assessing the strengths and weaknesses of even one's own enterprise are difficult tasks, and subject to much disagreement.

Salter and Weinhold's particular contribution to resolving this problem is the 'Related Diversification Grid', set out in Fig. 13.2.

Their claims for it are circumspect. Using the grid 'requires a healthy dose of judgement *since there is no simple, useful system for assessing relative business position or relative industry attractiveness*'. (The emphasis has been added.) 'Nevertheless,' they continue, 'the grid does suggest some crude propositions that can channel thinking along the lines of the strategy model.'

They exemplify the types of proposition (or 'guideline') the have in mind in this manner:

1. No diversification

(i) Where a company is strongly placed in an attractiv industry (i.e. High BP/High IA), diversification is usuall unnecessary on purely economic grounds.

(ii) Medium BP/Medium IA indicates a company whic ought to develop its existing skills and improve its positio before contemplating diversification.

(iii) A Low BP/Low IA company's condition is unlikely t enable it to afford diversification, or attract merger part ners.

2. Related-complementary diversification

(i) Competing in a highly attractive industry with averag skills (Medium BP/High IA), or below-average skills (Lo BP/High IA), a company can be helped by R-CD to acquir functional skills necessary to improve its business position i that industry.

(ii) Even Low BP/Medium IA companies, that is weak one in industries of average attractiveness, can similarly benef from R-CD.

3. Related-supplementary diversification

(i) Both High BP/Medium IA and High BP/Low IA com panies can benefit, in terms of growth and profitability, fro 'committing existing functional skills and resources to nev more attractive markets'.

(ii) And Medium BP/Low IA companies – 'where that marke *has become* relatively unattractive' – can benefit in the sam way. [Emphasis added.]

What Salter and Weinhold call 'the message' of the strateg model is that managers are not in a position to think about the company's future needs until they have assessed each of i functional area strengths and weaknesses. Additionally, th model suggests that the best approach to diversification is t start by determining which strengths are transferable to othe product-markets and what weaknesses need to be correcte rather than 'by constructing measures of product-market attractiveness'.

Of the three celebrated product-market/portfolio models,[6] they concentrate upon the BCG[7] variant because it is easily used and the best known. Like the other two, it highlights the strengths of a firm's cluster of products or businesses; but, unlike them, it stresses the relationship between a business's cash flow and its 'market-share/market-growth characteristics'. Underlying it, they argue, are certain 'explicit assumptions about the behaviour of costs, prices, and profit margins in competitive markets' which are worth exploring since the prescriptive power of the model depends upon them. The first of these economic rules is 'that in a stable competitive marketplace, *prices will decrease as costs decrease*', in response to the experience curve effect. So, given constant margins, there will be a parallel decline in average industry costs and prices – the difference between them being equal to the margin percentage. This parallel relationship may not be evident in unstable markets when demand outruns supply, or prices have been set below average costs; but, eventually, it will re-emerge.

The second rule governing the behaviour of the model 'is that the average cost for an industry is greatly influenced by the costs of the dominant producer'. And this leads, in turn, to the third: 'profit margins are a function of sustained market share'.

But, underlying even these assumptions, Salter and Weinhold contend, 'is the notion that experience curve effects do drive business decision making'. Considerable support for this comes from microeconomic theory; though, they warn us, factors external to the firm, such as product obsolescence, technological innovation, and government intervention, may render the benefits of experience unobtainable.

Given these three assumptions, and the notion underlying them, what are the implications of the BCG variant for the diversification decision?

6. The others being the PIMS and the McKinsey/GE models.
7. The Boston Consulting Group.

All product-market/portfolio models aim to assist management in making discriminative investment decisions among those businesses which constitute the company's portfolio. The focus of the BCG variant is on cash flows: that is, on cash generation and cash use. Generation is 'a function of accumulated experience best summarized through relative market share'. Cash use (or investment) is a function of market growth. It follows that merely to maintain an existing share in a growing market will require cash – for working capital and capacity expansion; while to increase one's share of a growing market will demand even more. But, where is the cash to come from? Taking on debt is not debarred; but ideally – Salter and Weinhold argue – a company should strive to balance its portfolio so that Cash Cows[8] provide funds to enable Question Marks[9] to become Stars.[10]

From a diversification standpoint, therefore, 'the key criterion [to be satisfied] is the fit of the target company's cashflow characteristics [current and expected] with those of the existing portfolio'.

To achieve a portfolio of balanced cash flows might seem to indicate broadly based or unrelated diversification. But 'further reflection on the concepts underlying the model' suggests to Salter and Weinhold that there is more to be said in favour of related diversification. This is because of the latency of what they call 'overlapping experience curves': that is, the transfer of accumulated experience between businesses.

As they put it: 'When distinct product markets have overlapping experience curves, exposure to each alters the markets' cost curves.' In other words, the industry's experience curve will change (in line with what constitutes *relevant* cumulative volume) as one business's costs in its own product market reflect the experience of another's in its – and conversely.

---

8. Cash Cows are businesses in low growth markets whose accumulated experience yields more cash than it requires.
9. Question Marks need cash to increase market share in rapidly growing markets to accumulate experience and make profits.
10. Stars have large shares of growing markets and are therefore highly profitable, but need little or no cash.

The product-market/portfolio model can therefore help with both related and unrelated diversification decisions. In the first case, when overlapping cost curves are to be found; and in the second, by seeking balanced cash flows.

The guidelines it provides for related diversification resemble – in scope and content – those of the strategy model. However, those for unrelated diversification 'greatly expand the scope of possible analysis'.[11] In neither case, though, does the portfolio model indicate how cash flows can be invested in business operations most effectively. Developing policies to that end are the purpose of the strategy model. So the two models can be seen as complementary, the strategy model's analyses being applied to those businesses identified as capable of generating cash, justifying investment, by the product-market/portfolio model. Where the portfolio model (and, by implication, the strategy model) have a shortcoming – according to Salter and Weinhold – is in the field of relative comparisons.[12] But this they see as the contribution of the risk/return model.

'An amalgam of related concepts drawn from contemporary financial economics', the risk/return model 'reflects the interests and concerns of investors rather than operating managers'. It is based on four propositions, according to Salter and Weinhold. These are:

Investors are compensated for bearing the risk of security by receiving a return from it: the return being commensurate with the risk.

Investors can alter their levels of risk and return by putting together a diversified portfolio of securities.

Risk is of two kinds: systematic (or market-related) risk – that is the risk associated with the market for securities as a whole; and, unsystematic (or security-specific) risk – that is,

Remembering Salter and Weinhold's views as to the bias of the strategy model in favour of related diversification.

An example they give of this type of difficulty is when the relative attractiveness of two businesses with similar product-market *and* cash flow characteristics has to be assessed.

the risk which is unique to any particular security. *Only the latter can be diversified away.*

4. The market in securities (or the capital market) prices/values a security or an investment portfolio according to the level of systematic risk involved.

The first of these calls for little explanation, we are told, because it merely states the underlying condition of all competitive markets. However, as it is used in the model, risk is defined as 'the variability of returns'. More specifically, that means an uncertainty attaching to the receipt, at a future date, of the initial investment and a return upon it. The investor is, therefore, concerned with the variability of his dividends or interest, and capital appreciation. The company, on the other hand, concerns itself with the variability of its 'free cash flow': which is the cash left, at the end of an accounting period, after the productivity of its assets has been assured by reinvestment.

The notions of risk and return greatly help with comparative investment analysis, Salter and Weinhold argue. And they enable us to pose two questions critical to 'most investment decisions taken in market economies': as to whether the expected rate of an investment is proportionate to its risk; and what additional return justifies taking on an additional unit of risk.

The essential precondition for the model's second assumption to prove true is met when an investor sells part of his holding in a single security in order to purchase one or more other securities whose risk/return relationships are not perfectly correlated with that of the original investment. The advantage he is looking for from such portfolio diversification is obtained, for example, when, overall, he can derive a greater return for the same risk or the same return for a lower risk, than he did with his original portfolio.

The third assumption is particularly important because it is the basis for 'a widely accepted theory of how individual securities and diversified portfolios are valued by the capital market'.

13. This refers to the calculation of systematic and unsystematic risk using familiar regression coefficients, Beta and Alpha.

incorporates the notion of a 'risk-free' asset: that is, a US Treasury Bill or UK 'gilt edged' security. This provides the measure ('the efficient frontier') which investors strive to reach by diversification. However, it is only approached when every security available in the market finds a place in the portfolio, with each investment proportional to the security's market value. At that point the portfolio's risk is the one which is common to all securities and thus cannot be diversified away: systematic risk.

Following directly from this conclusion is Salter and Weinhold's fourth model assumption: 'that since investors can diversify away unsystematic risk in their own portfolios, securities will yield a return commensurate with their systematic risk instead of their total risk'.[14]

The imperative of the risk/return model is, of course, that any candidate for diversification by acquisition must be evaluated from an investment standpoint. The key issue they identify as being 'the free cash flow and systematic risk of the company to be acquired, and its impact on the risk/return complexion of the acquiring company'. This not only provides a basis for comparing one candidate with another – more than that, the model gives managers a strategic insight of general as well as particular (e.g. diversification) applicability. This is because the relevant risk they have to assess is the volatility of an asset's cash flows relative to the cash flows of all other assets in the marketplace: that is, systematic risk.

Now, while the model argues for the management of systematic risk in order to enhance the company's market value, managers – quite understandably – devote most of their energies to dealing with company-specific (i.e. unsystematic) risk in the form of, for example, 'competitive retaliation, labour relations, or even bankruptcy'.

But how is one to manage systematic risk? Salter and Weinhold believe that the model suggests three guidelines.

14. Students of financial theory will recognize this as the basis for the Capital Asset Pricing Model.

1. Strategies should be developed 'aimed at generating fre
   cash flows that have as little relationship to the level o
   activity of the economy as possible'. Ideally, they shoul
   decouple the performance of the company from that of th
   economy.
2. Systematic risk is reduced 'by shifting value into the future
   and this can be done by strategies that:
   (i) Lengthen the time during which cash flows can be gener
   ated, or
   (ii) Improve the latter's growth rate.
3. Managers should remember that cash flow forecasts deeme
   to be reliable in the marketplace are less severely discounte
   and therefore have a higher value.

In the case of diversification through acquisition, the risk/retur
model offers more specific guidance. It stipulates that 'corpor
ate diversification' only creates values for the shareholde
when, *as the consequence of combining the skills and resource
of the two companies*, there is: (a) an increase in return, c
(b) a reduction in systematic risk, compared with 'portfoli
diversification' brought about by simple investment in the sam
companies.

Relative to each of these desirable outcomes, Salter and Weir
hold set out three strategic guidelines.

An increase in return can be obtained when:
1. *Related diversification* results in lower unit costs and im
   proved margins through the better utilization of skills an
   resources. (In product-market/portfolio terms, this occur
   when experience curves overlap.)
2. *Unrelated diversification* leads to more investment opportu
   ities within the company, and this enables more high-retur
   projects to be launched.
3. 'Aggressive financial management' makes better use of wor
   ing capital within the diversified company, and employ
   more debt than was possible before.

A reduction in systematic risk can be obtained when:

Related diversification increases margins relative to the business's fixed costs, and thus reduces the variability of its cash flows.

Through better asset selection and management, the company can achieve either a faster growing or a more stable free cash flow than is obtainable from 'a comparable portfolio of businesses'.

The degree of corporate diversification arrived at enables managers to adopt high risk business strategies – with their concomitant, large organizational and financial costs – in order to obtain (now, or later) low systematic risk.

considering these guidelines, Salter and Weinhold argue, anagers should perceive that the benefits of corporate diversification 'are much more limited in scope and magnitude' than had een generally accepted. Nor is such an acquisition to be judged lely in comparison with portfolio diversification. For only hen its discounted cash flow – once it is integrated into the quirer – is greater than the price paid for it (that is, its 'market lue plus tender premium plus transaction costs plus integration sts'), can value be said to have been created for the diversifier's areholders.

Each of the three models described above has in common a eoccupation with the creation, and maintenance, of value – nether value is seen from a manager's or an investor's stand-int. And this makes it possible to integrate them into one ialytical framework, Salter and Weinhold contend.

The 'two critical variables' which affect the assessment of lue in the eyes of the capital market are cash flow, and risk – measured by variability of return.

As we have seen, like the risk/return model, the product-arket/portfolio model is concerned with cash flow: or more curately, in the language of Salter and Weinhold, free cash w. On the face of it, the strategy model is concerned with ofit; and this would seem to set it apart from the other two. t, our authors argue, much has happened in the last twenty ars to destroy the old, straightforward correspondence be-een profit and the cash a business has for disposal once its bills are paid. Consequently, when using the strategy mode[l] analytical approach, managers now 'prefer to think in terms [of] cash flow rather than accounting profits'.

The thrust of the strategy model is either towards cost redu[c-] tion, or the premium-pricing that can result from the deployme[nt] of a distinctive competence (or competitive advantage). Eith[er] way, there will be greater cash flow. The model's perspectiv[e,] however, is that of the operating division or single busine[ss.] And this provides a basis for the product-market/portfolio mod[el] to build upon.

The latter's thrust is towards increasing cash flows by aggre[s-] sively investing in growing businesses so as to secure a domina[nt] industrial position, and, therefore, ultimately the lowest u[nit] costs. As the industry matures, the effects of accumulated expe[ri-] ence generate large free cash flows to be reinvested in oth[er] product-markets with high potential.

In the drive for increased cash flow, the models compleme[nt] each other – Salter and Weinhold contend – since both seek [to] exploit market opportunities, and obtain dominant competiti[ve] positions. Indeed, 'distinctive competence' and 'accumulated e[x-] perience' play equivalent parts in the achievement of mark[et] power. While the portfolio model says invest in market sha[re,] the strategy model shows how to invest most effectively. Wh[at] the portfolio model adds beneficially to the strategy model is [a] multi-business perspective: 'a portfolio of product-market oppo[r-] tunities, some growing and some dying'. And all will be well – [in] terms of market value – so long as new business investmen[ts] yield a greater return than the cost of investment funds: t[he] determination of which is the focal point of the risk/retu[rn] model.

Turning to Salter and Weinhold's second critical variab[le,] risk, we find Fig. 13.3, entitled 'Perspectives on Risk Suggest[ed] by the Three Models'.

Because each model addresses a different level of econom[ic] activity, they argue, each defines risk differently.

The strategy model – with its single-business (i.e. 'operati[ng] level') perspective – permits two approaches to risk assessme[nt:] the 'judgemental', and the 'forecasting'. The first describes t[he]

Fig. 13.3 Perspectives on Risk Suggested by the Three Models

	Level of analysis	Principal risk measure
trategy	Operating level	Total risk (environmental, managerial, financial)
roduct/market-portfolio	Corporate level	Business portfolio risk
isk/return	Capital market level	Market-related or systematic risk

ubjective judgement by its managers of their particular busi-
ess's variability of return; and the second, their ability to
redict – through budgeting and resource allocation – the busi-
ess's future financial performance. On the assumption that
hose businesses whose financial performance characteristics are
asiest to predict are the least risky, then risk can be measured
n the basis of the accuracy of budgets, the role of the general
nanager being to control variations in profitability by dealing
vith its underlying determinants.

Since the portfolio model assumes a corporate level of analy-
is, dealing with a cluster of products or businesses, risk is
efined 'as the predictability and stability of cash flows associ-
ted with a portfolio of businesses that has been assigned a
argeted (or expected) growth rate'.

And finally, as we have seen, the risk/return model 'adopts
he perspective of the rational investor operating in a reasonably
fficient market'. Here 'sophisticated statistical expression[s]'
an be employed to measure the volatility of past returns as
basis for assessing the risks attaching to current and future
ctivities.

Taken together, the three models thus provide an ascending
cale of economic analysis; while their measures of risk follow a
ational progression from the intuitive and subjective to 'a more
bjective, market-related concept'.

Not only do the models complement each other, however – as
he discussion of cash flow and risk, summarized above, indicates
they are closely related. All three:

1. 'Are useful in defining and measuring the attractiveness of future value.'
2. 'Treat return in an absolute sense, and risk in a relative sense.'
3. Are 'concerned with the difficult problem of managing future cash flows so that current market value can be maximized'.

Salter and Weinhold regard the last point as especially important. Each of the models, they tell us, is useful to the manager who wishes to reduce the impact of the unforeseen on the particular assets for which he is responsible. The key insight of the risk/return model is that he should focus on the relationship between the returns on those assets and returns for the economy as a whole. Also, and by implication, the model suggests that he should strive to increase his control over future returns and cash flows. Significantly, it is precisely with these objectives that the methodology and concepts of the other two models can help him.

The analytical framework Salter and Weinhold propose (that is, 'the power of the three models, taken as a complementary package of concepts'), is not just its utility in terms of assessing the benefits and costs of diversification by acquisition – it has a wider strategic application. It may challenge some common presumptions about such diversifications. But it also reinforces others which for long have been intuitively appealing to experienced businessmen – e.g. the conclusion of all three models that the related route is safer than the unrelated.

Bibliography

Malcolm S. Salter and Wolf A. Weinhold, *Diversification Through Acquisition: Strategies for Creating Economic Value*, The Free Press, 1979.

14

Oliver E. Williamson

—

Oliver Williamson's first degree was in engineering (at MIT), and his PhD was in industrial organization (at Carnegie-Mellon). He has lectured at the Universities of California (Berkeley), Pennsylvania, Warwick, Kyoto, and Yale – where he is currently Professor of Economics of Law and Organization. An energetic researcher and a prolific writer, he has still found it possible to fit into a crowded life service with the US Government (advising on antitrust issues), and with Mayor Lindsay of New York (in connection with cable TV franchising).

At the heart of Williamson's thinking is *transaction cost economics* (TCE), which he has described as 'an interdisciplinary undertaking that joins economics with aspects of organizational theory and overlaps with contract law'. Of the three disciplines, perhaps the most surprising to the newcomer is the last. But it is of fundamental importance to TCE – not least because its perspective coheres with Williamson's view of economics, which can be illustrated by the use he makes of this quotation from J. Buchanan: 'economics comes closer to being a *science of contract* than a *science of choice*'.

Viewing economic activity from a contractual standpoint invites the question: what is the nature of the relationship between the parties to a transaction? Williamson's answer is dependent upon further questions about the state of the attributes which, he contends, all transactions have: uncertainty; how frequently they recur; and, whether they call for any specialized (what he calls **asset-specific**) investment.

Asset-specific investment occurs when a buyer induces a supplier to purchase plant or equipment, or recruit/train people, in order to engage in the transaction. Effectively, this binds the supplier to the buyer; but, the converse is also true. The buyer is bound to the supplier – since he cannot readily, or on such favourable terms, find alternatives from unspecialized suppliers. Transactions of this kind Williamson terms idiosyncratic.

Idiosyncratic transactions pose problems for both parties. How long will the relationship last? (Crucial to justifying the supplier's original, and perhaps continuing, investment.) How will any incremental gains (from experience curves, or scale economies), or additional costs (from product modifications) be shared? Ideally, any agreement between the parties to the transaction would include a general clause to the effect – as Williamson expresses it – that: 'I will behave responsibly rather than seek individual advantage when an occasion to adapt occurs.' But, he argues, two things stand in the way: 'the unenforceability of general clauses', and **bounded rationality** – which Williamson following H. A. Simon, assumes best describes human economic behaviour.

Bounded rationality takes it that economic actors are '*intendedly* rational, but only *limitedly* so'. Williamson insists that both parts of the definition (i.e. those emphasized) should be respected, since the first elicits 'an economizing orientation', while the second, by accepting that there are limits to our cognitive powers, encourage the study of organizations. This latter thought is especially important to his theorizing because, he argues, the profit maximizing tradition of neoclassical economics – to which he is largely opposed – suppresses the importance of the individual nature of organizations in economic decision-making. Instead, it holds to the view that 'firms are production functions, consumers are utility functions, the allocation of activity between alternative modes of organization is taken as given, and optimizing is ubiquitous'.

To man's limited powers of knowing and conceiving which bounded rationality acknowledges, Williamson adds – to complete his explanation of human conduct – **opportunism**; by which he means, 'self-interest seeking with guile'. More often than not, opportunism involves subtle forms of deceit – both active and passive. But it also includes more blatant activities such as lying, stealing and cheating.

TCE relies, as Williamson puts it, 'on the conjunction of (1) bounded rationality; (2) opportunism; and, (3) asset specificity'. If any one of these conditions is missing, then 'the world of contract is vastly simplified'. To explain what he means by this (and to demonstrate the reasoning he employed to arrive at his 'conjunction' proposition), we must examine four cases.

'The world of contract,' Williamson asserts, 'is variously described as one of: 1. planning; 2. promise; 3. competition; and, 4. private ordering.' And the applicability of these descriptions will depend 'on the behavioural assumptions which pertain to an exchange, and on the economic attributes of the good or service in question'. For example:

Planning applies where 'the parties are opportunistic, the assets are specific, but economic agents have unrestrictive cognitive competence' – that is, *un*bounded rationality. Williamson's rationale is that, because of opportunism, a formal agreement will have to be concluded ahead of the transaction; but that the agreement will be completely comprehensive because of unbounded rationality. The consequence will be that contract execution problems will not arise – on the presumption that legal adjudication ('court ordering') of disputes will be efficacious.

Promise applies where opportunism is absent, assets are specific, but rationality is bounded. In this case, Williamson argues, the parties can trust each other absolutely. However, because of bounded rationality, any contract will be incomplete. Nevertheless, a remedy is to hand: a self-enforcing general clause pledging the parties to act currently in a 'joint profit-maximizing manner', and to seek only fair returns in the future when the contract is renewed.

Competition applies where there is opportunism, bounded rationality, but no asset specificity. In this world, the parties have no continuing interests in each other, markets are fully contestable, and fraud and contract deceits are deterred by court ordering.

Finally, we turn to **private ordering** (what Williamson alternatively terms **governance**). This is the world which concerns TCE: the one where – as we know – opportunism, bounded rationality, and asset specificity come together. Here, because of bounded rationality, planning is incomplete; opportunism rules out promise; and court ordering, thought no longer to be effective, is replaced by private ordering – which (as the name suggests) is when the parties *themselves* devise contracts and resolve disputes, here in the context of asset specificity.

In the world of governance, Williamson contends, the **organizational imperative** is: 'organize transactions so as to economize on bounded rationality while simultaneously safeguarding them against the hazards of opportunism'.

It will have been noticed that the only difference, identified here, between the worlds of competition and private ordering (or governance) is asset specificity. Williamson's argument, at this point, is that this condition is far more widespread than has been generally realized to date. This is not to say that 'recurrent spot contracting' – where open competition, subject to court ordering, sets the prices and terms of transactions – does not occur. Far from it. TCE does, however, maintain that what could start out in this fashion may well be superseded by private ordering where 'transaction-specific human or physical assets' are invested in, to the benefit of both buyer and supplier. And, we might add, it is then – when this new relationship of shared dependency occurs – that Williamson's organizational imperative comes into play.

His principal economic assumption about the firm is that it is **transaction-cost economizing** or, in other words, that it is 'an efficiency instrument'. He does not deny that firms sometimes seek to monopolize markets; or that their managers pursue personal objectives, rather than corporate ones. But an extended period neglectful of efficiency is dangerous to the well-being of the firm; and this threat curbs management's self-indulgent decisions. Additionally, Williamson contends that since cost economizing is socially valued, the firm serves 'affirmative economic purposes'. The position he adopts therefore enables him to avoid some of the opprobrium attaching to the profit-maximizing theory of the firm, with its natural corollary monopoly. But, simultaneously, he abandons the notion of market competition as a check to monopoly power. This is so, not only because such power must eventually accrue to the most efficient firm, but also because his perception of the firm-market relationship is radically different to that of the neoclassical economist.

Williamson views the firm and the market as optional governance structures – that is, 'explicit or implicit contractual framework[s] within which a transaction is located'. More accurately, he sees a continuum of governance structures stretching between the firm at one end and the market at the other – with what he terms 'mixed modes' (e.g. franchising), positioned between. At its simplest, the firm has the choice of either standardizing a supply-item (and thus taking advantage of competitive tendering among many prospective suppliers), or – if this is impossible (or undesirable) – continuing to do business with its asset-specific supplier, or – alternative to this – bringing the transaction within the firm.

The economics of this familiar 'make-or-buy' decision can be forbiddingly difficult to resolve. But, Williamson argues, as transactions become more idiosyncratic – that is, as already-specialized human skills and physical assets are increasingly dedicated to but a single use – 'economies of scale can be as fully realized by the buyer as by an outside supplier'. The decision then comes down to assessing which 'mode [make or buy] has superior adaptive properties'.

Williamson's prime arguments for TCE may be simplified and summarized as these:

. The firm is primarily a cost-economizing (and not a profit maximizing) entity.

. It is constrained by bounded rationality; and, for the most part, subject to opportunism – within and without.

. Asset specificity has become an increasingly important factor in its affairs.

. Where bounded rationality, opportunism and asset specificity occur together, transactions (which represent a significant proportion of all costs) are better mediated by the private ordering (rather than the court adjudication) of contracts.

. In the conditions described by (4) above, the firm and the market should not be seen as being necessarily in some form

of opposition to each other, but as being alternative locations
for such transactions; and, therefore,

6. The focal points for transaction-cost economizing.

TCE has an enormously wide application. This is because it
amounts to 'a theory of the firm'. Its inclusion here is not
merely because of its general importance to all business thinkers,
but also because of the way Williamson uses it to explain the
development of modern corporations (in the US), and his sugges-
tive view as to how they should be judged, relative to their
collective contribution to society.

Williamson contends that while both economists and laymen
consider the modern corporation to be 'an important and complex economic institution', our poor understanding of the economic factors which have brought about its present shape, size
and performance can be put down to the explicatory failures of
two intellectual traditions. The first, already referred to, is 'the
neoclassical theory of the firm that populates intermediate theory
textbooks', which – being indifferent to its structure – treats the
firm as merely a profit maximizing production function. And
the second, which Williamson calls 'the inhospitality tradition'
one maintained by many public policy analysts who largely
accept the market-efficiency stance of the first tradition, and
therefore believe a firm's distinctive structural features to result
from anti-competitive 'intrusions into the market process'.

'In the beginning, so to speak, there were markets,' Williamson
tells us.[1] Their importance – in terms of the effect they had on
organizational design – can be judged by S. Bruchey's view

1. Indeed, both bureaucratic and production-cost considerations combine to
lend force to the proposition that 'transactions will be organized in markets
unless transaction-cost disabilities appear'. (The emphasis has been added.)
Williamson's 'bureaucratic' argument is that market exchange (buying) involves fewer 'distortions' than internal exchange (making). Those for
production-cost are that it is better to buy rather than make when: the firm
needs are small relative to the market – for total cost reasons; the firm can
secure the 'risk-pooling benefits' of markets which aggregate uncorrelated
demands; the firm can take advantage of any 'economies of scope' available
to the market, but not to it.

(which he quotes) that late eighteenth-century US merchanting firms had much in common with their counterparts in quattrocento Venice. Basing his position on A. D. Chandler Jr's later historical studies, Williamson argues that it was the 1840s which saw the start of that spasmodic evolution of organizational forms which culminated in the multinational enterprise (MNE) – for that was the decade when the railway arrived in America.

The 'natural' length of any rail system seemed initially to be about fifty miles. Typically, it would employ some fifty people who were managed on a functional basis: that is, in what Williamson terms a U-form, or unitary, structure. Where lines ran in parallel, classic competitive conditions applied. The future lay, however, with end-to-end systems which enabled greater numbers of people and larger quantities of freight to be transported over longer distances. Contractual relationships sprang up between, and among, end-to-end operators caused by the needs, on the one side, to co-ordinate their work activities, and on the other, to concert their policies relative to winning the custom of travellers and shippers using the whole system, and to reduce intra-system price competition. These arrangements proved only partially successful – seriously breaking down when the volume of through traffic fell away, as a consequence of the depression of 1873, and price cutting ensued.

The railway companies reacted constructively. They determined, as Chandler tells us, to 'transform weak, tenuous alliances into strong, carefully organized, well-managed federations'. Even then, court ordering – to maintain, notably, price discipline – proved ineffective: since the backing of Federal legislation could not be obtained. And it slowly became apparent that, in the words of Albert Fink – a major player of the time – it was not possible to 'rely on the intelligence and good faith of railroad executives'. (So, clearly, opportunism reigned.) The final step was merger. Eventually, systems which initially comprised fifty miles grew to control hundreds, even thousands, of miles of track by the 1880s.

During the course of this massive industrial transformation, a remarkable organizational revolution was taking place. It began, according to Chandler, with the Western and Albany company.

This system was made up of three units, each separately managed on a functional basis, covering, in total, over 150 miles of track. It experienced such managerial difficulties that, for the first time in the US, Chandler has asserted, a 'formal administrative structure manned by full-time, salaried managers' was created to deal with them. This 'decentralized line-and-staff' innovation was steadily improved upon until, by 1893, it was employed in the management of ten of the nation's largest railway companies, controlling upwards of 50,000 miles of track.

This organizational innovation (in US business) was not only the essential precursor to the multidivisional (**M-form**) company, as Chandler sees it; it also – to Williamson – constitutes an application of 'the principles of efficient hierarchical decomposition' which Simon propounded, in part, to deal with problems of bounded rationality.

Finding, in Chandler's account of the early development of rail in the US, the conjunction of bounded rationality, opportunism, and asset specificity upon which TCE relies, it is not to be wondered at that Williamson concludes:

> Confronted, as they were, by the contractual dilemmas that arise when highly specific assets are in place and by complexities that exceeded, perhaps by several orders of magnitude, those that had been faced by earlier business enterprise, the managements of the railroads supplanted markets by hierarchies of a carefully crafted kind.

Again basing himself upon Chandler's research, this time into the development of the M-form, or multidivisional, firm (*Strategy and Structure*), Williamson concentrates on the transformations of Du Pont and General Motors. Immediately before, the former's structure was U-form – that is, centralized with functional departments; while the latter was a holding company (H-form).

He quotes Chandler as identifying Du Pont's 'inherent weakness' as being the incapacity of senior managers to discharge their long-term entrepreneurial responsibilities efficiently, when the operational activities of the company became so complex as to make the administration of them too intricate. This in turn caused the function managers – now unguided by corporate objectives – to pursue their individual departmental goals instead. Williamson's 'translation' of this is instructive:

In the language of TCE, bounds on rationality were reached as the U-form structure laboured under a communication overload while the pursuit of sub-goals by the functional parts (sales, engineering, production) was partly a manifestation of opportunism.

He sees General Motors, under its creator, W. Durant, as afflicted with 'partisan decision-making': a species of opportunism. In general, such H-form (holding) companies may also suffer from opportunism when their subsidiaries can retain profits to invest in their own activities – rather than returning them to the centre; or when, in the absence of any effective headquarters' monitoring of their results, they act as their own judge and jury. In the first case, the self-investment may not be in the interests of the company as a whole; and in the second, cost control can become undisciplined.

But for opportunism, Williamson argues, the H-form structure might have proved the solution to the difficulties experienced by U-form companies when sheer size unbearably magnified their decision-making requirements. The structure is already 'decomposed', in conformity with Simon's ideas. That is, crudely expressed, operational and strategic decisions have been separated – thus enabling the problems of bounded rationality to be dealt with. However, the solution is more apparent than real, since the typical H-form company had such a small headquarters staff that it could neither attend to strategic matters, nor even monitor current performance effectively.

As we now know, thanks to Chandler, the answer lay with the M-form structure. Characterizing it in TCE terms, Williamson says that it serves 'both to economize on bounded rationality . . . and safeguard the internal resource allocation process against the hazards of opportunism (which is what the general office concept adds)'. As we now also know, its adoption – and therefore the displacement of the U-form structure in large US firms – was gradual, until after the Second World War. By comparison, the development of two of what Williamson calls its 'applications' was breakneck. These were the **conglomerate**, and the MNE (multinational enterprise).

(Williamson distinguishes between the M-form, and other forms, of conglomerate. However, since instances of the latter are few in number, we shall ignore his analyses of them.)

Despite their almost simultaneous adoption of the M-form structure, General Motors and Du Pont followed two different strategic routes. Under A. P. Sloan, Durant's successor, the former remained essentially – Williamson contends – an automotive manufacturer. Du Pont, however, was potentially a conglomerate: that is, diversified. And it was this characteristic – the capacity to deal with breadth rather than depth – which he employs as a point of distinction between the mainstream M-form structure and its variant, the conglomerate.

Conglomerates, he believes, 'are usefully thought of as internal capital markets whereby cash flows from diverse sources are concentrated and directed to high yield uses'. While from a TCE standpoint, the conglomerate can be seen – *contractually* – 'as substituting an administrative interface between an operating division and the stockholders, where a market interface had existed previously'. The general office – on this interpretation – could then be considered as the agent of the shareholder in monitoring the constituent parts of his investment. And, by implication, it would appear that Williamson – far from regarding this as having undesirable anti-competitive consequences – finds in its favour: on the ground that the general management of the conglomerate is in a better position to know and act on that knowledge (by way of acquisition, divestment, or internal change) than the shareholder.

In the same vein, he speculates on whether the structure of the conglomerate may be said to have gone some way to resolve, if not end – at least in its own case – the 'problem of separation of ownership from control' which A. Berle and G. C. Means first identified in 1932.

Observing that US companies have long invested in activities abroad, Williamson suggests that the rapid spread of the MNE after 1945 would not have excited quite the puzzlement or alarm that it did had transaction-cost economizing and organization form issues been better understood.

Essentially, he argues that just as the M-form structure facilit ated the management of diversity (by the conglomerate), so it made possible the more effective management of foreign investment; and this, once again, was primarily because of the separation of strategic (in the case of the MNE, global) decisions, from those of an operational nature.

Williamson notes that these investments have been concentrated in a relatively small number of industries: e.g. chemicals, drugs, car manufacture, food processing, electronics, machinery, and so on. He next draws on research studies which demonstrate that – for the most part – the MNEs were heavy investors in R & D, and technological innovators at the time of their initiatives abroad. The inference he then makes is that they were confronted with all the difficulties of technology transfer – difficulties, one is left to presume, which were rendered more acute by the advanced nature of that technology.

His detailed arguments at this point centre upon the familiar TCE governance structure question: bilateral trading or self-manufacture? That the companies concerned chose the latter is evidence to Williamson that they were merely responding to the demands of transaction-cost economizing, rather than to some anti-competitive drive towards monopoly. And that those MNEs were largely American stemmed from nothing more sinister than the advantage conferred upon US companies, ahead of the rest of the world, by the development of the M-form structure: a structure which made possible the efficient management of foreign divisions and thus, in turn, the decision to make instead of buying.

Bibliography

Oliver E. Williamson, *The Economic Institutions of Capitalism*, The Free Press, 1985.

Oliver E. Williamson, *Economic Organization – Firms, Markets and Policy Control*, Wheatsheaf Books, 1986.

15

Robert A. Burgelman and
Leonard R. Sayles

—

Robert Burgelman is Associate Professor of Management at the Stanford University Graduate School of Business. Leonard Sayles is Professor of Business at Columbia University's equivalent institution, and the author of a number of works dealing with the relationship of technology to management.

Burgelman and Sayles came together when the former was preparing his doctoral dissertation under the latter's guidance. In the course of the next five years, they married some of Burgelman's research findings and concepts with Sayles's more extended work in the writing of a book which examined 'the complexities and subtleties involved in managing corporate entrepreneurship, innovation and venturing'. The book was *Inside Corporate Innovation*.

Its research setting was a 'multibillion dollar, diversified, US-based, high technology firm'. Traditionally a volume producer and seller of various commodities, the company had diversified in order to get closer to the end-user or customer and add value as it went downstream. In the 1960s it had done this using its existing divisions. But, early in the next decade it created a separate 'new-venture division' (NVD) to pursue such projects. The structure of this division, its functioning, departmental 'charters', reporting relationships, co-ordinating mechanisms, reward systems, and the role it played in the execution of the company's strategy of unrelated diversification, lay at the heart of their longitudinal study. Altogether, six 'internal corporate venturing' (ICV) projects[1] were studied – ranging from one embryonic enough to require the definition of its objectives, to another already turning over $35m.

The company represented what Burgelman and Sayles have called 'a most difficult case' example of the strategic renewal which is being urged upon US firms in the face of intensifying world competition. The difficulty here stemmed not from any ineptitude on the part of the company; nor from any threat of bankruptcy. To the contrary, it resulted from success. The issue was how 'a truly massive corporation', with large commitments and great strengths in the routine production and marketing of commodities, could move into novel markets and areas of technology, where its existing skills, knowledge and culture were of little value – and could even prove inhibiting.

To describe the ICV process,[2] Burgelman and Sayles adopt J. L. Bower's distinctions: **definition**, **impetus**, and **structural context**.[3] They then add a third, first made by Burgelman: **strategic context determination**. This sub-process, under the continuing pressure of **impetus**, brings about an accommodation of current strategy to new business activities, and overcomes any hindrances that the firm's structural context (which, of course, was related to that strategy) might occasion.

They illustrate the ICV process with Fig. 15.1, showing the 'key and peripheral activities' involved.

Bootlegging is unauthorized research. Gatekeeping is not defined.

The process begins, as Burgelman and Sayles saw it, in the bottom left hand box of the model. It may be the consequence of a technical development within or without the company's R & D laboratory. But, whatever its origin, product innovation

---

[1]. The titles given to these were: fermentation products, fibre components, improved plastics, farming systems, environmental systems, and medical equipment. The first and last, respectively, are those referred to in the text.

[2]. This they define as: 'the activities and management by which R & D developments are moved through and evolve into commercially viable products (or stumble and fail to achieve that viability)'.

[3]. See **Joseph L. Bower**, pages 110–119.

Fig. 15.1

□ = Key activities **Levels**	**Core processes**		**Overlying processes**	
	Definition	Impetus	Strategic context	Structural context
Corporate management	Monitoring	Authorizing	Rationalizing	Structuring *Selecting*
New venture division management	Coaching Stewardship	Strategic building *Organizational championing*	Delineating	Negotiating
Group leader/ Venture manager	Technical and need linking *Product championing*	Strategic forcing	Gatekeeping Idea generating Bootlegging	Questioning

starts when an individual or a group synthesizes or integrates a number of items of this new knowledge into something which looks capable of commercial exploitation. It is their combination – not the items themselves, novel though they may be – which constitutes the product, and 'gives rise to the distinctive, creative, innovative early **definition** stage' of the process.

They found that the most promising circumstances for this to happen were when a technically trained, entrepreneurially inclined manager performed two 'linking' tasks: 'technical linking' – where the new items of knowledge were combined into a problem-solving product or process; and 'need linking' – where the resulting solution could be shown to meet an existing market need 'or one that can be induced'.

At the **definition** stage, and bridging into **impetus**, 'product championing' has to begin. This is because innovations die without support and resources. Being most closely concerned with definition, group leaders – assuming they are strongly motivated and have the social skills – are best placed to perform

his work. In addition, they will be required to improvise and
ake risks in order to maintain the innovation's **impetus**. Their
dilemma originates from the nature of the product: it frequently
does not fit the categories of offering specified by existing
strategy, so existing customers cannot readily evaluate it. Investment is therefore difficult to justify; yet, without sufficient
resources, demonstrating its potential is equally difficult: a veri-
able catch-22.

What Burgelman and Sayles call 'effective product champions'
adopt a variety of stratagems to maintain **impetus** in the face of
these troubles. For example: they will disguise the project so
that it appears consistent with the company's accepted product
domain – until it has had a chance to prove itself and secure an
encompassing extension of that domain; they will rob other
projects to support it; and they will engage in illicit marketing
from the R & D department. Their objective is to gain 'venture
status' for the project and thus have it moved into the NVD –
thereby acquiring a general manager, organization, and budget.
The decision to accord a project venture status, despite screening
models and the whole apparatus of quantification, is highly
subjective. 'Much depends,' we are told, 'on the selling abilities
of the product champion – both inside the corporate hierarchy,
and outside in the marketplace.' In the studies that Burgelman
and Sayles made, he went with the project to become the 'new-
venture manager'. His technical background might seem to
militate against such a general management appointment. But
they found that many of the individuals concerned were eager to
take the step: a fortunate outcome when a company cannot
readily find a generalist with his product or market knowledge
to fill the post. For, training a newcomer to take up the reins
can slow a venture's momentum at a time when corporate
management – looking for early evidence of success – may
become discouraged and withhold the support essential for a
successful launch.

To overcome this type of corporate scepticism, successful
venture managers quickly learn to look like winners. They
engage in what Burgelman and Sayles have called 'strategic
forcing': that is 'showing impressive, consistent growth *at almost*

any cost'. (The emphasis has been added.) This not only retains support high up in the company, it also secures the co-operation of those lower down who may the more readily provide materials, parts and services – and, in this way, contribute to the possibility of success.

But along with strategic forcing goes 'strategic neglect': that is, the deliberate failure to develop a suitable administrative structure for the venture. Things are done 'on the cheap'. Where management specialists are called for in, say, purchasing or manufacturing, existing generalists are pressed into service to cover as many functions as possible. And when, eventually, the need for the former becomes undeniable, their arrival is likely to be resisted by the venture manager – since his concentration is on short-term issues (e.g. increasing share), rather than the building of a business. Nor is strategic neglect confined to administration. It can even extend to the development of new or complementary products, and their associated services.

Unless the venture manager can ultimately take a more rounded view of his responsibilities, the moment will arrive when he will have to be replaced. This is an all-too-familiar outcome. Indeed, Burgelman and Sayles contend that the more successful he is at increasing sales, the less likely it is that he will develop the administrative mechanisms required to support them.

Those ventures they observed, which eventually matured into commercial successes, owed much to what they term 'strategic building'. Usually performed by the venture manager's manager, this consists of the application of orthodox strategic thinking and techniques to the embryonic business. The preoccupation with the sales growth of the core product is abandoned. Top management is furnished with plans, central to which is the notion of completing the line with related products and technologies. Some of these products and technologies may well come from elsewhere in the company; some from outside – by acquisition. But, in either case, those on high must be convinced of the wisdom of what is proposed: and conviction will depend upon the history of the venture to date.

Burgelman and Sayles discovered that the **impetus** process

ly represented a combined effort by the venture manager and
s superior when the latter engaged in 'persistent-coaching' and
e former was receptive. And they record that, in most instances
ey came across, coaching was not persisted with. As a conse-
ence, the venture manager was overwhelmed by strategic
rcing (and its concomitant, neglect), and finally replaced.

The manager who brings the venture manager in under his
ng and engages in strategic building also takes on the 'organiza-
nal championing' of the venture. This is largely a political
tivity, occasioned by the need to maintain top management's
nfidence in the venture during those times when its record
oks ambiguous. It requires a reputation-risking commitment
the organizational champion's part. If he is by nature 'cau-
us but astute', he will make sure that any venture he sponsors
s in with 'the existing predispositions' of his superiors. But
ose Burgelman and Sayles call 'more brilliant, or more risk-
one' try to change such predispositions in favour of the new
siness field the venture affords an entry to. Successful cham-
oning, therefore, depends to a degree on the individual's
wers to enthuse, explain, and justify. But he also needs to be
le to conceive of the venture in strategic terms (rather than just
hnically, as in the case of the product champion), and devise
ong-run strategy for it.

It is at this point that Burgelman's **strategic context deter-
nation** comes into play.

Effectively, organizational champions change the company's
erall direction by getting senior management to accept the
ccessful new venture, and its strategic implications. As he and
yles put it: 'Thus, relatively autonomous, unplanned initiatives
m the operational and middle levels of the organization help
shape corporate strategy.'

The thrust may come from below, but top management 'sets' from among the initiatives – and, by doing so, legitimizes
m. Three reasons are given for this necessary modification to
ategy. They are:

From the standpoint of existing strategy, the new venture
may be illicit.

2. It may also bring with it activities and values – even a who
   culture – which are inimical to the established ones.
3. Existing strategy may be inadequate; yet while this is realize
   senior management does not know how to alter it.

To summarize: new types of business for the company a
'delineated', because certain middle managers work for the str
tegic accommodation of initiatives made by operating manager
who are pursuing new ventures *from within*.

Burgelman and Sayles's findings are especially important f
what they contribute to the debate about the formulation
strategy – relative to internally generated innovation. What th
observed was a bottom-up process, consisting of experiment a
selection – rather than top-down planning imposed from abov
Moreover, because of the dynamics of the process, they disco
ered that strategy was modified *after* the venture had prov
successful, rather than *before* its launch.[4]

They conclude that the picture which emerges is far mo
hopeful and realistic than that of 'the traditional model'.
deed, they question whether 'much real innovation' cou
ever take place in large companies if it depended upon 'chang
being foreseen and preordained by the prescient plans' of t
management.

Given that corporate management's role in **strategic conte
determination** is largely reactive, how does it attempt to cont
the ICV process? The answer which the study provides
through **structural context determination**.

This consists, unsurprisingly, of such moves as setting up
NVD as a separate unit, defining the posts and their responsib
ties within its departments, appointing individuals with eith
administrative or entrepreneurial inclinations to those pos
and establishing performance criteria for the venture and
manager.

The guiding force behind these choices (or, as Burgelman a
Sayles describe them, 'manipulations') is the view taken

---

4. This is termed 'retroactive rationalization'.

orporate level, from time to time, of what emphasis should be placed on expanding the mainstream business, as against diversification. And, for the most part, it would appear that they are aimed not at directing ICV efforts with a well-conceived strategy, but at restricting them to certain levels of activity.

As seen in the study, **structural context determination** was a rather crude tool for influencing ICV efforts', and resulted in venture managers believing that the criteria for survival were fast growth and large size.

Burgelman and Sayles believe that their process model can help management understand '*better and more completely* the deeply rooted problems and . . . the "perverse dynamics" generated and encountered by internal corporate venturing'. They identify four 'major problem areas in the strategic management of ICV' it can assist with. Two have already been mentioned.[5] The third is what they call 'indeterminateness in the strategic context'.

This becomes evident when corporate management limits its strategic guidance to declarations about an interest in broad areas, such as 'health' or 'energy'. Or again, when its concern for ICV fluctuates widely. (What Burgelman and Sayles call 'a now we like it, now we don't approach'.) It is as though new ventures were seen as insurance policies, should the mainstream business falter – rather than as strategic endeavours which are legitimate in their own right. Even more than at the **impetus** stage, the strategies of the different levels of management can show a lack of coherence during the **determination of strategic context**.

The fourth problem area concerns the 'perverse selective pressures' which structural context imposes on the venture to grow

These are: (i) the vicious circle (or catch-22 position) the product champion can find himself in at the **definition** stage when first technically, and later commercially, he cannot demonstrate the venture's feasibility without more resources – yet he must, if he is ever to get any; and (ii) at the **impetus** stage, when the venture manager must reconcile sales growth with business development, and his manager (the organizational champion) has to spend time expanding the scope of the new business, as well as coaching his protégé.

quickly – adding to the external pressures it is already subjected to. As has been noted, fluctuations in top management's strategic preferences for ICV activity (consolidation versus expansion) appear to lead to reactive restructurings of the NVD. So, given the popular view within the company that the NVD's future is always precarious, this promotes a 'now or never' attitude on the part of its staff – and, once again, impels them toward faster growth.

Bibliography

Robert A. Burgelman and Leonard R. Sayles, *Inside Corporate Innovation – Strategy, Structure, and Managerial Skills*, The Free Press, 1988.

PART FOUR

The Developers and Teachers

Preface

It has been truly said that if you want to learn, teach. But equally, it is the case that if you want to learn, apply. Both teaching and application demand more, by way of education, than is required of the successful student. For him, or her, an easy familiarity with the subject, a tenacious memory, and a knowledge of examination technique will suffice – more often than not. But if you are going to present concepts, facts, and theories in a form coherent enough for others to learn from you – or, in management, for others to practise what you preach – then you need much more.

It is for this reason that we include the writers in this section. Each of them has striven to bring order out of the conflict of ideas which characterizes strategic thought, and to put forward an internally consistent, understandable, and practical approach to strategy. Apart from the need they have to satisfy their own critical standards, their work has been scrutinized for its defects by their peers, by their students (and no one is more unforgiving than the average masters student), as well as by those companies who hire them having come to the end of their own intellectual resources. So it can be said that their learning has qualified them as teachers *and* practitioners.

Do they all arrive at the same conclusions? Of course not. As Ansoff[1] has pointed out, 'strategy is an elusive and somewhat

---

1. See **H. Igor Ansoff**, pages 15–33.

abstract concept'. What the reader will find, however, is an emerging consensus about the value of certain constructs and perspectives.[2] While the particular appeal of each writer will depend, we suspect, upon the lacks and predispositions of the reader.

Les Digman's views, for instance, on how strategic decisions are actually made, and the human responsibilities of general management, will resonate for those who have learned to look behind systems and procedures.

Jay Galbraith and Rob Kazanjian (more developers perhaps than teachers) have much to say to the strategist exploring vertical integration; and especially to the individual fascinated by TCE.[3]

The sheer lucidity of Charles Hofer and Dan Schendel's prose style illuminates corners left dark by other writers. Could there be a better introduction to the subject; or one which traces its development more informatively?

Jack Pearce and Richard Robinson perceive strategic management as a process. Their model of it, which they claim to be 'representative of the foremost thought', would alone merit their inclusion.

And in the work of Art Thompson and Lonnie Strickland we find not only such insights as their 'key success factors', but a structured clarity which must surely have done much to make it the most popular book of its type in the US.

2. For example, portfolio theory and Porter's five-box schema.
3. Transaction Cost Economics. See **Oliver E. Williamson**, pages 173–183.

16

Lester A. Digman

—

s Digman is the Leonard E. Whittaker/American Charter
ofessor of Management at the University of Nebraska. A
olific writer and contributor to scholarly journals, he has an
ernational reputation in consultancy as a specialist in strategic
anagement and decision-making, technology management, and
ecutive development.

Digman defines strategy as 'the organization's preselected
eans or approach to achieving its goals or objectives, while
ping with current and future external conditions'. Goals, he
es as 'broad directions the firm wishes to pursue, or results it
shes to accomplish within its mission'. While objectives 'pro-
de more specific ends to be met within the framework of the
oader goals, and . . . involve specific time frames for accom-
shment'. And a firm's mission 'is a broad statement, providing
general direction for business activities and a basis for the
herent selection of desired ends (goals and objectives), and
e] means to achieve them (strategies)'.[1]

Along with many other strategic thinkers,[2] he considers that
y strategy has four components. Modifying the formulation
C. W. Hofer and D. E. Schendel, he lists these as:

The *scope* or domain of action within which the organization
tries to achieve its objectives.

aving clearly distinguished between ends and means in this way, it is curious
hat he categorizes decisions about the firm's mission as strategic.

ee, for example: **Kenneth R. Andrews**, pages 5–14; **H. Igor Ansoff**,
ages 15–33; **Charles W. Hofer and Dan Schendel**, pages 216–229.

Fig. 16.1 Strategy levels

Strategy types	Applies to	Focus
Enterprise	All organizations	Mission, purpose, role in society
Corporate	Multibusiness organizations	Which businesses and their interrelationships
Business unit	All organizations	How to compete most effectively
Functional/ operating	All organizations	Functional and operational business-un support

2. The skills and resources that the organization will use achieve its objectives – its *distinctive competence.*
3. Advantages the organization expects to achieve over its co petitors through its skill and resources deployments – *competitive advantage.*
4. *Synergies* that will result from the way the organizati deploys its skills and resources.

There are, moreover, four levels of strategy: enterprise, c porate, business-unit, and functional/operating. Their appl ability, and main distinguishing features, are shown in Fig. 16.

Whether it is made explicit or not, all organizations have enterprise strategy,[3] Digman contends. This is because th have, from time to time, to consider why they exist; what th are trying to provide for, and how they function in, socie what is the form of their ownership; even who is on the dire orial board. This type of strategy is especially influential determining the relationships the firm has with its 'stakeholder that is, with those who have a stake (or interest) in what t organization does, and how it does it. Expressed more general the firm's enterprise strategy 'acts as a framework or envelo within which other, more specific types of strategy will operate

Corporate strategy is concerned with diversification, n ventures, acquisitions, divestments, and the like. This is beca it addresses portfolio issues such as the types of business

3. A term introduced by H. I. Ansoff, referring to a firm's societal relationship

rm is/will be in; how they relate one to another; and what hould be the appropriate allocation of resources among them.

Business-unit strategy (which is essentially the same for ingle-business companies and divisions of multibusiness comanies) deals with the nature of competition facing the firm's roduct(s) in market or industry terms. It considers how best utilize the firm's distinctive competence(s), and what can e done 'to integrate the various functional areas of the busiss (notably product design, manufacturing, and marketing) to roduce a competitive advantage'.

Functional and operations strategies should support igher-level strategies. Indeed, people in charge of functions and perations frequently make the difference between the success d failure of those strategies – just by the way they implement em. At the same time, functions and operations strategies nphasize 'resource productivity, by capitalizing on any possible nergies and distinctive competences that the firm may possess'.

It follows from Digman's identification of these four levels of rategy that (where they are to be found) many people are volved in strategic decision-making at any one time. Yet, he gues, most strategic decisions emanate from the corporate and siness-unit levels. The explanation for this apparent paradox s in the *way* that they are made.

His essential contention is that 'a "decision" is the result of a ream or sequence of inputs and actions by a number of ople': so very few decisions are made by just one individual. be sure, the choice – from among competing recommendans – is made by the chief executive officer (CEO), or a siness-unit manager. Yet everyone engaged in the process has aped that decision. The CEO is therefore held to be responsle (along with his board and senior colleagues) for major ategic decisions. But his 'prime strategic function' is, arguably, provide strategic leadership' for people below him: by selectg the right team, setting its agenda, and allowing its members come to their own conclusions. The role of top management thus becoming, as Digman interprets it, more one of changing ngs – 'so that the firm can achieve competitive advantages in ch of [its] businesses', than running things.

Classing both CEOs and people in charge of business-units
general managers, Digman says of them that their jobs a
qualitatively – rather than quantitatively – different to those
middle or executive level managers. Merely working hard
(which will enable many of the latter to get by) is not enough,
their case. They have, for example, to be able to recognize whi
issues confronting them are important, what kinds of risk a
involved (and how much to accept), and whether a subordina
is truly capable or not. More specifically, he itemizes three k
general management functions.

1. Managing the strategic process – which he sees as bei
   responsible 'for *creating* the structure and systems so that t
   organization's objectives are met effectively and efficientl
   and . . . resources are allocated properly'.
2. Managing relationships – which is more a matter of wh
   they should be, 'rather than how to live with them'. (At t
   corporate level, the relationship with business-unit manage
   is of major importance; while that with the board must
   'productive'.)
3. Managing executive development – since the quality of corp
   ate and divisional managers ultimately determines what su
   cess the firm will have.

Digman adopts the schema developed by R. H. Rock and I
Eisthen to illustrate the distribution of strategic decision-maki
roles and responsibilities within the company. It is set out
Fig. 16.2.

Strategic decisions are rarely clear-cut or simple, he tells
This is because:

1. They rest upon intangibles and assumptions.
2. They involve value judgements, risks and uncertainties.
3. Usually they are for high stakes.
4. Their typically long-term consequences are difficult to evalua
5. Many people may have an interest in them, yet, typically,
   individual or group possesses enough knowledge or skill
   deal with them unaided.

Add to these characteristics the probability that the company

Fig. 16.2

Hierarchy of strategy	Decision level			
	Board of directors	CEO	Corporate management	Division management
Enterprise				
Formulation	Primary			
Assessment		Primary		
Implementation		Primary	Contributory	
Monitoring	Primary			
Corporate				
Formulation	Contributory	Primary		
Assessment	Primary			
Implementation			Primary	
Monitoring	Contributory	Primary		
Business				
Formulation			Contributory	Primary
Assessment		Contributory	Primary	
Implementation				Primary
Monitoring			Primary	

pursuing more than one objective at a time, and it becomes
clear how many are the interrelated factors contributing to their
complexity.

Digman regrets the tendency of some writers to portray
strategy-making 'as a "rational", specific step-by-step process'.
While acknowledging that he is proposing a systematic approach
to its elements, for use in large companies, he asserts that the
most effective decision-makers are usually creative, intuitive
people, 'employing an adoptive [*sic*], flexible process'. Moreover,
since most strategic decisions are event driven, rather than
preprogrammed, they are unplanned. Accordingly, they should
be more often seen in terms of 'preferences, choices, and
matches',[4] than as exercises 'in applied logic'.

What is therefore required, he contends, is 'the proper integration of analysis and intuition'. But here he finds a contradiction.

4. Here Digman follows A. Van Cauwenbergh and R. Martens.

Formal planning is necessary for the management of strategic decision-making in complex organizations, but its very existence inhibits creative thinking. His resolution of the difficulty depends upon us reminding ourselves that strategy-making is about correct decisions, and not about the preparation of detailed plans!

He suggests that it is also helpful to consider strategic decisions from the perspectives of planning and control.

Taking his cue from J. M. Juran, he argues that management's ultimate goal is to achieve a higher level of performance for the firm. It follows, therefore, that any economically justified attempt at performance improvement must be given precedence over control – a temporary reduction in which may be expected before the firm breaks through to the planned, higher level.[5]

He simplifies how he sees the relationships of strategic decision-making, planning and management, one with another, in this way: if point A is where the company is now, and point B is where it needs to be, then: strategic decision-making determines how to get from A to B; strategic planning determines the details of getting from A to B; and strategic management controls the whole process and its accomplishment.

Digman considers that strategic management 'represents the intersection ... of organization theory, microeconomics, and industrial organization'. He defines it as a 'continuous process that involves attempts to match or fit the organization with its changing environment in the most advantageous way possible. It clearly includes adapting the organizaton itself (via internal changes) to fit the external environment'. It has to be continuous because today's conditions are changing faster, and becoming more complex, than ever before. Moreover, the rate of change is accelerating. No longer can the modern manufacturer complete a programme of investment in some new technology and look forward to a lengthy period during which he can exploit that investment. Paradoxically, as conditions become more unstable

---

5. An interesting indication of Digman's approach is that he perceives control as 'a reactive, problem-solving activity', and performance improvement as an 'opportunity-finding' one.

planning becomes more difficult. Yet for the same reason it becomes more essential. Consequently, to deal with these greater magnitudes of change, their increasing rapidity, as well as commensurate rises in risk, more strategic decisions must be made, and made more frequently.

His 'integrated model of strategic management' is set out in Fig. 16.3.

Fig. 16.3

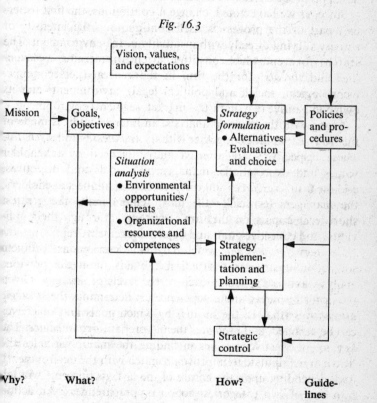

As the model indicates, the formulation of strategy begins with the establishment of the company's *mission*. This broad statement flows from the *values and expectations* of stakeholders, defining why the company exists, and guiding what it should be doing. The next step is to lay down *goals* and *objectives* – which are applicable at enterprise, corporate, business-unit, functional and operational strategy levels. (See above, pages 196–197, for definitions.)

So that the company may relate productively to the world about it, it must understand the general and competitive conditions confronting it – as well as its own organizational characteristics. This process Digman terms *situation analysis*.

Since, as we have noted, change is continuous, the first (external) part of the process is itself continuous – the intensity of activity varying directly with instability in the environment. The search is for events which constitute current, or emerging, *opportunities* and *threats*[6] for the firm in the general (i.e. economic, technological, social, and political/legal) environment, and its own competitive (e.g. industry, market, segment) environment.

Along with the external analysis, an internal audit is made of the firm's capabilities, together with its *weaknesses* and *strengths*. These, respectively, are 'affected' and 'influenced' by stakeholder values and expectations, management's goals and objectives, and the firm's *resources* and *competences*. Of all the stakeholders, the managers (especially the most senior) make the greatest short-term impact on the firm's strategy – through their individual and collective goals and objectives.

Strategy formulation, which Digman describes as 'problem solving in unstructured situations', builds upon the previous analysis and is applied to each of the levels of strategy. Given the firm's resources and competences, it determines the *strategic alternatives* (that is, the means) by which goals and objectives can be attained, and *evaluates* them – preparatory to *choice*. The key to its effectiveness 'lies in finding the major variables the firm can manipulate to improve its match with the environment' and, depending upon the nature of the last, its outcome will fall into one of two categories: action or preparedness. An action strategy is developed for 'initiating actions' relative to an environment where change can be reliably anticipated. If, on the other

---

6. Determining whether an event qualifies as either an opportunity or a threat 'depends on how accurately the firm diagnoses and understands the change and its significance, as well as what [it] decides (and is able) to do about it'.

hand, change is too rapid or the environmental conditions too complex, 'response actions' are called for. These are contingency plans – prepared in advance – which can be introduced when circumstances dictate.

'After a strategy has been evaluated and selected, the critical *implementation* phase begins.' For this a master *plan* is developed. It is the basis for more detailed and shorter-term planning at lower operational levels. (See below.) It specifies 'any structural, system, process, or personnel changes' necessary for implementation, in addition to budgetary and resource requirements. Unlike formulation and evaluation, which may be conducted outside the operating structure of the firm, implementation, which is primarily an administrative task, is always performed within it. This means that there is a transfer of responsibility for implementation – 'critical to the success of the strategy' – to those individuals who are already familiar with existing organizational procedures.

(In addition to strategic planning, Digman distinguishes three other planning levels: tactical; operational; and scheduling and dispatching.[7] The most specific form of planning is the last: scheduling and dispatching. In this, the manager is concerned 'with the assignment and sequencing of specific existing resources ... to manufacture or deliver given quantities of products' during the next operational period. Operational planning 'allocates tasks to specific existing facilities to achieve particular objectives in each planning period'. Tactical planning, however, relates directly to strategic planning. This is because it 'deals with the implementation and support of longer-range plans'. It 'is often concerned primarily with future facilities, or product planning'; and as such, it includes capital budgeting, optimal pricing patterns, facility provision, expansions and closures.)

The *strategic control* process monitors the implementation of strategy, and then determines whether it is yielding the desired results. Because internal and external conditions may have changed since the strategy was formulated, it also re-evaluates both – to signal the need for, and to facilitate, corrective action.

7. Here Digman adopts the categorization of D. S. Hirshfield.

In this context, Digman regards *policies* 'as constraints guiding strategy formulation and selection'; and *procedures* as 'the specific [day-to-day] expressions of policies'. (The relationship between the two, he sees, as analogous to that between strategy and tactics.) A firm, for example, may have a policy of not diversifying into unrelated businesses. The effect is, thus, to preclude such an option at the formulation stage of any new strategy. So desirable may be an opportunity of this kind that the firm will revise the policy. However, generally 'the major direction of influence is from policies to strategies' – hence the solid line/dotted line interaction of the model.

Digman follows orthodox US practice in suggesting that, where there is a planning staff, its role is to assist with, rather than make, planning and strategy decisions. But he points out[8] that Japanese companies, on average, employ more people[9] who help initiate and formulate strategy. They in turn work with a much larger group[10] than is usual in the States; and one, moreover, which is solely responsible for general management and strategic decisions, and has few, if any, operational duties.

The Japanese approach is – for the most part – top-down; while in the States (and reflected in Digman's model), strategic planning is 'primarily a bottom-up process for implementing the CEO's vision of the future'. Plainly, either approach can bring success. Citing research into ten British companies by M. Goold and A. Campbell, Digman concludes that 'if corporate development and [the] co-ordination of individual businesses is [*sic*] the key objective, headquarters should make the strategy and accept the fact [?] that the motivation of managers and [the] performance of their units may suffer. If unit financial performance matters most [*sic*], headquarters should let unit managers determine strategy, and accept less co-ordination between businesses.' A third position – 'a balance of the two' – would mean 'increased ambiguity'.

8. Quoting research by Toyohiro Kono.
9. Twelve, as against 3 to 5 in the US.
10. Eight to 10, as against 3 to 5.

Bibliography

Lester A. Digman, *Strategic Management – Concepts, Decisions, Cases,* Richard D. Irwin, Inc., 2nd edn, 1990.

17

Jay R. Galbraith and
Robert K. Kazanjian

—

Jay Galbraith is a Professor of Management and Organization and a senior research scientist at the Center for Effective Organizations, University of Southern California. A consultant with an international reputation, his researches and publications concern organizational design, change and development and their relationships with strategy at all levels. Robert (Rob) Kazanjian is Associate Professor of Organization and Management at Emory University, Atlanta. His first degree was in economics; but thereafter, his masters and doctoral theses (which were gained at Wharton, Pennsylvania) concerned organization and strategy. His numerous publications have, in recent years, dealt *inter alia* with technology transfers, non-bureaucratic structures, and stages of growth.

Galbraith and Kazanjian found their joint work, *Strategy Implementation – Structure, Systems and Process*, upon three definitions – pertaining, respectively, to strategy, structure, and process. Since they are writing in co-operation with them, they adopt Charles W. Hofer and Dan Schendel's[1] definition of an organization's strategy as:

the fundamental pattern of present and planned resource deployments and environmental interactions that indicate how the organization will achieve its objectives.

They view structures as:

1. The book is a component of the West Series in Strategic Management which is edited by Charles W. Hofer.

e segmentation of work into roles such as production, finance, marketing, and so on;

e recombining of roles into departments or divisions around functions,
products, regions, or markets;

d the distribution of power across this role structure.

nd they define processes as:

e direction and frequency of work and information flows linking
e differentiated roles within and between departments of complex
ganization.

he principal contention of their work (which is of interest to
) is that – perhaps because of the wealth of research which
as been devoted to strategy-structure relationships – too little
tention has been given to other features of organizational
esign which must also be brought into line with strategy if
onomic success is to be attained. More specifically, it is that
ch 'dimensions' as the processes of resource allocation and
oss-departmental decision-making, and systems governing
areer paths, information flows, and rewards, must match one
other *and* structure *and* strategy in a 'fit, a consistency, or
congruence' – the achievement of which they regard 'as
e most important contribution of organization to economic
fectiveness'.

On the way to arriving at this contention, they set out an
dmirable review of much of the empirically-based strategy-
ructure literature available today.[2] From this they elicit the
llowing 'guidelines for managers' – three of which are ex-
ressed, interestingly, in imperative (i.e. 'should statement')
rm:

Single-business and dominant-business firms should be organized in a functional structure.

Related diversified firms should be organized into a multidivisional form.

Including findings by: A. D. Chandler Jr, B. R. Scott, L. Wrigley, O. E.
Williamson, D. A. Nathanson, J. Cassano, R. P. Rumelt, H. K. Christenson
and C. A. Montgomery.

- Unrelated diversified firms should be organized into a holdin company structure.[3]
- An early adoption of a strategy-structure fit can comprise competitive advantage.

These particular propositions are preceded by a more genera proposition (also derived from their literature review):

- Performance is the product of multiple factors, but two ar primary:
  (a) Matching strategy to industry structure and core skill and
  (b) Matching organizational structure to strategy.

Relative to (b), Galbraith and Kazanjian's complaint (if such is) is that research into strategic change has tended to concentrat on diversification: a surprising outcome considering how man strategic changes firms make which are 'not of this nature Central to any study of diversification is the concept of relatec ness: and, therefore – as a starting point – what constitutes a individual business. Typically, they argue, three 'prime mode: have been used to define such a business: resource separatenes market discreteness, and product differences. The modes hav then been matched with some overall assessment of diversit Whatever its merits, this type of approach has left largel unexplained 'issues related to the shift in strategic emphasis an importance that the firm places across existing businesses, an the associated implications for implementation'.

What Galbraith and Kazanjian therefore propose is a fram work which is 'more implementation oriented': one where relatec ness is seen 'in a more operational, functional manner'. There i moreover, the need for such a framework to deal with 'emergin strategies yet to be addressed', they contend. These are strategic being followed by certain upstream commodity companies i

3. This structure they see, typically, as having a minimum of staff at t corporate level, which is the locus for centralized finance, accounting, a legal functions, capital allocation and control mechanisms, and decisio pertaining to acquisition and divestment.

Fig. 17.1 Supply stages in a manufacturing industry

Raw materials	Primary manufacturer	Fabricator	Product producer	Consumer marketer	Retail	
●	●	●	●	●	●	Consumer

Supply flow ──────⟶

the US which have moved the emphasis of their businesses downstream to specialized activities – a move, they describe, as neither vertical integration nor diversification.

Galbraith and Kazanjian argue that, despite the considerable variety that is to be found in management practices among vertically integrated companies, the differences between upstream and downstream companies have largely been ignored. To help repair this omission, Galbraith has introduced the concept of a firm's 'centre of gravity': a concept which, incidentally, can be applied to firms making a strategic change that is neither further vertical integration nor diversification.

Essentially, the new concept marries two others (Tregoe and Zimmerman's 'driving force',[4] and Nathanson and Cassano's 'nexus'), to 'the value-added industry supply chain'. The last is illustrated with Fig. 17.1.

Industries differ in the number of stages in their chains – service industries, typically, having fewer than manufacturing. Taking those in the figure to be representative of the latter, Galbraith and Kazanjian describe stages to the left of the central dividing line as upstream, and those to the right as downstream. They then assert that the differences between the two segments are more striking than differences between, and among, stages. This is because upstream stages add value by

---

4. For further information, see **Benjamin B. Tregoe** and **John W. Zimmerman**, pages 81–89.

Fig. 17.2 Contrasting characteristics of upstream and
downstream companies

Upstream	Downstream
Commodity	Proprietary
Standardize	Customize
Maximize end users	Target end users
Low-cost producers	High margins
Sales push	Marketing pull
Line-driven organization	Line/staff
Process innovation	Product innovation
Capital budget	R & D/advertising budget
Capital intensive	People intensive
Technological know-how	Marketing skills
Supply and trading/manufacturing and engineering	Product development/marketing

reducing the variety of raw materials to a small number of
'flexible, predictable raw materials and intermediate products',
whereas downstream stages convert these 'standard commodities' into a variety of products designed to meet any number of
consumer needs – value being added by advertising, product
positioning, distribution and R & D. Thus, 'upstreamers have a
divergent view of the world', and downstreamers a convergent
one.

This distinction is not, however, universally true since some
specialized chemical companies, for example, offer differentiated
products in what they term 'the broad market', and are not
therefore commodity producers. But where it holds good – and
that is in the majority of cases – 'upstream and downstream
companies face very different problems and tasks'. As a consequence, the management processes and experience, the success
factors, the dominant functions, the organizational structures
and, of course, the cultures are quite different in the two types
of company.

Some of these 'contrasting characteristics' they identify in
Fig. 17.2.

Galbraith and Kazanjian argue that, in its formative years, a company develops an integrated organization (in terms of its structure, processes, rewards, and people) that is appropriate to the upstream or downstream stage where it has its beginning and its early success; and that this forms the company's centre of gravity. Since changing a centre of gravity – as the figure above suggests – can be extremely difficult, the concept provides an explanation as to why strategic moves which do not call for such changes (e.g. related diversification) are easier to introduce, and can be shown historically to have been more successful than those which do – upstream or downstream.

In addition, they claim that the concept extends the discussion of strategic change in new ways, a point they illustrate by examining it relative to vertical integration, various types of diversification, and shifts in the centre of gravity itself.

The key to successful vertical integration, it emerges, is to maintain, and indeed support, the firm's existing centre of gravity. So any moves up or downstream should be subordinate to its principal stage activities. For example: in a comparative analysis of five companies in the paper industry – each 'centred' in a different stage, Proctor & Gamble is described as 'driven by the advertising or marketing function'. Like the other four, it owns woodlands and operates pulp mills. But the woodlands operate as suppliers to the mills. They do not constitute a 'stand-alone profit centre'. And to emphasize the point, Galbraith and Kazanjian argue that career progression to the top of Proctor & Gamble is via brand management, not by excelling further up the industry chain in woodlands or pulp mill management.

Taking the types of diversification in ascending magnitudes of strategic change, difficulty (in making the change), degrees of diversity and consequent decentralization, they first deal with 'by-product diversification'.

This category applies to a firm which appears to have diversified outside of its industry – to judge by where its sales are made, but is just intelligently looking for additional revenues and profits. It is still committed psychologically to its industry and its centre of gravity, and has actually changed neither. So it continues to be dependent on a single industry in a way which would have been impossible 'with real diversification'.

Related diversification is defined as occurring when a 'company moves from its core industry into other industries that are related to the core industry'. Galbraith and Kazanjian's contribution to the continuing debate about the nature (and degrees) of relatedness between industries[5] is to proffer the centre of gravity concept as the distinguishing criterion. In other words, a firm can be said to have engaged in related diversification if it has ventured into another industry, *but only if* the entry has been via a business 'at the same centre of gravity' as the firm already has.

Again using Proctor & Gamble as an exemplar, they recount how the company's early diversification moves took it from soaps (of various kinds) to shortening and cooking oils, later to flour, cake mixes and biscuits, and then into toothpastes – culminating in the introduction of Crest. Each of these new businesses they describe as being similar to soap – in terms of product and process technologies, central purchasing capability, line packaging, delivery logistics – as well as sharing the same selling and distribution channel arrangements. However, what was most important about each of these moves, they argue, was that they 'resulted in a branded product, sold primarily by advertising to the homemaker, and managed by a brand manager'.

Later in its history, Proctor & Gamble moved into yet more industries. However, since the centre of gravity of the new businesses – whether acquired or created – remained the same, the company was still adjudged to be a related diversifier. Even so, many of the 'functional aspects'[6] of the new businesses were different from those to be found in the earlier ones. On the basis of this and similar examples, Galbraith and Kazanjian suggest that these functional differences could perhaps be used to form

---

5. See **Richard P. Rumelt**, pages 145–154.
6. Nineteen of these are itemized by Galbraith and Kazanjian. They are: process technology, product technology, product development, purchasing, assembly, packaging, shipping, inventory management, quality, labour relations, distribution, selling, promotion, advertising, consumer/customer, buying habits, capital (fixed), working capital, and credit.

scale by which degrees of relatedness might be measured. Judgement, as to which functions were related or not, would then be exercised; with a majority either way determining the overall assessment.

Such an assessment is required, they argue, in order to estimate the magnitude of any strategic change that is envisaged. For the greater the unrelatedness, the greater are: the difficulty of implementation; the likelihood that diversification should be by acquisition, rather than internal development; the political problems to be surmounted; and, the degree of decentralization.

Intermediate diversification (which they liken to Rumelt's Related-Linked category) is the classification they apply to companies 'whose businesses are somewhat related, but operate at a number of – usually a few – centres of gravity'. There are two 'dimensions' to this type of strategic change: (1) the number of centres of gravity; and (2) the distance(s) between them.

Galbraith and Kazanjian hypothesize that taken together these indicate a greater amount of strategic change (and subsequent operating difficulty) than is the case with either by-product or related diversification. The first, because 'the company must learn not only new businesses, but also new ways of doing business'; and the second, because 'the differences between ways of doing business is proportional to the distance on the industry supply chain'. And partial confirmation comes from a study by Nathanson (using a concept similar to that of a firm's centre of gravity) which shows that the larger the number of centres, the poorer is the company's performance.

Considering the previous discussion, it is no surprise to find that unrelated diversification applies to companies which 'have several centres of gravity, operate in many industries, and actually seek to avoid relatedness'. Moreover, they 'have no psychological commitment to any industry, or group of related industries'; and they always rely on acquisition and divestment when making strategic changes.

Galbraith and Kazanjian assert that changing the firm's centre of gravity is probably the most difficult of all strategic moves. This is because it 'requires a dismantling of the current power

Fig. 17.3 Strategies and associated structures

Strategy	Structure
Single business	Functional
Vertical by-products	Functional with profit centres
Related businesses	Divisional
Intermediate businesses	Mixed structures*
Unrelated businesses	Holding company

* These forms, often transitory, are difficult to classify.

structure, rejection of parts of the old culture, and establishing all new management systems'.

As evidence for this view, they cite the record of those oil companies which after the 1973 'oil shock', and again during the gluts of the 1980s, sought profits downstream of their traditional activities. The shift meant that power moved from the 'engineers, geologists ... supply and distribution people' to marketing – with consequent turmoil. Those that succeeded were companies which began with downstream centres of gravity. Some of the upstreamers have since sold their downstream operations and attempted to diversify into unrelated areas. Yet others have moved, at their centre of gravity, into different extractive industries such as coal and uranium mining. These have had trouble operating multiple businesses; but Galbraith and Kazanjian consider that, in the long run, they should outperform their fellow upstreamers.

Their 'alternative framework for conceptualizing strategic diversity' occasions a review of strategy-structure relationships according to Galbraith and Kazanjian. The reader may find it interesting to compare the summarizing Fig. 17.3 above with the 'guidelines' noted earlier.

Bibliography

ay R. Galbraith and Robert K. Kazanjian, *Strategy Implementation – Structure, Systems and Process*, West Publishing Company, 1987.

18

Charles W. Hofer and
Dan Schendel

—

Charles (Chuck) Hofer is a Professor of Management at th
University of Georgia; Dan Schendel holds a similar cha
at the Krannert Graduate School of Management of Purdu
University.

Hofer and Schendel's principal collaborative work, *Strateg
Formulation: Analytical Concepts* – which is prescriptive rathe
than descriptive in emphasis – was published in 1978 and ha
been reprinted more than a dozen times in the intervening year
It has two main purposes: 'to define the concept of strategy
explaining 'the reasons for its central role' in the managemen
of companies; and 'to describe the various analytical concept
models, and techniques' useful for strategy formulation at the
corporate and business levels. We shall deal mainly with the fir
purpose in order to bring out the authors' particular contributio
to the development of strategic thought.

Alfred Marshall was the first economist to see that Charle
Darwin's theory of evolution could be employed to explain wh
certain companies survive and others do not. Hofer and Schend
introduce their subject using the same approach. By analog
they argue, the fittest companies survive because they are selecte
by their environments on the basis of the acceptability of good
and services they can produce at a profit. However, unlik
organisms, which cannot change their essential characteristics

---

1. Neo-Darwinism depends, in part, upon randomness of genetic mutation: th
   is, the accidental arrival of characteristics suitable for survival when condition
   occur that are hostile to life for members of the species which have n
   mutated.

organizations can consciously adapt to the world about them; though, as Hofer and Schendel tell us, it is perfectly apparent that not all of them do.

The adaptations they can make are of two types: those that affect the relationship between them and their environment; and those which change their structures and ways of working. Typically, the first type has a greater impact on the organization's *effectiveness* (where this is defined in terms of the degree of correspondence between actual and desired outputs) than the second. While *efficiency*[2] (as measured by the ratio of outputs to inputs[3]) is more greatly influenced by the second than the first.

On a day-to-day basis, management's energies are mostly devoted to matters of efficiency. But in the long term, Hofer and Schendel contend, a company's survival and success depend much more on its effectiveness – that is, on relating satisfactorily to its environment. Indeed, while a company should strive to be both efficient and effective, in any conflict over the two, 'priority usually should be given' to the latter.

Determining how to stay effective, however, is by no means always obvious to practising managers at any one time. This is because 'major environmental shifts that influence effectiveness occur relatively infrequently . . . while the organization . . . must stay at least moderately efficient in the meantime to survive'. Moreover, these shifts 'usually start small and develop slowly'; so it is difficult to decide what proportions of the company's resources should be applied to increasing effectiveness rather than efficiency. And even when it is possible to distinguish the really critical shifts from among the multitudes of environmental changes that are simultaneously taking place, there still remains the problem of specifying how the shifts may evolve. Essentially, therefore, Hofer and Schendel conclude, 'a critical aspect of top management's work today involves matching organizational

2. This distinction between effectiveness and efficiency, which owes much to C. Barnard (as Hofer and Schendel readily acknowledge), informs a great deal of their thinking on strategy – as we shall see.
3. These definitions will be familiar to students of general systems theory.

competences[4] with the opportunities and risks created by environmental change in ways that will be both effective and efficient over the time such resources will be deployed'.

The 'basic characteristics' of this match are what they *initially* term the organization's strategy. Defining strategy in this way makes no assumptions about the quality of the match, or even whether it has been arrived at in a formal manner. Thus, all organizations can be said to have a strategy. Nevertheless, we are told, 'if strategy is important' then its formulation should be managed: that is, it should be the consequence of 'formalized, analytical processes'. Eight justifications are given for these. They can help in:

1. 'The formulation of organizational goals[5] and objectives.'[6]
2. 'The identification of major strategic issues.'
3. 'The allocation of discretionary strategic resources.'
4. 'The development and training of future general managers.'
5. 'Forecast[ing] the future performance of the organization.'
6. 'The evaluation of senior and middle management.'
7. 'Stretch[ing] the thinking of top management.'
8. 'Guid[ing] and integrat[ing] the diverse administrative and operating activities of the organization.'

These processes may help in formulating goals and objectives, but does strategy include goals and objectives?

In one of the most interesting historical accounts of strategic thinking to be found in the literature, Hofer and Schendel trace

---

4. Competences is the collective term Hofer and Schendel use to refer to internal resources and skills.
5. Goals are 'the ultimate, long-run, open-ended attributes or ends ... [an] organization seeks'. By this definition, goals (such as profit maximization) are 'unbounded' – because one cannot tell if any unpursued option might have yielded more profit. They, therefore, 'are not achievable'.
6. Objectives are 'the intermediate-term targets that are necessary but not sufficient for the satisfaction of goals'. They have four components: the goal/attribute sought, an index for measuring progress, a target, and timing. (Hofer and Schendel see constraints as objectives where 'some minimum level of performance is to be exceeded'.)

Fig. 18.1

	Andrews	Ansoff	Hofer and Schendel
Breadth of strategy concept/definition	Broad (i.e. inclusive of goals and strategy)	Narrow (i.e. strategy alone)	Narrow
Components of narrow concept	N/A	Product-market scope; growth vector; competitive advantage synergy	Domain or scope; resource deployments; competitive advantage; synergy
Differentiates between goal formulation, and strategy formulation, processes	No	Yes	Yes

the development of the concept of strategy from its putative birth in 1954 (with some thoughts of P. Drucker), to the year of their book's publication (1978). According to their analysis, the two authors (K. R. Andrews and H. I. Ansoff) who first explicitly examined the concept, and its related processes, differed on three major points. First, the concept's breadth: that is whether it includes ends (goals/objectives) as well as means (strategy). Second, whether strategy-as-means (which Hofer and Schendel term 'the narrow concept') has any components; and what they are. And third, the inclusiveness of the formulation process: that is, whether goal setting is part of strategy formulation.

These three points of disagreement remain unresolved among strategists. In a table identifying thirteen separate characteristics, Hofer and Schendel set out the views of thirteen writers on the concept of strategy and the strategy formulation process. Fig. 18.1 is a much reduced tabulation showing merely how they

compare with Andrews and Ansoff relative to the three major
points.

As Fig. 18.1 indicates, Hofer and Schendel elected to adopt
the narrow concept of strategy. They give three reasons for this.

1. They instance research into structured problem-solving which
   showed that most people perform the processes involved
   better when they separate them into their constituent parts
   (e.g. goal setting, and strategy formulation), address each in
   turn, and then combine the results.[7]
2. They argue that 'it is clear that there is a narrow concept of
   strategy, and that it does have components'. (This raises the
   question of what name to give it to distinguish it from the
   broad concept. They decide upon 'strategy', calling the latter
   'grand design'.)
3. They contend that 'for many organizations . . . goal setting
   and strategy formulation . . . are separate and distinct'. Therefore, in those cases, it is less confusing to give each process a
   different name than 'to acknowledge that the two processes
   are intimately intertwined in other organizations'.

Even though, as they concede, their initial definition of strategy – as 'a statement of *fundamental means* [an organization
will use . . . to achieve its objectives' – is broad, it is circumscribed in two ways. One, in taking any action the organization
will use up resources. And two, in order to realize any of its
objectives, it will have to interact with the world about it.
Strategy statements must reflect these imperatives, they argue,
so they refine their definition of an organization's strategy to be:

the fundamental pattern of present and planned resource deployment
and environmental interactions that indicates how the organization will
achieve its objectives.

This definition, and the need to be both effective and efficient,
lead directly, they contend, to the conclusion that an organization's strategy has four components:

7. They add, significantly, that they are unaware of any similar research into *unstructured* problem-solving; but they believe the findings 'would be the same'.

. **Scope** (sometimes called **domain**), which specifies the extent of present and planned organization/environment interactions 'in ways that are most pertinent to [the] organization'.[8]

. **Resource deployments**[9] (sometimes called **distinctive competences**), which are 'past and present resource and skill deployments that will help [the organization] achieve its goals and objectives'.

. **Competitive advantages,**[10] which are the 'unique' competitive positions an organization develops 'through its pattern of resource deployment and/or scope decisions'.[11]

. **Synergy**, which is 'the joint effects' the organization seeks by its resource deployment and/or scope decisions.

Taken together, the first three components determine the organization's effectiveness. Synergy, however, is the prime determinant of its efficiency. All four 'can be used to operationalize the concept of strategy'; and are to be found in all strategies, good or bad, whatever their organizational level.

For their purposes, Hofer and Schendel distinguish three major levels of organizational strategy: **corporate**; **business**; and **functional area**.

Corporate strategy mainly addresses questions relating to the businesses the company should be in. The primary strategy components called into play are, therefore, scope and resource deployments. Synergy and competitive advantage are more important in related product than in conglomerate firms. In the case of synergy, this is because the issue is whether, and how, the businesses can reinforce each other. At this level, the two

. This could be in terms of product/market segments, geography, technology, or distribution channels. The term is broadly applied by Hofer and Schendel to cover combinations of products and markets, which 'when matched create a business'.

. and 10. They hold that resource deployments and competitive advantages are possibly more important than scope in determining success: an unusual view at the time of their writing.

. When such advantages stem from resource deployments, they are more important to business level than corporate strategy; while the converse is true for scope (e.g. product-market positioning).

major types of functional area policy decisions[12] which are o
universal importance are: financial structure, and the designs o
organization structure and processes.

Business strategy is principally concerned with how to com
pete in industry or product-market terms. Consequently, it
most important components are distinctive competences and
competitive advantages. Scope's preoccupations are with segmen
tation choices, and with 'the stage of product-market evolu
tion'.[13] It is thus less important at the business level than at th
corporate; and also less important here than synergy – which i
to be found in the integration, within each business, of differen
functional area activities. Functional area policy decisions dea
with choices covering the product line, market development
distribution, finance, staffing, R & D, and the design of majo
manufacturing systems.

Functional area strategy is mainly directed at 'the maximiza
tion of resource productivity'. Here again scope is of lesse
importance: the key components being distinctive competences
and synergy – arising out of 'the co-ordination and integratio
of activities within a single function'.

While all three types of strategy are distinct, they should forn
a coherent whole if the organization is to be successful in th
long run, Hofer and Schendel tell us. Each level is 'constrained
by the others. Which essentially means that corporate strateg
constrains business strategy, which in its turn, constrains func
tional area strategy.

Fig. 18.2 sets out 'some basic characteristics' of the thre
types of strategy.

12. Hofer and Schendel categorize certain major decisions, which guide an
render consistent repeatedly-made decisions, into **functional area polic
decisions**, and **operating policies**. The distinction between the two is on th
basis of timing. The first (e.g. to do with capital structure, or geograph
scope) may be changed only after a period of years – and influence effectiv
ness. The second (e.g. stock write-offs, or price discounting) are altered mo
frequently – and usually only affect the efficiency of strategy execution.

13. Here they follow P. Kotler in preferring a theory of market evolution to th
conventional product life cycle concept.

Fig. 18.2

Level	Corporate		Business	Functional
Goals and objectives	Survival		Constrained	Constrained
	Purpose and mission		Product-market segment	Market share, technological leadership, etc.
	Overall growth and profit objectives		Growth and profit objectives	
Relative importance of strategy components	C*	RP*		
Scope	***	***	**	*
Distinctive competence	*	**	***	***
Competitive advantage	*	**	***	**
Synergy	—	*	**	***
Characteristics of strategy components				
Scope	Scope of business portfolio and conglomerate diversification		Product-market segment matches and concentric diversification	Product-market development and product form and brands
Distinctive competences	Primarily financial, organizational, and technological		Varies with stage of product-market evolution	Varies by functional area, stage of product-market evolution, and overall competitive position
Competitive advantage	v. industry		v. specific competitors	v. specific products
Synergy	Among businesses		Among functions	Within functions

continued overleaf

Fig. 18.2 continued

Level	Corporate		Business	Functional
Major functional policy decisions	C* F, O*	RP* F, O, D, T, & M/B*	Manufacturing system design, market development, R & D, and distribution policies	Pricing, promotion, production scheduling, stock control, staff and labour policies
Nature of resource allocation problem	Portfolio problem		Life-cycle problem	Functional integration and balance problem

Key

C = Conglomerates	D = Diversification policies	*** Very important	
RP = Related product, multi-industry firm	T = Technological policies	** Important	
F = Financial policies	M/B = Make or buy policies	* Occasionally important	
O = Organizational policies		— Not important	

To help visualize strategy at all three levels, Hofer and Schendel set out a number of constructs. We shall confine ourselves to those applicable to two levels: **corporate** and **business**.

At the **corporate level** (for all companies bar those diversifying from single product line businesses, and dominant product line firms whose secondary businesses are closely related to their principal business), two of the three constructs they discuss are dealt with elsewhere.[14] Accordingly, we shall only set out their critiques of them here; and expand upon their own offering.

In connection with BCG's matrix, Hofer and Schendel raise three objections:

14. These are the Boston Consulting Group (BCG)'s growth/share matrix, and the McKinsey/GE business screen. See **Robert D. Buzzell and Bradley T. Gale**, pages 59–71; **Bruce D. Henderson**, pages 72–80; and **Richard G. Hamermesh**, pages 120–130.

The four-cell structure is 'too simplistic', since companies can occupy middle positions, as well as highs and lows.

Overall industry attractiveness is inadequately described by its growth rate alone. (Some industries, for instance, have experienced high growth and low profitability, because supply has outstripped demand.)

Market share is an inadequate descriptor of competitive position, because 'it depends so heavily upon a definition of the market' (e.g. Mercedes has a small total market, but a high segment, share).

They consider that the McKinsey/GE business screen over-
mes most of these difficulties. It can also forecast the com-
ny's future position; so that 'present and forecast matrices
ay be] used to help describe the firm's scope and competitive
sition,[15] and to identify some of the more important strategic
ues facing the firm'. However, they find fault with its capacity
depict effectively the positions of new businesses starting to
ow in new industries. To deal with these circumstances, they
offer their own 15-cell matrix adapted from an individual
oject of Hofer's, and shown in Fig. 18.3.

If for no other reason, this matrix[16] commends itself for
clusion because it embodies one of their most interesting
ncepts: the stages of product/market evolution. However,
ofer and Schendel do not propose it as superior to either
the other two. Indeed, they see the desirability of it being
ed as an alternative to the screen in a two-phased portfolio
alysis.

They suggest a tentative plot with the BCG matrix: largely
cause it is the least demanding of data, and the simplest. This
ould indicate those businesses requiring more analysis – either

---

and 17. 'Competitive position' is a term Hofer and Schendel prefer to the original 'business strengths' (which Hamermesh calls 'business unit position'), since it enables them to make direct comparisons with the BCG matrix and their own.

. Similar to the business screen (though not illustrated in the section on Hamermesh), the circles represent the sizes of relevant industries, and the pie wedges business market shares.

Fig. 18.3

Stage of product-market evolution	Competitive position[17]		
	Strong	Average	Weak
Development		◔	
Growth	◕		◔
Shake-out	◕	◕	
Maturity ↓ Saturation		◕	
Decline		◔	

17. See note 15, p. 217

because they are important, or because the results are anomalous. At this point (the second phase), the screen is utilized, if 'most of the businesses represent aggregations of several product-market segments'; or the 'product-market evolution matrix', if the portfolio consists of 'individual or small groups of related product-market segments'.

To help visualize **business strategy** (once again excluding those companies barred in connection with visualizing corporate strategy), they propose three constructs – two of Hofer's devising:

1. A 'product-positioning' matrix which plots the competitive positions of the company's, and its rivals', major products in each of its major market segments. 'Assuming no change

business strategy' by the firm or its relevant competitors, similar matrices – covering the past and the future – will 'help define the scope components' of everyone in the industry.

. A set of decision trees showing functional area policy decisions, for the company and its competitors, 'sequenced according to their relative importance' to the firms in question. This should enable the company to determine what the remaining three of its strategy components ought to be; and, in the case of synergy, whether these policy choices reflect a pattern of consistency, or a 'common thread', among its activities.

. A 'functional area resource deployment' matrix which, used in conjunction with the policy decision trees, will indicate 'the relative importance of the firm's ... functional area policies', and how it hopes to create competitive advantages.

Both the corporate and business strategies of the two categories of companies excepted above (i.e. those diversifying from single product line businesses, and dominant product line firms whose secondary businesses are closely related to their principal business) are difficult to visualize – using any of the constructs already mentioned – because of inequalities in the size and importance of their established and emerging businesses.

In their place, Hofer and Schendel suggest the employment of two others: H. I. Ansoff's 'growth vector components', and his growth vectors in diversification'.[18] Thereafter, their own matrix can be applied. This will then show the relationships between the companies' principal and secondary businesses, in terms of nance and growth. And they add that it is often useful to develop policy decision trees and resource deployment matrices for the principal business, and any related businesses which contribute in the region of 10 per cent of overall revenues or profits.

One of Hofer and Schendel's most illuminating contributions to strategic thinking is to do with strategy statements. They

8. About which they say: 'Together, these ... matrices indicate the nonfinancial relationships that will exist among such [firms'] businesses'. For more information, see H. Igor Ansoff, pages 15–33.

Fig. 18.4

	Broad	Precise
Functional terms	Transportation business	Long distance transportation of low-value, low-density products
Physical terms	Railway business	Long haul, coal carrying, railway

argue that such statements, to be considered complete, ought to possess four characteristics. They should:

1. Describe each component of the organization's strategy (i.e. its scope, distinctive competences, competitive advantages - '*and how they will be produced*', as well as its '*intended synergy*'). (Emphases have been added.)
2. Indicate how the strategy will realize the organization's objectives.
3. Describe the strategy in functional,[19] not physical, terms.
4. Be as precise[20] as possible.

To illustrate characteristics (3) and (4) they give us Fig. 18.4 commenting that the upper right quadrant contains what is required.

They also append a model strategy statement which is worth quoting in full.

H & S International's strategy for the next four years is to compete in the high-price segments of the digital watch and calculator business with a limited line of high-quality products sold on the basis of state-of-the-art technology and their high quality in terms of performance and appearance. During this period, H & S will not diversify into other businesses.

19. Functional: in order to meet T. Levitt's well-known arguments in *Marketing Myopia*.
20. Precise: so as to avoid P. F. Drucker's and H. I. Ansoff's objections that Levitt's formulation could be too broad to be useful.

Finally, in the course of some not unexpected remarks about
the need for strategy to be carefully described – so as to avoid
inconsistencies and misunderstandings, they give us this warning:
'it is not always wise to communicate the company's plans
completely or precisely to middle and lower management for
various political and social reasons'.

Bibliography

Charles W. Hofer and Dan Schendel, *Strategy Formulation:
    Analytical Concepts*, West Publishing Company, 11th re-
    print, 1986.

19

John A. Pearce II and
Richard B. Robinson Jr

—

Jack Pearce has the Eakin Endowed Chair in Strategic Manage
ment at the George Mason University, Fairfax, Virginia. Aside
from heading the university's department of management, he
consults widely and has contributed to most of the best known
US management journals.

Richard Robinson is Professor of Strategy and Entrepreneur
ship at the University of South Carolina. Like his co-author, he
is an active consultant and writer, specializing in the strategic
management of growth ventures.

Pearce and Robinson contend – such has been the increase in
the sophistication and complexity of decision-making within
businesses since 1945 (caused, principally, by intensifying com
petition, the ubiquitous activities of government, and the
demands of international trading) – that there is a need for the
'all-encompassing approach ... known as strategic manage
ment'. This, as they define it, is:

The set of decisions and actions resulting in [the] formulation and
implementation of strategies designed to achieve the objectives of an
organization.

And by 'strategy' they mean:

Large-scale, future-oriented plans for interacting with the competitive
environment to optimize [the] achievement of organization objectives.

Typically, they tell us, 'strategic issues' (that is, those decisions
which 'deserve strategic management attention') have six charac
teristics (or 'dimensions'). They:

Require top-management decisions.

Involve the allocation of large amounts of company resources (i.e. people, physical assets, or money).

Are likely to have a significant impact on the long-term prosperity of the firm.

Are future-oriented.

Have major multifunctional or multibusiness consequences.

Necessitate considering factors in the firm's external environment.

what they call the multibusiness firm, Pearce and Robinson stinguish three levels of strategy: corporate, business, and nctional. (The single-business firm has two – the upper level nsisting of a combination of corporate and business levels.) roadly, as one would expect from items 1, 2, 3, and 5 of the six

Fig. 19.1 Characteristics of strategic management decisions at different levels

aracteristic	Level of strategy		
	Corporate	Business	Functional
pe	Conceptual	Mixed	Operational
asurability	Value judgements dominant	Semi-quantifiable	Usually quantifiable
equency	Periodic or sporadic	Periodic or sporadic	Periodic
aptability	Low	Medium	High
lation to sent activities	Innovative	Mixed	Supplementary
k	Wide range	Moderate	Low
fit potential	Large	Medium	Small
st	Major	Medium	Modest
ne horizon	Long range	Medium range	Short range
xibility	High	Medium	Low
-operation uired	Considerable	Moderate	Little

Fig. 19.2 Hierarchy of objectives and strategies

Ends (What is to be achieved?)	Means (How is it to be achieved?)	Strategic decision makers			
		Board of directors	Corporate managers	Business managers	Function managers
Mission, including goals and philosophy		**	**	*	
Long-term objectives	Grand strategy	*	**	**	
Annual objectives	Short-term strategy policies		*	**	**
Functional objectives	Tactics[1]			*	**

Key ** A principal responsibility * A secondary responsibility

characteristics above, strategy formulation predominates at t corporate level; and strategy execution is the principal conce of functional level managers – that is, those responsible f 'product, geographic, and functional areas'. At the middle lev managers 'translate the general statements of direction a intent' they receive from above into decisions about how b their SBUs (strategic business units) can compete. And t involves looking to 'secure' that 'fairly [*sic*] unique piece of t total market . . . the business can claim and defend because competitive advantages'.

Fig. 19.1 sets out in more detail the characteristics of ea level of strategy.

Ideally, the strategic management process (SMP) is carried o by a team drawing managers from each level, supplemented planning staff members (assuming that degree of corpora

---

1. This is the only mention to be found of 'tactics' in the text – except for argument asserting the superiority of a 'holistic', as against a tactical, approa to strategic management. The latter would, of course, be a contradiction terms.

ophistication), and 'lower-level managers and supervisors' whose contributions are to provide data, and put strategy into ffect). Despite this wide involvement of people throughout the ompany, 'strategic decisions . . . can only be made' by the most enior of managers. Fig. 19.2 shows Pearce and Robinson's view f the distribution of strategic decision-making responsibilities.

The SMP is described as interactive and iterative.[2] Interactive n that, while it is 'overseen by top managers' (because of their broad perspective' of the firm and its environment), it is de-igned to involve managers at all levels – as we have noted, and lso stimulate contributions from 'creative, skilled, and know-dgeable people' throughout.

Following P. Lorange, Pearce and Robinson illustrate its terative' nature by detailing five 'loops' where, for example (in oop 1), the Chief Executive Officer (CEO) may ask for a vision of some of the 'emerging portfolio pictures' sent up om his SBU managers, and/or change his 'original tentative bjectives' a number of times, until an acceptable reconciliation etween the two has been reached. Or again (in Loop 5), the EO may demand implementation plan changes to secure 'a nal overall fit'.

Pearce and Robinson proffer what they consider to be an clectic model which is representative of the foremost thought n the subject of the SMP. It is set out in Fig. 19.3.

The essential features of the model's eleven 'key components' re summarized below.

The **company mission** 'describes the product, market, and chnological areas of emphasis for the business in a way that *flects the values and priorities of the strategic decision makers*'. he emphasis has been added.)

The **company profile** is derived from an internal analysis hich identifies the firm's 'performance capabilities' on the basis f its available resources, actual or accessible. The profile has ree aspects: (1) it sets out the quantities and qualities of those sources, 'financial, human, and physical', at any particular

---

Pearce and Robinson see this as meaning that 'strategic decisions are usually reached only after trial and error'.

Fig. 19.3 Strategic management model

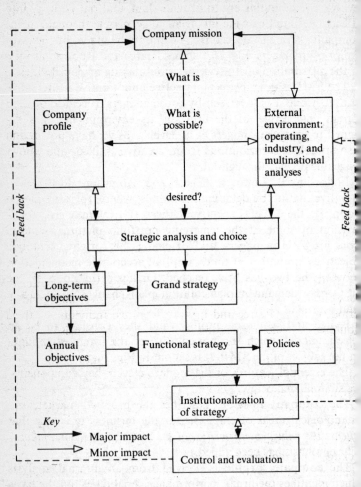

time; (2) it evaluates 'inherent' management and structur[
weaknesses and strengths; and (3) it attempts to identify t[
firm's future capabilities by contrasting its past successes a[
management's 'traditional values and concerns' with its prese[
capabilities.

The **external environment** is comprised of two 'interactive and interrelated segments': operating, and remote. The first consists of those industry and competitive operating 'conditions and forces' which affect the choice and attainment of the firm's rational 'objective/strategy combinations'. The remote environment is made up of those general forces and conditions (economic, political, social, and technological) that provide the framework within which all firms compete.

Strategic analysis and choice, as the name suggests, comprises two related activities. The first, by comparing the findings which constitute the company profile with those that emerge from the environmental analysis, attempts to answer the question 'What is possible?' In the second, these results are then sifted – the company mission being used as a screen – so as to provide answers to the question, 'What is desired?' The overall intention is to produce a possible *and* desirable ends/means combination of long-term objectives and 'grand strategy' which will enable the firm to relate successfully to its environment in accordance with its mission.

Long-term objectives 'are a statement of *what* is expected from pursuing a given set of business activities' over an extended period of years, Pearce and Robinson tell us. Individually, they should be specific, measurable, achievable, and consistent with one another. And they are applied, typically, to such features of the business as return on investment, competitive position, technological leadership, productivity, employee relations, public responsibility, and employee development.

Grand strategy is the 'comprehensive, general plan of major actions through which a firm intends to achieve its long-term objectives'. Although each grand strategy is a 'fairly [*sic*] unique package of long-term strategies', there are twelve 'basic approaches: concentration, market development, product development, innovation, horizontal integration, vertical integration, joint venture, concentric diversification, conglomerate diversification, retrenchment/turnaround, divestiture, and liquidation'.

Annual objectives apply to activities similar to those for which long-term objectives are specified. The former, however, can be – and need to be – cast in more precise terms.

Functional Strategies, which must conform to the gener.
framework of the grand strategy, are the integrative plans
action each distinctive business function or division needs
specify *how* it will attain its annual objectives. Alongside the
are developed the company's budgetary proposals, to ensure th
the planning process may be specific, practical, and accountable

Policies (sometimes called 'standard operating procedures
guide the implementation of strategy by standardizing routi
decisions and limiting operational discretion.

Institutionalizing the strategy is required to ensure that
shapes the day-to-day life of the firm. In the long term, thr
organizational elements bring this about: structure, leadershi
and culture.

Control and evaluation are necessary: (1) because manage
need to know whether their strategic plans are being followe
and (2) since strategy formulation is 'largely subjective', strateg
managers require early evidence as to its success or failure.

Conceiving of strategic management as a process – whic
Pearce and Robinson do – brings with it a number of implic
tions that they are careful to point out.

1. The flows of information, or the directions of impact, are,
   the majority of cases, two-way – as the arrows in th
   model indicate. This reciprocity means that a change in o
   component will affect a number – perhaps all – of the oth
   components.
2. Formulation and implementation are sequential. Howeve
   the apparent rigidity of the sequence (from the top, compo
   ent by component, to the bottom of the SMP model) will b
   modified by: (1) a major change, internal or external, whi
   affects company performance (e.g. the death of a boa
   member, or the arrival of a new competitor); and (2) th
   absence of the need to give each component equal attentic
   every time the planning cycle begins. A stable environmen
   for instance, may not require exhaustive analysis every, sa
   five years.
3. The feedback (dotted lines) loops of the model enable strat
   gic managers to consider, at the formulation stages of th

process, what the effects of their strategies, once implemented, are likely to be – and modify those strategies (or even the company mission) accordingly.

Formal planning tends to freeze perceptions. Treating strategic management as a process is to recognize that its components' constituents are always evolving: and must be constantly monitored. In other words, the SMP is a dynamic activity.

a section discussing the practical limitations of their own
MP model, Pearce and Robinson advocate a dynamic approach
it, as well. It cannot be shown to be ideal, they concede.
deed, they argue, 'no model should be seen as providing a
escription for the way strategic planning should be done'.
ialytical in character, theirs describes the steps 'many busi-
sses actually use in their strategic activities'; though 'it does
t describe the routines or procedures necessary to carry out
ch step'. It should be 'treated as a dependable outline for [the]
instruction of individualized planning systems'; and as such
ers . . . should be continually alert to the need for occasional
ditions or deletions'.

Bibliography

hn A. Pearce II and Richard B. Robinson Jr, *Strategic Management – Strategy Formulation and Implementation*, Richard D. Irwin Inc., 1988.

20

Arthur A. Thompson Jr and
A. J. Strickland III

—

Arthur Thompson is the John R. Miller Professor of Busine
Administration at the University of Alabama where he specializ
in strategy formulation, competition and market analysis. Lonn
Strickland is Professor of Strategic Management at the san
university. Their work, *Strategic Management – Concepts ar
Cases*, which is but one of three books in the same field they ha
co-operated on, is the most popular text of its kind in U
colleges and universities.

Thompson and Strickland do not define strategic managemer
– except ostensively. That is, they show us what they consider
consists of; they tell us why it is a continuous process; the
describe those who participate in it; and they talk about i
benefits. But they do not capture its essentials in a pithy senten
or two. About strategy they are more direct, however.

Strategy is the pattern of organizational moves and manageri
approaches used to achieve organizational objectives, and to pursue tl
organization's mission.

Strategy is, therefore, a means: and carefully distinguished fro
ends (i.e. mission and objectives). Strategic management, on tl
other hand, is concerned with all three – and two other 'compo
ents' beside – in what they call the 'five Tasks of strateg
management'. They are illustrated in Fig. 20.1.

Developing a mission (or, management's 'vision') is the fir
of three of these five Tasks which are termed 'direction-setting
(By implication, it should result in the production of a writte
'mission statement'.) There are three 'distinct aspects' to tl
Task which distinguish the firm's identity and character fro
those of its competitors:

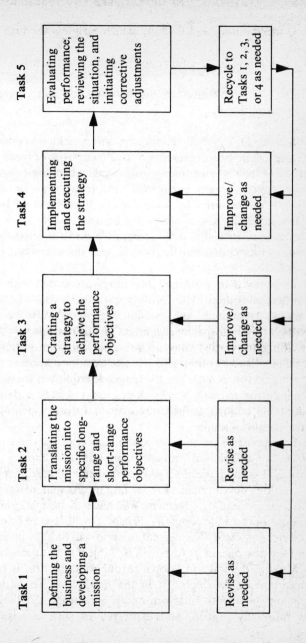

Fig. 20.1

Task 1

Defining the business and developing a mission

Revise as needed

Task 2

Translating the mission into specific long-range and short-range performance objectives

Revise as needed

Task 3

Crafting a strategy to achieve the performance objectives

Improve/ change as needed

Task 4

Implementing and executing the strategy

Improve/ change as needed

Task 5

Evaluating performance, reviewing the situation, and initiating corrective adjustments

Recycle to Tasks 1, 2, 3, or 4 as needed

- Understanding and defining which business the firm is *reall* in.
- Deciding when to change the mission and the firm's 'strategi course'.
- The communication of the mission in 'clear, exciting an inspiring ways'.

Following D. F. Abell, Thompson and Strickland consider tha business definition comes down to a 'composite of three factors customer needs; customer groups; the technologies used, an what functions are performed. In answering the question related, respectively, to these factors (that is, *what* needs ar being satisfied? *whose* needs are being satisfied? and *how* ar they being satisfied?), management's gaze is directed outward while concepts of what the firm is, and does, are being forme internally.

There are two principal difficulties associated with definin the firm's business. The formulation can be too broad, or to narrow. Essentially, the mission statement must be 'narro' enough to pin down the *real* arena of business interest', becaus anything too broad 'has no practical direction-setting value (The emphasis has been added.) The exception appears to be th diversified company, when the language employed should delim 'their customer-market-technology arenas', but be expansive an adaptable enough to accommodate a future widening of th firm's business scope.

Entrepreneurship enters into the second of the three 'aspects since 'a well-chosen mission prepares a company for th future'. Looking ahead to where innovational customer-marke technology developments are leading means that, at some poin an entrepreneurial judgement will have to be made about th options open to the company. Prospects will need to be explore and risks assessed. The current mission will have to be amende and the new one, in its turn, will be subject to time constraints.

Making the mission known throughout the firm is nearly important as developing it in the first place. To be effectiv mission statements must win minds and hearts. So they shou be rationally argued, and expressed in such concise, simp terms as to leave no doubts about the direction that has been chosen, and why. Moreover, the message should be repeated often enough, in inspiring language, to 'begin the new organizational march'.

The second direction-setting Task is that of **establishing objectives**,[1] both long- and short-range. These breathe life into the mission by 'training the energies of *each part* of the organization on what needs to be accomplished'. Specified for each 'key result' deemed necessary for success, the 'areas' where they are usually required include: size, industry ranking, growth in sales and earnings, return on investment, dividend increases, market share, product quality and/or technological leadership, stock exchange status, degree of diversification, 'bad weather' performance, financial strength, customer service, and cost competitiveness.

Long-range objectives have two purposes: (1) they raise the issue of what to do *now* in order to reach distant targets; and (2) they cause managers to consider the implications, for the long term, of today's actions. Short-range objectives indicate speed, as well as performance levels. (What Thompson and Strickland call 'how much by when'.) The most distinct difference between the two types of objective occurs, in their view, when a long-range target of raising organizational performance cannot be met in one year, and short-range objectives have to be set as 'steps' on the way to that target.

Whether long- or short-range, objectives should be stated in measurable terms, and 'contain a *deadline for achievement*'. In these ways strategic decision-making becomes purposive, and provides the means for control. They must 'meet the criterion of being *challenging but achievable*'. And they must also satisfy the external demands made on a company which is to be successful in the face of prevailing industry and competitive conditions.

The process of setting objectives has to be 'more top-down than ... bottom-up', if strategic thinking is to penetrate all

---

. To avoid any semantic confusions, Thompson and Strickland eschew the use of 'goals', and speak only of 'objectives' – which they equate with 'performance targets'.

levels in a company. Indeed, if the converse were the case – and overall objectives came from the aggregation of lower level objectives – the result might be neither coherent nor representative of senior management's priorities.

Crafting a strategy is Thompson and Strickland's third direction-setting Task. In their view, four levels of strategy making stand out: corporate, business, functional, and operating. At each of these, strategic decisions, that is 'decisions about what approaches to take, and what new moves to initiate' in order to meet objectives and realize the company's mission, are made. Set out in Fig. 20.2 is a summarized version of their depiction of the 'strategy-making hierarchy', and its responsibilities.

Each managerial level, Thompson and Strickland argue, has to have a strategic 'game plan' so that it can meet the objectives set at that level. However, the company's direction-setting Tasks are not finished until the 'separate pieces and layers of strategy making' are brought together into a coherent whole. And, this harmonization 'usually occurs via the review and approval process'. The key to the table opposite highlight that process. Yet more informative of their view about this is Fig. 20.3, which reveals what they call the 'networking of missions, objectives and strategies' throughout the hierarchy.

Strategy-making is not 'truly successful' – to which Thompson and Strickland add, even more carefully, 'as a rule' – unless three criteria are met: (1) it brings together the factors, internal and external to the firm, in what they call a 'goodness of fit'; (2) it helps create a sustainable advantage; and (3) it raises performance.

They group the factors under six heads: three internal and three external. A simplified version of how Thompson and Strickland see them shaping the choice of company strategy is given in Fig. 20.4 on page 245.

Their three external factor groupings are:

1. Societal, political, regulatory, and citizenship considerations.
2. Industry attractiveness and competitive conditions.
3. Specific company opportunities and threats.

Fig. 20.2

ategy l	Primary strategy development responsibility	Strategy-making functions and areas of focus
porate	Chief Executive Officer (CEO), other key executives[a]	• Building/managing a portfolio of business units. • Finding synergies among related business units, and converting them into competitive advantages. • Allocating resources to businesses with the most attractive opportunities. • Reviewing/revising/unifying business unit managers' major strategic proposals.
e-of-iness	General manager/head of business unit[b]	• Devising moves/approaches to compete successfully and gain competitive advantage. • Forming responses to changing external conditions. • Uniting strategic initiatives of key functional departments. • Addressing company-specific issues and operating problems.
ctional	Functional managers[c]	• Crafting functional/departmental moves/approaches to support business strategy and achieve own objectives. Functional strategies apply to such areas as: R & D/technology; production/manufacturing; marketing and sales/distribution; finance; and human resources. • Reviewing/revising/unifying strategy-related moves/approaches proposed by lower-level managers.
erating	Field unit heads/lower-level managers within functional areas[d]	• Crafting yet narrower, more specific approaches/moves to support functional and business strategies, and meet field unit/department objectives.

Letters refer to superscripts in figure above. Typically, decisions are ewed/approved by: (a) the Board; (b) a senior corporate executive, usually CEO; (c) the business unit head; (d) a functional area head/department d.

Fig. 20.3

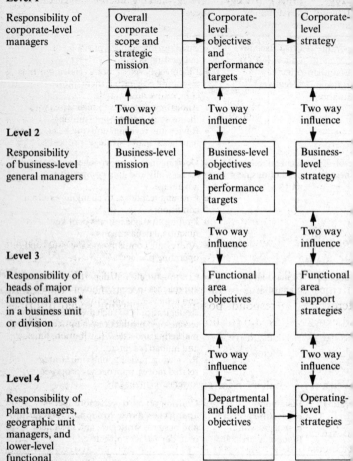

Level 1

Responsibility of corporate-level managers

| Overall corporate scope and strategic mission | → | Corporate-level objectives and performance targets | → | Corporate-level strategy |

Two way influence / Two way influence / Two way influence

Level 2

Responsibility of business-level general managers

| Business-level mission | → | Business-level objectives and performance targets | → | Business-level strategy |

Two way influence / Two way influence

Level 3

Responsibility of heads of major functional areas * in a business unit or division

| Functional area objectives | → | Functional area support strategies |

Two way influence / Two way influence

Level 4

Responsibility of plant managers, geographic unit managers, and lower-level functional managers

| Departmental and field unit objectives | → | Operating-level strategies |

* Manufacturing, marketing, finance, etc.

Fig. 20.4

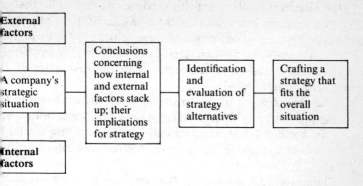

roadly, they argue, strategic choice is always bounded by all
ur aspects of the first of these. To make strategy socially
sponsible, it is necessary: (a) to ensure that the company's
tivities are in line with general perceptions of the public
terest; (b) to respond 'positively to emerging social priorities
d expectations'; (c) to show, by anticipatory action, a willing-
ss to avoid 'regulatory confrontation'; (d) to balance share-
lders' and society's interests; and (e) to behave as a good
tizen should.

Without a belief in an industry's long-term attractiveness,
her prospects for investment should be sought. Given that
lief, then strategic options will depend upon such specific
nditions as: what brings about change in the industry; its
rice-cost-profit' characteristics; the competitive forces at work;
e strategies and likely reactions of rivals; and the determinants
competitive success – which Thompson and Strickland term
ey success factors', or K S Fs.

K S Fs are 'the specific outcomes crucial to success in the
arket place, and the functional skills with the most direct
aring on company profitability'. In a list of the most common

types, they itemize forty KSFs grouped under seven headings. This sizeable number notwithstanding, we are told that an industry seldom has more than three or four KSFs at any time, with perhaps only one or two of these proving critically import ant. Strategists should therefore be discriminating in any listing they make – always remembering what the first letter of th acronym stands for: *Key*.

The identification of the particular opportunities open to th company [3] and any threats facing it, is a priority consideratic for the company. Indeed, essentially, strategy-making should l directed at exploiting the former, and putting up a defen against the latter.

Thompson and Strickland's three internal factors (which sha strategic choice) are:

1. Organizational strengths, weaknesses, and competitive cap bilities.
2. The personal ambitions, business philosophies,[4] and ethic beliefs of managers.
3. The influence of shared values and company culture.

Strengths are activities a company is good at, or things (skill assets, competences etc.) it possesses to its advantage. A wea ness, unsurprisingly, is an activity it performs poorly, or som thing it lacks. Both can be strategically unimportant, howeve since what confers importance is the capacity to compete succes fully.

A 'trade secret' of strategic management, they tell us, is

2. By way of example, one of these groupings is set out below.
   Distribution-related KSFs
   - A strong network of wholesale distributors/dealers.
   - Gaining ample space on retailer shelves.
   - Having company-owned retail outlets.
   - Low distribution costs.
   - Fast delivery.
3. Thompson and Strickland distinguish between 'company opportunities', a 'industry opportunities', on the ground that not all of the latter can be tak advantage of by every company.
4. Philosophy here appears to mean conventional practice, rather than ideolog

urning a company strength into a 'distinctive competence': that s, into 'something a company does especially well in comparison vith its competitors'. Distinctive competences are important to trategy-making because of what they afford the firm in exploit- ng an opportunity, the competitive edge they give it in the narketplace, and their potential to act as 'cornerstones of trategy'. Moreover, when a distinctive competence relates to a ESF it can be more easily developed into a 'competitive advant- ge' – always assuming the firm's rivals have 'no offsetting ompetences', and cannot match it without a heavy investment f time and money.

'Crafting a strategy is rarely so dominated by objective ana- ysis as to eliminate any room for the subjective imprint of nanagers.' Thompson and Strickland's general view – buttressed y research – is that, since managers quite normally have indi- idual notions about strategy and entertain ambitions for their ompany and its reputation, their decisions are likely to be ffected by these. In particular, their personalities and value ystems will, respectively, influence corporate attitudes towards isk and what constitutes ethical conduct.

As well as these purely personal factors, the company's own ulture can make an impact upon strategy – especially where ertain practices, policies, values, and types of behaviour have ecome deeply ingrained.[5]

Moving from the three direction-setting Tasks of Strategic Management to the remaining two (implementation/execution; nd what we may call control), is to enter a very different world f managerial endeavour, according to Thompson and Strick- and. While the crafting of strategy is largely entrepreneurial in haracter – involving 'heavy doses of vision, analysis, and . . . udgement', its implementation is 'primarily administrative', and lependent for its success upon inter-personal skills, 'culture- uilding, and creating strong fits between strategy and the way

. At this point, Thompson and Strickland deal with ethics in relation to strategy-making. Simultaneously, they abandon their more usual descriptive style and become normative. The reader can gain an impression of the change from the first proposition of their argument: 'Strategy ought to be ethical.'

Fig. 20.5

Component	Specific tasks
Building an organization capable of executing the strategy	<ul><li>Creating a strategy-supportive organizational structure.</li><li>Developing the skills and distinctive competence upon which the strategy is grounded.</li><li>Selecting people for key positions.</li></ul>
Establishing a strategy-supportive budget	<ul><li>Seeing that each organizational unit has the budget to carry out its part of the strategic plan.</li><li>Ensuring that resources are used efficiently 'to get the biggest bang for the buck'.</li></ul>
Installing internal administrative support systems	<ul><li>Establishing and administering strategy-facilitating policies and procedures.</li><li>Developing administrative and operating systems to give the organization strategy critical capabilities.</li></ul>
Devising rewards and incentives that are tightly linked to objectives and strategy	<ul><li>Motivating organizational units and individuals to accomplish strategy.</li><li>Designing rewards and incentives that induce the desired employee performance.</li><li>Promoting a results orientation.</li></ul>
Shaping the corporate culture to fit the strategy	<ul><li>Establishing shared values.</li><li>Setting ethical standards.</li><li>Creating a strategy-supportive work environment.</li><li>Building a spirit of high performance into the culture.</li></ul>
Exercising strategic leadership	<ul><li>Leading the process of shaping values, moulding culture, and energizing strategy accomplishment.</li><li>Keeping the organization innovative, responsive, and opportunistic.</li><li>Dealing with the politics of strategy, coping with power struggles, and building consensus.</li><li>Enforcing ethical standards and behaviour.</li><li>Initiating corrective actions to improve strategy execution.</li></ul>

the organization does things'. Implementation is also more diffi-cult and time-consuming than formulation.

By way of definition, they say that 'implementation entail

onverting the strategic plan into action, and then into results'.
nd its goal (*sic*) 'is to unite the total organization behind
rategy accomplishment, and to fit the organization's conduct
f its operations to the requirements for successful execution'.

In Fig. 20.5 is set out – in slightly altered format – what they
rm 'the administrative components' of implementation. Taking
ese together with the elements of the fifth (control) Task –
valuating performance, reviewing the situation, and initiating
orrective adjustments', indicates why Thompson and Strickland
ontend that 'strategic management is a process filled with
onstant motion'.

Bibliography

rthur A. Thompson Jr and A. J. Strickland III, *Strategic
    Management: Concepts and Cases*, Richard D. Irwin, 1990.

PART FIVE

The Incrementalists

Preface

n 1959, Charles E. Lindblom upset the scholarly consensus
bout the means-ends nature of complex decision-making with
he article briefly anatomized here.[1] Its title may be seen as an
xercise in irony, an oxymoron, or both. In more serious vein, it
as a footnote which describes its subject matter as 'the incremen-
al method', because of its resemblance to the use of incremental,
r marginal, analysis in economics. Afterwards, Lindblom came
o call it 'disjointed incrementalism'.

Some twenty-one years later, James Brian Quinn subtitled his
ook *Logical Incrementalism*; and, as the reader will discover,
his was not a nominal coincidence. Indeed, it could be said that
Quinn's work complements Lindblom's in the sense that it
rgues for the value (even the inevitability) of such a method in
he complex decision-making of companies, just as Lindblom's
rticle did for the public sector – and, it should be added, our
rivate lives.

Now while Lindblom's title may be thought witty, Quinn's
ubtitle is troubling. It is, of course, possible that he was reacting
a touch too gravely?) against the notion of 'muddling through'
s descriptive of the workings of the large corporations he
esearched; and that he wanted to convey, as emphatically as he
ould, the cerebral, systematic, and practical character of these –

For a more comprehensive discussion of his work as a whole, see *Writers on Organizations*, Penguin, 1989.

as he perceived them. But such an intention would not justif
the application of the term 'logical' to them.

That logic would be marshalled in argument, *as part of thes*
methods, we can be sure – in order to avoid the absurdities o
contradiction; or, so that the mind may be freed from th
limitations of conventional wisdom, by considering what i
'logically possible'. But logic, of itself, tells us nothing about th
world. Its usefulness depends upon the *empirical truth* we inves
in its propositions; and such truth, as Lindblom and Quin
frequently remind us, is hard come by.[2]

Far more usually, strategy discussion centres upon cause an
effect; and causation is a scientific, not a logical, concept. Whe
this occurs, formal theory is appealed to. Or, more accuratel
theor*ies* – often competing – are considered. Assuming that on
of these is chosen to shape discussion (and that cannot b
guaranteed), the tendency is for it to be supplemented with wha
often replaces it: judgement based upon experience, expertis
and intuition. And judgement, so essential to good management
is not an activity constrained by the rules of logic.

Because resemblance does not confer identity, one shoul
beware of describing a decision-making method as being logica
or 'having a logic', merely because it possesses certain propertie
in common with a logically valid argument. Both may be said t
be structured, and governed by a system of rules. A logicall
valid argument has a compelling quality: a thrust from premise
to conclusion which seems, indeed frequently is, intellectuall
inescapable. And some well worked out methods, systems an
procedures have the same imperative feel to them. But there th
similarities end. An argument is *validated* by its conformity t
the rules of logic. A method is *verified* by its results. If
logically valid argument leads to an empirically absurd conclu
sion, you *change the content* of the argument. If a method yield
disastrous results, you *change its rules, or its structure, or both.*

2. The reader who is unfamiliar with the elementary principles of formal log
   may yet be aware of the GIGO (garbage in, garbage out) aphorism o
   computer science – the machine language and programming of which ar
   based on those principles.

Both Lindblom and Quinn contend that the conventional view of how complex policy/strategy decisions are made is just plain wrong. And from their different standpoints they describe what actually happens, and what the structure and rules should look like.

21

James Brian Quinn

—

the mid 1970s, James Brian Quinn, who is the William and sephine Buchanan Professor of Management at the University Dartmouth, discovered a paradox. Indeed, it was the same radox which C. E. Lindblom[1] had come across before him: at large, well-managed organizations changed their strategies ways which bore little resemblance to the planning prescriptions usually found in management literature; and that the tionale for what they were doing – 'incremental strategy formution' – was not an instance of failure, but probably constituted e best normative model' for this type of decision-making.

In terms of personal revelation, Quinn's discovery recalls the ama of what happened to Saul on the road to Damascus. For ll over a decade he had subscribed to the 'step-by-step formal nning systems approach' – contributing to its literature, and, nsequently being hired by firms and government agencies to tall it. An increasing unease led eventually, in 1977, to the unting of a carefully constructed programme of research ich resulted in the publication of *Strategies for Change* three ars later.

The programme was centred upon very large, strategically namic, diversified companies[2] whose activities, as a whole, ve the sample breadth (in terms of industry types), and variety

Lindblom's work was, of course, relative to organizations in the public sector. ee **Charles E. Lindblom**, pages 263–270.

hose firms which 'generously co-operated' were: Chrysler, Continental Group, Exxon (Esso), General Mills, General Motors, Pilkington Brothers, illsbury, Volvo and Xerox.

(in terms of technology, 'time horizons', and national/inte
national characteristics). After secondary data surveys of eac
company, Quinn devised standardized questionnaires which l
used as the basis for two-hour interviews with ten or more of tl
people concerned with the strategy changes to be studied. Mo
of the interviews were taped; and for those where this was n
possible he made shorthand notes. He next brought this inform
tion together into a 25–35-page case history for each compan
The cases were compared with both primary and secondary da
sources, as well as checked and cleared by individual respon
ents, and on behalf of the companies. As this intensive proce
was completed for each company, the cases were publishe
collectively forming a data base for the programme.

To aid clarity, maintain consistency, and for the sake of rigo
Quinn set out definitions of the terms he used throughout l
research programme.[3] They are of interest beyond its immedia
scope.

3. (a) **Strategy** 'is the *pattern* or *plan* that *integrates* an organization's *ma*
goals, policies, and action sequences into a *cohesive* whole'. Well formulat
it 'helps to *marshal* and *allocate* an organization's resources into a *unique c
viable posture* based upon its relative *internal competences* and *shortcomin*
anticipated *changes in the environment*, and contingent moves by *intellig
opponents*'.

(b) **Goals/objectives** 'state *what* is to be achieved and *when* results are to
accomplished'.

(c) '**Policies** are rules or guidelines that express the *limits* within which act
should occur.'

(d) '**Programmes** specify the *step-by-step sequence of actions* necessary
achieve major objectives.'

(e) **Tactics** 'are the short-duration, adaptive, action-interaction realignme
that opposing forces use to accomplish limited goals after their initial conta

(f) **Influence** 'enables a manager to shape the actions of one or more person

(g) Influence stems from sources of **power**, such as individual ability; perso
'charisma'; conformity to an individual's, or a group's, norms (i.e. 'refere
power); role or position (i.e. 'legitimate power').

(h) **Formal authority** is 'the delegated right to use legitimate power'. T
is distinguished from **informal authority**, which arises out of aspects of
personality.

(i) **Political behaviour**, which is 'normal for any ambitious person', 'cons
of activities undertaken primarily to increase an individual's or grou
referent or legitimate power'.

He begins his account by analysing the formal planning approach to be found almost everywhere in the literature on strategy. It includes, he says, twelve 'main elements'. (These are so familiar to the reader that they hardly need recapitulation here.) 'Although excellent for some purposes', the approach unduly emphasizes 'measurable quantitative forces' at the expense of the 'qualitative, organizational, and power-behavioural factors that so often determine strategic success'. Moreover, it can so easily become a rigid routine – principally useful for financial control, and inimical to strategic creativity.

In practice, the larger organizations supposed to employ this approach rarely write down their complete strategy; and, typically, construct it with processes[4] which are 'fragmented, evolutionary, and largely intuitive'. To be sure, one can find – here and there among the fragments – examples of the employment of sophisticated, formal analysis. But what Quinn calls 'the real strategy' usually *evolves* from the consensus among top management which is created by an interaction between internal decisions and external events. 'In well-run organizations', he adds, managers are active in guiding actions and events towards strategies which embody the 'military-diplomatic principles' he discusses later.

What we may call, though Quinn does not, the structural base for strategy formulation is a series of subsystems.[5] The nature of their work places them in one of two categories: 'hard data' and 'soft'.

Hard data subsystems, which Quinn merely touches upon because of the extensive coverage the decisions they deal with have been given 'in the analytical literature about business

---

Process, as used by Quinn, is 'the sequence of steps, relationship transformations, and interpersonal and intellectual transactions needed to reach an end state or outcome'.

A **subsystem** 'is a grouping of activities and decisions interacting principally toward the accomplishment of one major strategic goal'. While each has its own timing and information 'imperatives', it is dependent upon other subsystems – which are staffed by other people (except for some top managers who may be members of a number of subsystems), and are perhaps pursuing another such goal.

strategies'), handle such matters as product-market segmenta
tion, make-or-buy issues, plant locations, and internal alloca
tions of finance.

There were eight 'soft' changes most often cited by the com
panies he researched:

1. Degree of diversification.
2. Divisional controls and divestment.
3. Structure/management style.
4. External relationships (domestic government, intere
   groups).
5. International posture, and foreign governmental relations.
6. 'Innovative capabilities or personnel motivations as affecte
   by growth.'
7. Employee relationships relative to changed values and soci
   expectations.
8. Capacity to deal with past or future technological co
   ditions.

On investigation, he discovered that: (a) neither quantitati
modelling nor financial analysis was suitable for dealing wi
most of these issues; (b) although companies used differe
subsystems to formulate strategy for each issue (including ha
data ones), the subsystems 'were quite similar' despite the co
panies' varied industrial settings; and (c) 'no single form
analytical process could handle all these strategic variabl
simultaneously on a planned basis'.

The reason for (c) being the case is what Quinn has term
'precipitating events': that is, events (either internal or externa
outside of management's control which could precipitate 'urger
piecemeal, interim decisions that inexorably shaped the co
pany's future strategic posture'. Because their arrival, th
impact, even their character cannot be foreseen, Quinn ca
them 'unknowable'. And since premature measures to cope wi
them can be hazardous – perhaps irreversible – senior manage
of the companies studied approached them incrementall
making only broad and tentative commitments of a kind whi
could be revised later. Even when hard pressed, they wou
choose to delay making decisions, or would keep them vague.

Three purposes were served by this deferment: (1) more information could be obtained in the meantime; (2) the participation
of subordinates could be encouraged; and (3) 'a commitment to
solutions' could be built. Items 2 and 3 were important because
senior executives were 'sensitive to organizational and power
relationships' among their key constituents – constantly striving
to improve their 'dynamics'. As Quinn puts it: 'added information *had to be* combined with phased political moves to secure a
desired outcome'. (Emphasis added.) At such critical times,
therefore, when an incremental approach was the only one
possible, it met 'the organizational, psychological, and informa-
tional imperatives' of the company.

The essentials of Quinn's findings can be summarized, therefore, as being that 'the most effective strategies of major enterprises tend to emerge' from an iterative process which:

> Leads to incremental commitments that enable the enterprise
> to experiment with, and learn about, an otherwise unknow-
> able future; and
> Coheres with the power political and 'organizational-psycho-
> logical' aspects of collective decision-making.

However, this summary oversimplifies. Overall strategy results
from the 'development and interaction' of major subsystem
strategies which, themselves, emerge by way of processes characterized by A and B, but responsive to their own 'unique needs'.
They have to cater to their own needs because no one can
predict how any subsystem will evolve, or interact with others to
create the strategy of the enterprise as a whole. It then becomes
the continuing task of strategic management to reconcile subsystem strategies with each other so as to produce an integrated
enterprise strategy. And in order to do this it deals, 'consciously
and simultaneously', with the three factors contributing to the
quality of strategic decisions and the likelihood of their successful execution: information-analysis, power politics, and organization psychology.

Quinn is emphatic that, despite appearances, this process is
not 'muddling through'. It is, by contrast, 'a conscious, purpose-
ful, proactive, executive practice' – when properly managed. He

terms it 'logical incrementalism'. Its incremental character goes
without saying. He believes it to be logical because it proceeds
'flexibly and experimentally' from broad concept to particular
commitment, using delay to acquire more information and thus
reduce risks.

As well as arguing for the displacement of today's formal
planning systems by 'the realities of logical incrementalism',
Quinn contends that business leaders could benefit enormously
from studying the literature of 'military-diplomatic strategy
formulation'.

Drawing principally upon the campaigns and writings of a
sizeable number of outstanding figures,[6] he sets out the following
'essential insights'.

1. 'Effective formal strategies' contain three elements:
    (a) 'the most important *goals*';[7]
    (b) 'the most significant *policies*';[8]
    (c) 'the major *programmes*' [or action sequences];[9]
2. Such strategies 'develop around a *few key concepts and
    thrusts*'. These provide 'cohesion, balance, and focus'.
3. Strategy deals with the *unknowable* – not just the unpredict-
    able. The essence of strategy, therefore, is to '*build a posture*
    selectively strong enough and flexible enough for the organiza-
    tion to attain its goals regardless of the unforeseeable inter-
    actions of external events.
4. In the manner of the military – with strategies for each of its
    spheres of operation (e.g. grand, theatre, area, and battle) –
    complex civil organizations should have a hierarchy of re-
    lated, and supporting, strategies: each more or less complete
    and appropriate to its level of decentralization.

Ultimately – if, for example, one can disregard luck, overwhelm-
ing resources, or the incompetence of the combatants – the
criterion by which a strategy should be judged is its success. But

6. Including Alexander the Great, Napoleon, Sun Tzu, Foch, Jomini, Lenin,
   Von Clausewitz, Mao Tse-tung, Liddell Hart, Von Bulow, Machiavelli, Montgomery and Von Scharnhorst.
7, 8, 9. See page 256, note 3.

vhat criteria can be used 'to define an effective strategic struc-
ure' in advance of any test? In dealing with this question,
Quinn itemizes some ideas already familiar to managers.[10] He
hen adds nine other 'critical factors and structural elements'
vhich, at a minimum, should also be present. They are:

Clear, decisive objectives. Major goals need not be in written
form, or 'numerically precise'; but they must be understood,
since – if achieved – they ensure the integrity of the organization as a competitive entity.

Maintaining the initiative. The strategy should promote a
proactive attitude to determining the course and timing of
events.

Concentration. Having determined what confers superiority
on the organization (e.g. a distinctive competence), the strategy applies that superior power to the place, and at a time, so
as to make the application decisive.

Conceding selected positions. This is the obverse of the
previous factor, in that the strategy – to bring about
concentration – specifies where it can best afford to lose.

Flexibility. The strategy should identify what 'resource buf-
fers' and 'reserved capabilities' the organization can deploy in
order to be able to outmanoeuvre competitors – either offen-
sively or defensively.

Co-ordinated and committed leadership. Since strategic
success 'require[s] commitment, not just acceptance', responsible leaders, whose 'interests and values match the needs of
their roles', must be chosen for each of the organization's
major goals.

Surprise. Use should be made of speed, secrecy, and (industrial) intelligence to 'wrongfoot' exposed competitors.

Security. The strategy should 'secure resource bases and all
vital operating points for the enterprise'. This is to be done by
developing an effective intelligence system (to prevent the

). 'Clarity, motivational impact, internal consistency, compatibility with the
environment, appropriateness in light of resources, degree of risk, match to
the personal values of key figures, time horizon, and workability.'

organization being surprised by competition), logistics planning (to support its major thrusts), and coalitions (to 'extend the resource base and zones of friendly acceptance').

- **Communications.** The strategy should develop broad, clear, and uncomplicated plans together with the networks 'to adjust these effectively'. (Quinn's rationale for this is that strategies have failed in the past, not over structural defects, but because: (1) they were insufficiently well understood; (2) they suffered from 'human errors', which were neither perceived nor corrected in time; (3) they did not lend themselves to coordinated implementation; and (4) they could not be adjusted rapidly enough to cope with unexpected competitive moves.)

There is, Quinn tells us, nothing rigid or dogmatic about these tenets. Rather, the strategist should use them to check that his organization's emerging strategy has not disregarded them – as so frequently happens, whether it has been 'formally derived' or constructed incrementally. In this view he finds himself at one with C. Von Clausewitz, who says in his classic work, *Vom Kriege*: 'All that theory can do is give the artist or soldier points of reference and standards of evaluation ... with the ultimate purpose of not telling him how to act but of developing his judgement.'

It is a quotation Quinn seems especially fond of, since he employs it twice: commending it not only to working strategists, as above; but also to reading strategists – including those who have studied logical incrementalism.

Bibliography

James Brian Quinn, *Strategies for Change – Logical Incrementalism*, Richard D. Irwin, Inc., 1980.

22

Charles E. Lindblom

—

Charles Lindblom's distinguished career culminated with his appointment as Sterling Professor of Economics and Political Science at Yale University. The focal point of his work has been organizations in the US public sector. However, his study of decision-making with D. Braybrooke,[1] and his famous article, 'The Science of "Muddling Through" ', which is dealt with here, continue to merit the attention of manager-students everywhere.

Lindblom's starting point is a paradox. He contends that, in the literature dealing with complex decision-making in the public sector, writers continue to advance one particular approach – which he terms the 'root' method – while both acknowledging mankind's intellectual shortcomings in attempting to practise it, and accepting that policy formulation[2] is *inevitably* carried out by employing an entirely different approach – which he terms the 'branch' method.

The persistence of the paradox is in part due, he argues, to the records of operations research, statistical decision theory and systems analysis. Each of these – like the root method – is typified by 'clarity of objective, explicitness of evaluation, a high degree of comprehensiveness of overview, and, wherever possible, quantification of values for mathematical analysis'. But, by clear implication, Lindblom considers that their undoubted successes should not be allowed to buttress support for the root method. This is because their employment is only appropriate to

---

1. *A Strategy of Decision*, The Free Press, 1963.
2. For 'policy' we can today read 'strategy'.

Fig. 22.1

Root (or Rational-Comprehensive)	Branch (or Successive Limited Comparisons)
1a. Clarification of values or objectives distinct from, and usually prerequisite to, empirical analysis of alternative policies.	1b. Selection of value goals and empirical analysis of the needed action are not distinct from one another but are closely intertwined.
2a. Policy-formulation is therefore approached through means-ends analysis: first the ends are isolated, then the means to achieve them are sought.	2b. Since means and ends are not distinct, means-ends analysis is often inappropriate or limited.
3a. The test of a 'good' policy is that it can be shown to be the most appropriate means to desired ends.	3b. The test of a 'good' policy is typically that various analysts find themselves directly agreeing on a policy (without their agreeing that it is the most appropriate means to an agreed objective).
4a. Analysis is comprehensive: every important relevant factor is taken into account.	4b. Analysis is drastically limited: i. Important possible outcomes are neglected. ii. Important alternative potential policies are neglected. iii. Important affected values are neglected.
5a. Theory is often heavily relied upon.	5b. A succession of comparisons reduces or eliminates reliance on theory.

relatively small-scale problem-solving, where there are few vari‑
ables and value issues are straightforward – rarely, if ever, th‑
characteristics of public policy formulation.

In the manner above (Fig. 22.1) he sets out the distinctiv‑
differences of each method, described in what he regards as th‑
simplest terms.

Lindblom uses an explanatory analysis of the branch (succes‑
sive limited comparison) method to demonstrate: (1) that this i
'how most administrators do *in fact* approach complex ques‑

ions'; (2) that the root (rational-comprehensive) method 'is *in fact* not workable for complex policy questions'; and (3) that, because of (2), 'administrators *are forced* to use the [branch] method'. (The emphases have been added.)

Dealing with each section in turn, he says, in connection with (1a) and (1b), that there are three difficulties impeding the successful application of (1a) of the root method to complex social problems.

First: on many 'critical' values (e.g. freedom, security, better schools) and objectives (e.g. road siting, pest control, minimum wages), there is no consensus among politicians, citizens or administrators. Nor can majority preferences be readily appealed to, since they have often not been ascertained; and, prior to public debate, may not even exist.

Second: should the administrator be tempted to employ his own value preferences to guide decision-making, he will not know how to rank them if they conflict with one another – 'as they usually do'. So, typically, he will have to make a choice from among policies (i.e. the means by which objectives and values are realized) that 'combine' these values in different ways.

Third: circumstances change the relative values of social object-ves.[3] Lindblom illustrates the point by picturing an administra-tor who values highly both good public relations and the quick completion of projects. In an abstract sense, he argues, it hardly matters which of these possibly conflicting values the administra-tor favours. But, in policy terms, he may have to decide between the two: when, say, speed of working militates against the happiness of his clientele. So, his choice of policy will vary with circumstances.

This example, Lindblom contends, shows that the 'value prob-lem' is always one of 'adjustments at a margin'. And since, in practice, marginal values or objectives can only be stated in terms of particular policies, any attempt to rank values in some general way – 'so that they do not shift from decision to

3. Lindblom describes this as a 'subtle' difficulty which 'underlies ... the first two'.

decision' – is an academic exercise. As if to emphasize his position, Lindblom goes on to argue that were all administrators to agree on a set of values, objectives and constraints, and then agree on a ranking order within that set, it would still not be possible to formulate their marginal value choices when it came to making actual policy decisions.

'The process by which values are actually handled' has two aspects, he argues – by way of summary:

1. 'Evaluation and empirical analysis are intertwined; that is one chooses among values and among policies at one and the same time.'
2. In a 'related but distinct' activity, attention is focused on marginal, or incremental, values.

As a consequence, the administrator's 'need for information is drastically reduced as compared with the root method; and his capacity for grasping, comprehending, and relating values to one another is not strained beyond breaking point'.

Turning to the second section of both methods (2a and 2b). Lindblom reminds us that decision-making is usually formalized as an ends-means process, in the manner of (2a). But this is only practicable 'to the extent that values are agreed upon, are reconcilable, and are stable at the margin'; and, as he has already argued, such conditions do not characterize complex social problems. But, Lindblom observes, even granting such complexity, some people will find it unthinkable that a method of discriminating among policy options can work properly unless, like (2a) it attempts to measure their relative contributions to some predetermined value or objective. So how does one decide upon the best policy, using the branch method?

Lindblom deals with this question in his comments on the third section, (3a) and (3b).

It is still possible under the branch method, he argues, 'where objectives are defined only through the . . . incremental approach to values described above', to test whether a policy does meet the set objectives. However, 'a precise statement of the objectives takes the form of a description of the policy chosen, or some alternative to it'.

But what if there is no agreement on values or objectives? In this case, the root method can offer no test. For the branch method, regardless of agreement on values, 'the test is agreement on policy itself', arising out of a comparative discussion of all the policies which might have been chosen: a procedure many administrators will readily accept as being the most effective way of determining correctness.

'Agreement on policy thus becomes the only practicable test of . . . correctness.' (Indeed, attempting to win support for objectives as well as policies might be impracticable in that it could cause 'quite unnecessary controversy'.) And if this seems a poor substitute for an ends-means test then, as Lindblom reminds us, objectives themselves only acquire status through agreement. 'Hence, agreement is the test of "best" policy in both methods.'

The fourth section (4a and 4b) deals with analysis. As its alternative name suggests, the root method ideally leaves nothing out. However, limits to our cognitive powers and on the information available to us mean that no one can actually apply the rational-comprehensive approach to complicated problems, Lindblom tells us. Consequently, all administrators must look for ways 'drastically' to simplify complexity. The branch method systematically achieves this by two measures:

. It confines policy comparisons 'to those policies that differ in relatively small degree from policies presently in effect'; and,

. It ignores 'important possible consequences of possible policies, as well as the values attached to the neglected consequences'.

is immediately obvious how the first simplifies the administrator's task: by removing from consideration any option unlike those which are already familiar. Slightly less obvious is that this procedure – which Lindblom sees as the counterpart of the marginal comparison of values, described above – reduces the amount of new knowledge required to make decisions.

The latter feature gives the branch method a predictability which, typically, is missing from the non-incremental, root, approach. And predictability, in its turn, helps with the political processes of democracies – which also, according to Lindblom 'change their policies almost entirely through incremental adjust ments'. He, therefore, contends that the method of successiv limited comparisons has a 'relevance as well as [a] realism' no to be found with the rational-comprehensive.

The second simplifying measure could strike one initially as 'shocking shortcoming' of the method. But what may seem t some as 'random or arbitrary' exclusions, 'need be neither'. This is because, in societies like the US, 'almost every interes has its watchdog'; and the activities of such interest groups – b applying pressure to each other and to the administration, in process Lindblom terms 'mutual adjustment' – arguably contrib ute more to the safeguarding of society's values than systemati attempts at intellectual comprehensiveness ever could.

Indeed, while both methods (root and branch) exclude factor – as part of the unavoidable need each has to simplify – only th latter's exclusions are 'deliberate, systematic and defensible'.

In his commentary on the final section (5a and 5b), Lindblon tells us that policy-making is at best a very rough process, sinc no one yet has enough knowledge of the social world 'to avoid repeated error in predicting the consequences of policy moves' Wise administrators, therefore, expect to succeed only partially and are resigned to the arrival of unanticipated, and unwanted consequences. However, by proceeding via 'a *succession* of incre mental changes' serious and lasting mistakes can be avoided.

He gives four reasons for this to be the case. One: from th past, the administrator knows the probable consequences o moves similar to those he now proposes to make. Two: neve believing that what he does next will finally resolve the problem he need not attempt so big a step towards his goal that th outcome cannot be predicted. Three: effectively, therefore, h can test each past prediction as he moves along. And four: h can often correct mistakes quickly – certainly more quickly thar if he took bigger, wider spaced, steps.

4. Lindblom somewhat wickedly suggests that, even if they were, the resultin policies might 'be more intelligently formulated than through futile attempt to achieve a comprehensiveness beyond human capacity'.

By contrast, the root method relies heavily on theory – which Lindblom defines as 'general propositions which can be applied to specific situations'. Its advocates subscribe to the view that theory 'is the most systematic and economical way to bring relevant knowledge to bear'. But even granting that does not help when we have no theory adequate enough to apply to problems 'in any policy area'.[5] 'Comparative analysis, as in the branch method,' he concludes, 'is sometimes a systematic alternative to theory.'

Bibliography

Charles E. Lindblom, 'The Science of "Muddling Through"', *Public Administration Review*, American Society for Public Administration, Vol. 19, Spring 1959, pp. 79–88.

Though he does concede that theory can be of assistance in some areas (e.g. monetary policy).

PART SIX

The Analysts of Decline

Preface

Until Kathryn Harrigan's research into the strategies firms could adopt to deal with conditions found in declining industries, the subject had received little scholarly attention. This is understandable in the light of the long period of almost uninterrupted growth most market economies had experienced from the end of the Second World War until the early 1970s. This is not to say that neither products became obsolete nor markets disappeared during those decades. But it was the case – especially because of the increasing popularity of diversification – that strategic studies tended to concentrate on the search for new opportunities, which, at the time, seemed to stretch endlessly into the future.

In this venturesome climate the costs of divestment could readily – and for the most part, realistically – be ignored when compared with the advantages of a rapid investment, or reinvestment, of resources in advanced products. So, much academic effort went into examining ways of growing, the structural implications of growth, and the degree to which there should be compatibility within a portfolio of differing industrial activities.

The depredations of the Vietnam war, together with the oil crisis of 1973, signalled the end of these golden years. West Germany, and later Japan, had by then elbowed their ways on to the world stage: to be followed, respectively, by the rest of the EC and other Pacific Basin countries. Global competition was intensifying, aided by a general reduction in protective tariffs and a fashionable impetus towards deregulation. There was still growth to be found, but it was at lower rates and less predictable.

Instead of being nearly universal, it had to be sought for country by country, region by region, industry by industry, market by market, and niche by niche. Exit barriers began to be considered as seriously as those impeding entry; and the right hand half of that old scholastic standby, the product life cycle, was re examined for clues.

Here is Harrigan's starting point.

The cycle's literature is characterized by 'generalized truisms' she contends. This is unsurprising, in the sense that the cycle attempts to aggregate industrial behaviour. But that flaws it because – by its very nature – it cannot account for competitors who fail to behave in a Pavlovian manner to the common stimuli of falling demand, a disappearing consumer franchise excess capacity, and rising costs of transport and distribution eventually leaving their industry in the hands of an oligopoly And if competitors do behave differently, then what they do why they do it, and what can be learnt from their 'endgame strategies' (that is, strategies for coping with industrial decline) form the subject of worthwhile analysis.

Stuart Slatter is far less concerned with industries than with companies approaching collapse. To be sure, the former may cause the latter; but he examines more minutely the internal reasons for the company qualifying as a 'turnaround' (that is one needing a strategy to avoid bankruptcy), and how it can be restored to health.

If it can be said that Harrigan augments and refines our understanding of the macro aspects of decline, then Slatter adds to our practical, micro knowledge of how to effect a recovery.

23

Kathryn Rudie Harrigan

—

athryn Rudie Harrigan is Professor of Strategic Management Columbia University, New York.

Harrigan distinguishes between product revitalization and hat she calls the 'endgame environment'. The first occurs when reduction in demand is perceived to be temporary, and is ought capable of revival with the finding of new markets or w uses for the product. The second is when a firm is confronted ith substantially less demand for its products – perhaps because bstitutes have appeared which are held to be 'technologically, onomically, or culturally superior' – and must consider run- ng down production permanently (at which point, the best it n hope for is that sales will plateau – though at a much lower vel), or leaving the industry altogether.

The orthodox strategic response to the second condition is 'to rvest': that is, to exploit the remaining investment in the siness in such a way as to produce the highest possible cash w from it, until divestment becomes inevitable. Those who ng to the product life cycle (PLC) concept would approve of is response, believing, as they do, that all products have nited lives which, in their decline phase, tend to follow the me pattern.[1]

But might there not be circumstances when the firm would nefit from a greater rather than a smaller investment? Harrigan in no doubt that there are. Her work shows that firms in these

---

As volumes drop price cutting intensifies, reducing profits, causing expendi- ures on advertising and R & D to fall or be eliminated, and leading eventually to undifferentiated products of near-commodity status.

twilight industries can be as constructive with their 'endgame strategies (that is, strategies for dealing with industrial decline as they were in the halcyon days of growth. They will as questions about how to compete; whether it would pay to sta in and dominate; how to make the most of what opportunitie remain; which of their competitors are best equipped to continue and what would constitute their strengths in any battles t come. Equally, of course, they will consider when they shoul escape; and which of their exit barriers will be the most difficu to surmount.

Harrigan's quarrel with the PLC is not that it is alway inaccurate – indeed, it does fit some case histories – but that treats all declining industries in the same way, assuming that th behaviour of competitors in interpreting, and then respondin to, endgame conditions will be identical. Probably, as a conse quence, the literature has suggested few strategic options when firm is expected to suffer from relentlessly falling demand. Ther is not even, she argues, a 'framework' available to distinguis the truly hopeless business from the rest: a shortcoming no dissimilar to one she ascribes to the discussion of harvesting i academic journals (though not the business press), where n distinction is generally made between low-growth and declinin businesses.

By way of summary, she contends that the principal defect c past endgame discussions (whether scholarly or popular) is tha there have been no 'attempts to sort out the factors whic influence the strategic choices managers will face'. What stud there has been of declining demand has been cursory, an related only to PLC theorizing. Moreover, those discussion have 'espoused only one strategy alternative [sic] for copin with' it. All in all, therefore, what we have is 'a simplified vie . . . scarcely adequate for decision makers' needs'.

To help repair this intellectual omission, Harrigan tested tw key hypotheses:

1. That the characteristics of declining industries differ; an that, therefore, the endgame strategies companies adopt t deal with those differences, themselves, differ.

Fig. 23.1

oncentrated industries		
elatively high economic cit barriers	*Relatively low economic exit barriers*	
acuum receiving tubes	Synthetic soda ash	*Commodity traits*
ayon and cellulosic cetate extrusion	Baby foods	*Differentiable product traits*
ragmented industries		
elatively high economic cit barriers	*Relatively low economic exit barriers*	
cetylene	Leather tanning	*Commodity traits*
igars	Electric percolator coffee-makers	*Differentiable product traits*

. That in any one declining industry there are several appropriate endgame strategies.

he researched eight industries, but presented data (in the form f miniature case studies) from seven.[2] The eight were selected ɔ provide contrasts between industries with: (i) high,[3] as against ɔw, exit barriers; (ii) concentrated, as against fragmented, structures; and (iii) differentiated, as against commodity-like, endɑme products. Fig. 23.1 illustrates her taxonomy.

Adopting the perspective of a diversified parent company – to btain some distancing from the actual endgaming business – Iarrigan's fieldwork and questionnaire techniques brought her to contact with more than fifty companies. She cross-checked

Electronic receiving tubes, synthetic soda ash, baby foods, electric percolator coffee-makers, cigars, rayon, and acetylene industries.
Having 'capital-intensive technologies and undepreciated, business-specific assets'.

the responses of the managers most closely concerned not on!
with parent corporations, but also with buyers, suppliers, an
trade associations. The endgame period specified for the stud
was from a 'base year', which facilitated 'cross-sectional compar
sons' among the industries, to 1978.

Harrigan's researches verified her two key hypotheses (se
above). Importantly – at least from the standpoint of practisin
strategists – they also enabled her to discuss some of the polic
implications of her findings. As she observes, those findings ar
subject to certain qualifications and limitations.[4] Even so, if on
bears in mind their less than law-like qualities, they constitut
invaluable indicators as to future conduct.

Two general implications emerged:

1. In endgame conditions, firms unaccustomed to competin
   with one another are brought into conflict; and this cause
   price wars – with resulting low margins, or losses. Harrigar
   therefore, wonders whether managers should not spend mor
   time analysing endgame competitive behaviour.
2. Similar misconceptions about the nature of such competitio
   appear to have brought about badly timed exits from th
   industry, the uneconomic disposal of assets, and 'cons
   quently disruptive performances in [the] endgame'. Her sugge
   tion here is that it may be worthwhile examining the 'strateg
   postures of competitors' relative to the endgame, *but prior*
   it.

While among her other findings are these:

● The expectations of competitors, and those of their customer
relative to future demand, have not been sufficiently well reco
nized – in the past – as having a powerful influence 'upon th
nature of the competitive environment'. Just the fear of bein
without supplies can drive away customers, prematurely. An
companies which communicate poorly with their markets ma
rely upon otherwise uncorroborated forecasting to invest in th

---

4. That, for example, endgame activities were studied, and not the process
   leading to strategy choices.

owth of segments which are actually deteriorating rapidly. oreover, Harrigan argues, better information could reduce the cidence of price volatility.

On a slightly different tack, she speculates that some of the ratic competitive behaviour' she came across stemmed from a ck of general understanding about declining demand and the its underlying it. She therefore calls for better tools to help ms assess 'the potential evolutionary power' of technological, mographic or cultural changes relative to their industry's ucture. Such qualitative forecasting techniques as scenario alysis may help strategic managers (a) identify competitors st likely to remain in the industry; (b) estimate how quickly others will leave; and (c) determine what types of competitors ith some new technology, for example) might enter when mand for a product declines.

Where firms are not already offering substitute products, or ow little of the alternative technology's economics, Harrigan's rk strongly suggests that they should innovate in this way so to 'monitor the rate of commercialization of the new techno-y', and 'control the speed of transition' from endgame to bstitute product.

If, in the endgame, products become more 'commodity-like', n it is probable that all but the lowest cost competitor will e market share. However, declining products which are differ-tiable may well justify further investment to secure a more ourable position – always assuming that a 'true customer he' (that is, one where 'demand responds to differentiation') ists for the product.

Although a company may enjoy a large share of the market, indications are that it should make an early attempt to its endgame business to another competitor or a supplier, less it can boast the lowest operating costs in the industry, 'a ong distribution system, or a loyal niche of customers'. And s is particularly so if a large proportion of its assets is depreciated.

The attractions of such an offer to other competitors rest on the possibility of reducing the number of factors 'causing volatil ity in the endgame': for example, differing expectations abou demand, or excess capacity locked in by exit barriers. Firm therefore, which possess some strengths and believe that deman will be sustained (at least in some niches), might be well advise to acquire the assets of companies serving those niches in orde to reduce the numbers of competitors and plants. Shoul customers remain price-*in*sensitive, this strategy may eve become lucrative.

● Price levels stayed higher, and volatility lower, in industrie where:

(i) There were no cheaper, perfect substitutes.

(ii) Customers found endgame products difficult to replace be cause of high 'switching costs'.[5]

(iii) Buyers did not buy on price from manufacturers of declinin products.

(iv) Firms with excess production capacity did not feel compelle to cut prices in order to optimize the use of the whole of tha capacity.

● In general, it was preferable to compete in declining industrie where:

(i) There were few (as against several) 'strategic groups'[6] an high (as against low) 'mobility barriers'.[7]

(ii) The competitors' assets were fully depreciated, rather tha substantial, relatively new, and producing for the same seg ments.

● External events can prove to be 'particularly catastrophi if they occasion unavoidable and irrecoverable investment

5. These are incurred when a new product is sufficiently different from previous one to necessitate additional investment or expense (e.g. staff retrai ing) on the part of the customer.

6. A strategic group is a collection of rival firms which, essentially, compete the same manner.

7. A mobility barrier represents the initial costs a firm faces when it repositio itself within a market by, for example, extending its product range or changir its method of distribution.

rrigan cites pollution control and effluent standards legisla-
ı as having tended to encourage exits.
She also suggests that firms wishing to thin out competition
the endgame might invest appropriately – but ahead of any
ıl need, and then campaign for legislation! In a similar vein,
argues that 'it may not be out of order' if companies, having
ecast the effects of potential legislation on their own affairs –
luding departure from the industry, 'draw [the] attention' of
ıl politicians and 'affected residents' to their analyses in so
as decisions based upon them might make an impact upon em-
yment, rates, 'and other benefits associated with the presence
he business unit', thereabouts.)

Whether firms remain or exit is not necessarily determinable
economic calculation alone. When they are part of a diversi-
l company, their poorer than average returns may, for exam-
, be accepted for the sake of strategic relationships important
where in the corporate portfolio; or because the endgame
iiness is what the company started with. So, in predicting
iaviour, one should take into account (i) 'the patterns and
ent' of the parent's diversification; (ii) the history of the firm
hin the corporation; and (iii) the basis for its 'competitive
ture in the declining industry'.

her concluding remarks, Harrigan goes beyond the remit of
research in a most interesting manner: she discusses the
:nomenon of declining industries from what might be termed
ublic interest standpoint.
t may be that there is a need for a single 'viable and efficient'
n to survive in order to meet residual demand. As things
nd, if that demand is met at all it is frequently met by
nufacturers locked into the industry by high exit barriers –
l, most probably, enduring uneconomic prices and returns.
t any contrived attempt by these manufacturers to rationalize
ir excess capacity so as to bring about an orderly withdrawal
them in favour of a single survivor would lead to anti-trust
gation.
Neither US legislation nor 'the spirit of European anti-trust
:isions' makes provision for declining industries. But, if

market mechanisms do not 'in this instance permit ration
decisions regarding who should exit, and at what time, th
perhaps US anti-trust policy might be modified in this one sm
respect . . . to attain the desired rational behaviour'. Moreov
politicians 'who wish to encourage the mobility of resourc
from low-return to high-return industries should recognize t
stultifying impact of exit barriers' upon that mobility.

Bibliography

Kathryn Rudie Harrigan, *Strategies for Declining Business*
Lexington Books–D. C. Heath and Company, 1980.

Stuart St P. Slatter

—

_uart Slatter is a barrister with a Stanford MBA and a PhD in arketing. Prior to joining the London Business School, where : heads both business policy and small business management tivities, he was managing director of a UK public company bsidiary. He has a busy consultancy practice specializing in rategic management. Aside from his work on corporate recov- y, he has written on competition and marketing in the pharma- utical industry.

Slatter's _Corporate Recovery – A Guide to Turnaround Manage- ent_, was published in 1984 at a time when the UK's economy as still reverberating from the severest recession the country d suffered since the early 1930s. It therefore draws upon his ty-to-day experience of the period, together with research he as conducted on both sides of the Atlantic. The book addresses e imminence of an eventuality which the strategist rarely, if er, discusses: bankruptcy. It is a strange omission considering e frequency of corporate collapse in market economies. Nor n it be thought that strategy ends there; it merely passes into her hands: those usually of the Official Receiver – at least in e UK. Slatter stops short of advising him, concentrating sentially on four themes: the recognition of when the firm (or bsidiary) is in trouble, and needs a 'turnaround' strategy; the uses of the decline; the then available option(s); and its, or eir, implementation. Our interest is principally in the first and ird of these.

Slatter quickly tells us that there is no simple, agreed way of entifying a turnaround company – that is a company which eds a strategy to prevent it becoming insolvent. (Insolvency being when liabilities exceed assets.) There are those who lir the description to firms with an acute cash shortage. And, wh Slatter would agree that they are indeed 'turnarounds', he wisl to extend the definition to include organizations which exhibiting signs of failure but, as yet, have no cash crisis.

For the purposes of a major study of some 2,100 UK quot companies over the period 1961–76, which he made in 1978, defined a turnaround as a firm whose pre-tax profits (at consta values) had declined for three or more successive years. By t definition 20 per cent of the companies were revealed as tur arounds.[1]

Defining a 'successful turnaround' (a company which avoic insolvency) as one whose 'real' pre-tax income increased in fo out of the following six years, Slatter found that, on average, o in four of the original turnarounds qualified; the remainc going out of business or, more usually, being taken over. Acqui tion by another company was also the fate of about a quarter those which had been turned round. This discovery leads him distinguish between firms which escape insolvency but strugg to make adequate returns – perhaps then failing – and tho which achieve 'sustainable recovery': that is, ones 'maki "good" profits, and ... unlikely to face another crisis in t foreseeable future'.

'Almost anything a firm does wrong ... is potentially indicator that all is not well,' Slatter tells us. However, t major **symptoms** of decline that he has observed are ten number.

1. *Decreasing profitability.* By this he means downward tren in pre-tax and trading profits (adjusted for inflation, to more informative), as well as reducing sales margins a rates of return on capital.

2. *Decreasing sales volume at constant (i.e. inflation-adjuste*

---

1. Slatter quotes a study by D. Bibeault showing that 27 per cent of US quo companies, analysed over a ten-year period, could be classed as turnaroun Bibeault's criteria were a loss, or an 80 per cent decline in profit, in a sin year.

prices. These are to be judged, he recommends, against some appropriate industrial criterion: e.g. sales per square foot, in retailing.

Increase in debt. That is in gearing, or leverage.

Decrease in liquidity. As measured by the usual working capital ratios such as current, 'acid test', debtor days, stock turn, etc.

Restricted dividend policy.

Accounting practices. The introduction of 'unacceptable' practices, undue delays in publishing accounts, and a change of auditors, are all suspicious signs.

Top management fear. In crises, Slatter asserts, managers may become 'totally incapacitated' – even failing to deal with the mail.

Rapid management turnover.

Declining market share.

Lack of planning / strategic thinking.

tter stresses that his listing is not exhaustive; and that, gen-
lly, one should be looking for a combination of such
nptoms before predicting that a turnaround condition exists.
sting doubts on the value of employing financial ratios
ne, he suggests that, if such an approach is adopted, it is best
ne on a comparative basis using equivalent data from major
npetitors.

nternally, the perspective is somewhat different. At some
nt in the decline of the firm (which may be brought about by
cess, e.g. through overtrading, as well as by failure) there will
what Slatter calls 'a severe crisis'. Following C. F. Hermann,
defines this as when the very survival of the company is
eatened, bringing with it restrictions on the time available to
surprised managers for adequate responses – and, conse-
ntly, 'high levels of stress'. Intense stress adversely affects
nagers' ability to deal with the new complexities arising out
the crisis, he argues; so, ultimately, crisis tends to reinforce
1 accelerate the decline.

Slatter contends that typically there are four Stages in the
elopment of a crisis. These are illustrated in Fig. 24.1.

Fig. 24.1

Stages	Typical organizational behaviour
1. Crisis denial	Complacency: signals completely over-looked
2. Hidden crisis	Crisis explained away; belief that it will disappear. No need for action
3. Disintegration of organization	Some action taken, but need for action underestimated
4. Organizational collapse	Inability to take action
Recovery Failure	

Passage through the stages, not unnaturally, varies; but whe
the crisis is brought on by rapid growth, some stages may b
very short.

As the title suggests, Stage 1 is characterized by managemen
ignorance – frequently caused by inadequate financial and en
vironment-monitoring control systems. Complacency is nor
mal; and there may even be a certain arrogance about the firm
capabilities and market standing.

With the onset of Stage 2 (that is, when the signs of crisi

ear), management's tendency is to explain it away. Two
uments then commonly heard are: that the firm is suffering,
only temporarily, from some recent changes in, say, products
capital investments; or, that short-term eventualities outside
firm and beyond its control (for instance, exchange rate
tuations) have adversely affected it. Significantly, neither
ument calls for action by management: which Slatter inter-
ts as being effectively a denial that a crisis exists; or, at least,
t nothing different need be done.

Vhere managers do not genuinely believe that the company's
rent strategy is correct, their denial of anything being amiss
y stem from a wish either to avoid blame (and possible
mployment), or radical change which may threaten their
ce in the firm's power structure. In both cases, they may
ort to 'creative accounting' to improve the appearance of
vant data.

Delays in taking proper restorative action bring about a
ntegration in the company's systems and structure; and Stage
rives. Management now acknowledges that there is a crisis,
acts – but underestimates the magnitude of what has to be
e. Decision times shorten, and stress takes its toll. Managerial
cracy increases, and with it decision-making groups become
ller. The conventional wisdom of the company tends to
er support – at the expense of alternative viewpoints and
se who hold them. But, Slatter argues, such actions do little
re than slow down the process of decay. And, all the while,
imistic propaganda pours forth: typified by 'the classic
keystick forecast (a short period of continuing decline
owed by a sudden and prolonged up-turn in performance)'.

he organizational cracks continue until eventually Stage 3
s way to Stage 4 (Collapse). Slatter lists, but again not
austively, some of the processes which are at work during
Stage.

An actual decrease in decision-making is accompanied by
uch talk about the need to be decisive.
ndividual managers pay more attention to their own, rather
han the organization's, goals.

- Steps taken in the Third Stage (e.g. budget cuts, reorganiza tion) bring about power struggles which undermine co operative moves and increase centralization.
- There is an increased expectation of failure – which tends become self-fulfilling.
- The average level of competence drops as the most able leave

As he then puts it: 'These processes reinforce one another. Th management becomes incapacitated and morale declines to all-time low, causing an even further decline in efficiency . The result is almost certain to be insolvency unless an approp ate recovery strategy can be adopted.'

Existing management, according to Slatter's findings, is un likely to be able to effect a successful turnaround from qu early in the development of a severe crisis. Long before becomes incapacitated (Stage 4) – indeed it could be at Stage assuming this persists for any length of time – it is rare capable of taking the drastic action which may be necessary.

Usually the initiator of change is not internal to the compa but external: a bank or lending institution. The sequence events is:

| Bank expresses concern | → | Bank expresses deep concern | → | Bank refuses to extend overdraft | → | Bank appoints a receiver |

Banks are, in the main, reluctant to appoint a receiver – princ ally because of the damage this may do to their reputatio They will on occasion demand that a new CEO is appoint but they may have to settle for an accountant who enjoys th confidence; or insist that the firm be supervised by turnarou specialists. Whichever course they follow – and the reco of UK clearing banks in initiating management change poor – there is still the need to find and adopt a turnarou strategy.

Just as he identifies four Stages in the development of a cris Slatter finds that corporate recovery falls into four Phas

arting with the assumption that recovery 'begins when the new
E is appointed' (and that it will have ended when 'normal'
anagement activities resume), he describes the first Phase as
nalysis'. This may last from a few days to six months, depend-
g upon the size and complexity of the firm, and how severe is
e crisis. During it problems will be defined, the mix of turn-
ound strategies for short-term survival decided upon, and an
tion plan devised.

The Analysis Phase is not followed neatly by the next, 'emer-
ncy', since this can start on the new CE's first day – always
suming he immediately installs improved financial control
stems. The Phase, which typically continues for six to twelve
onths, is the time for 'cash generation, cost reduction, increased
ices and increased selling effort'. Organizational change may
cur. But, as Slatter puts it, the Phase 'is often characterized by
rgery': with the disposal of subsidiaries, plant closures, redund-
cies, firings, stock reductions, sales of obsolete items, and
e dropping of unprofitable products, all actions which are
signed to conserve cash and stop losses. Simultaneously, the
E may look for extra funds to support his recovery strategy.

The third Phase, 'strategic change', can begin once the firm's
ort-term survival is assured, and the longer term can be
ntemplated. The emphasis will be on 'product-market reorienta-
n'; a process which should have begun in the preceding
ase when those 'segments where the firm has most competitive
vantage' were identified. This third Phase is when it may be
alized that the firm's future is dubious; or that recovery
oks too costly to justify the risks. The search is then on for a
rchaser. But, if all appears well, there should be a greater
ive for profits, going alongside the earlier search for liquidity;
erational efficiency seeking; and, organization building.

Finally – if the balance sheet shows the company to be
althy – the fourth Phase, 'growth', arrives. It may then seek to
velop new products and markets, or consider acquisitions.

Despite appearances, the Phases are not discrete. They can
erlap with one another; and some turnarounds go through
o at the same time. Moreover, the duration of each Phase
ries according to the relative ease with which recovery is

possible. Companies in growth industries can reach the la
Phase quicker than those in declining industries – because th
find it easier to raise additional finance.

In Slatter's view, a successful recovery strategy consists of
combination of what he calls 'generic turnaround strategies'. I
has identified the following ten 'which firms commonly use'.

1. *Change of Management*

(a) Chief executive (CE). '. . . inadequate top management
the single most important factor leading to decline and stagn
tion.' Consequently, most turnaround companies need ne
CEs. Even if the outgoing individual were not to blame f
the disaster, his departure apparently reassures bankers, i
vestors and employees alike that something constructive
being done. And certainly, the new CE's arrival is symbol
punishment for his predecessor who jeopardized the firr
and therefore its stakeholders' interests.

'One useful concept to help us analyse the manageme
problem is the concept of industry 'recipes' [*sic*]. Adoptir
the term (recipe) which P. H. Grinyer and J. C. Spend
introduced to describe 'an industry's pattern of manageri
beliefs',[2] Slatter follows them in arguing that when a firm
recipe has become obsolete there are two ways of changing
by major innovation; or by imitation. The latter – important
for the turnaround company – is the quicker and safer of tl
two. And the quickest way to imitate is to bring in as C
someone from within the industry who has already demo
strated that he has a successful recipe. The move, however,
not a cure-all, Slatter argues, because a CE who is simply
turnaround expert may be preferable to a CE whose princip
resource is a knowledge of the industry. Indeed, in diversifi
firms – where additional complexities arise depending up
the organizational relationship between headquarters a
operating subsidiaries – this tends to be the case.

2. 'Recipe' has certain affinities with P. F. Drucker's 'theory of the business',
reader will have noted.

'The turnaround man needs to have special characteristics and skills that may be different from those required in a healthy firm.' Slatter notes these as being: 'considerable leadership and motivation skills; flexibility; the ability and courage to make rapid decisions based on a minimum of analysis; the ability to work long hours under stress; and, most importantly, the ability to implement the turnaround strategies in the shortest possible time'. As a personality – whether the style is abrasive or emollient – the successful turnaround CE is tough-minded, ruthless, and not afraid of unpopularity. Unsurprisingly, with characteristics and traits like these, Slatter has found that many individuals do not take their companies through all the phases of recovery. (See below.) They can become bored after the early excitements of the crisis; they may have no real industrial recipe to offer; and, they may well create organizational resistance to themselves.

(b) Other management. 'Views vary enormously ... as to the need for major management changes at the level below that of the chief executive.' At one extreme is the belief that such senior managers should be removed because they will cleave to the old ways, or that they will be unable to adjust to the new CE's approach. And at the other, the view is taken that only the CE has to change; it being incumbent on the new man as far as possible to work with the existing team. In Slatter's opinion, 'there is no single correct answer'. It is rare for there to be no changes, however. And since 'a lack of adequate control systems is the most common cause of failure, that usually points to the need to appoint a new finance director or controller', even if no one else is replaced. For Slatter, the key issues determining the need for management change are the 'causes and speed of decline' prior to the turnaround.

Strong Central Financial Control

'The introduction of strong, central financial control at the beginning of a turnaround is virtually a law ...' This is because, Slatter contends, 'the prevailing culture' of most turnaround companies is not characterized by such control. Even if the new system is less than ideal it is vital that it be operational in a matter of weeks. A participative approach is, therefore, not to be recommended. Any adverse management reaction to this autocratic imposition is something the CE must be prepared for.

3. *Organizational Change and Decentralization*

'Organizational change should *not* be contemplated as a short-term turnaround strategy, except under special conditions.' Slatter gives three reasons for this advice:

(a) The firm's 'appropriate' structure is determined at least in part by its product-market strategy; and until this has been formulated any sizeable organizational change is premature.

(b) The incoming CE knows little of the true capacities of his staff, and nothing about the 'informal organization' of his company. Without such information any structural change would be a purely theoretical exercise.

(c) 'Organizational change requires a considerable amount of learning on the part of the firm.' Both the time and managerial effort required for this are unlikely to be available early in the turnaround.

Slatter tells us that there are 'at least' four special conditions where his advice above does not apply. They are:

(i) When it may be necessary to restructure the company in order to divest it of a subsidiary.

(ii) When the CE widens his 'span of control' at the top of the company so as to develop a power culture and gain control rapidly: an approach which Slatter considers works well in a crisis.

(iii) When it is beyond the capacity of one individual to ensure that the day-to-day execution of strategy is properly carried out. This occurs, Slatter asserts, in very large companies where 'the dominant core business . . . is in trouble'. The CE will set the new strategy, but he needs competent managers to apply it. He will, therefore, need time to create a team; and if enough talented managers are not readily

available, then the firm's structure may require modification
to fit the skills of those who are.

(iv) When a centralized structure has been identified as a
major cause of decline. Decentralization – either to establish
a multidivisional structure, or so as to give first-line managers
more responsibility – is then in order. A consequence of
decentralization may be reductions in head office personnel.
Slatter sees this as being almost universally beneficial for
such turnaround companies. Indeed, the only headquarters
function he would retain would be finance.

New Product-Market Focus

(a) Product-market strategies for short-term profitability.
'Where survival is the key issue, the short-time horizon means
that product-market decisions are often of a surgical nature.'
Essentially, this means 'cutting back the business to its profitable core': dropping markets, segments, and customers which
are unprofitable, or where the return on the capital required
to serve them is too low.

A less drastic alternative is to concentrate effort on select
'product or customer groups where the short-term profit
potential is greater'.

(b) Product-market strategies for sustainable recovery.
'Growth-oriented strategies are only possible once survival is
assured, or in turnarounds of stagnant firms where there is
no financial crisis.' Slatter's argument is that the major strategic options, following H. I. Ansoff, are product development,
market development, and diversification. These are seldom
appropriate in crises because they divert 'attention from the
problem at hand, and often result in considerable extra revenue [*sic*] expenditure'.

Introducing M. E. Porter's three 'generic competitive strategies' (which he considers to be product-market strategies),
Slatter says that only a focused strategy 'is available to the
turnaround firm in the short term'. By concentrating on a
small number of segments, and withdrawing from others, the
firm may at least gain a breathing space – if not lay down the
base for recovery. But even this advice is highly qualified.

'Focus' still requires 'cost leadership' or 'differentiation' to b
successful. A commodity-type market militates against co:
leadership; and differentiation only works if the product
not obsolescent, and the industry is of such a type that sellin
is more efficacious than advertising (presumably because
the expense).

5. *Improved Marketing*

'The most commonly used elements of the marketing mix i
turnaround situations are selling and pricing.' The 'organiz:
tional slack' which typifies companies in crisis is especiall
evident in the sales force, Slatter tells us. Motivation tends t
be poor, sales planning non-existent, and management wea!
New, more competent management can often bring abou
sudden increases in volume – assuming that the firm has th
necessary stocks, and can afford to finance any increases i
them and concomitant debtor levels. Changes in the sal
force may also be required; though – given good managemei
– it is quite likely that something above half the people the:
will be capable of much better performance.

'Pricing strategy is usually a critical area for immediate to
management attention.' In only one circumstance shou!
prices be raised immediately, regardless of effects on volum
where the product's variable costs are not covered by i
price. Otherwise, generalizations are difficult. Much w:
depend upon the price-sensitivity of the market. Clear unde
pricing can be rectified by increases. But, Slatter contends,
'harvesting' approach (that is, when the firm sacrifices penetr.
tion to enhance short-term profitability), while immediate
attractive, 'is a liquidation strategy' and will not bring abo
a sustained recovery.

6. *Growth via Acquisition*

This is a 'somewhat surprising but quite common recove:
strategy'. It is principally applicable to turnaround firms whic
are stagnant: that is, producing poor results but in no fina:
cial danger. The prime objective is faster growth than can !
achieved by organic development; though it may be a way

improving competitiveness, when both companies are in related businesses. An unrelated business acquisition, which Slatter calls 'diversification', can provide the turnaround acquirer with access to fields where the growth and profit opportunities are superior to those currently available. But, whether related or not, acquisition represents largely the same dangers to a turnaround as to a healthy company – with the obvious exception of the former's greater vulnerability should the acquisition prove to be a poor one.

Asset Reduction

'An asset-reduction strategy is often part of product-market reorientation.' That is, when a company abandons segments, markets or customers certain fixed assets become redundant and are disposed of. A financial crisis may be so severe, however, that assets – even profitable subsidiaries – are sold to provide liquid funds. And when the firm is in this condition, asset reduction is more immediately beneficial than efforts to improve profitability since what is needed is cash, not cash flow. (Though Slatter has some difficulty distinguishing between the two.)

Aside from the disposal of assets, or subsidiaries, the working capital area (specifically, current assets) can be examined for reductions. Stock levels, debtors, and debtor days are obvious targets.

Cost-reduction Strategies

'Cost reduction can be strategic, or operational, or both.' Aimed at increasing margins, it can 'improve the firm's cost position relative to that of competitors' (strategic), or enhance efficiency 'and bring overheads in line with volume' (operational). It is essential to those loss-making turnarounds where costs play an important part in the calculation of prices; though its effects on profits are less immediately apparent than those resulting from price increases.

Investment

'Firms which remain independent during the recovery phase are rarely able to invest much in the business until any

liquidity crisis has passed.' Open principally to turnarou
companies that have been acquired by well-funded fir
therefore, investment strategies are directed at either c
reduction (through the replacement of plant and equipme
or growth (organic, or by acquisition).

However, Slatter argues, investment must not be thou
of purely in terms of assets – fixed and current: '... cert
revenue expenditures can also rank as investment strategi
For example, new product development and marketing m
qualify when a firm's decline can be traced to 'produ
market reasons'.

10. *Debt Restructuring and other Financial Strategies*

Turnaround firms with a cash crisis are usually too high
geared, Slatter tells us. Before they can be said to ha
recovered financially, they must reduce their debt/equ
ratios to 'acceptable industry levels'. Two financial strateg
are available to them: debt restructuring, and raising ad
tional finance. The first takes such forms as: converti
short-term debt into long-term debt, loans into preferei
or ordinary shares, unpaid interest into loans; even persua
ing lenders to forgo interest, or write down some of t
amount owed. These measures are more popular in the U
than in Britain, where raising new funds has been larg
dependent upon the confidence inspired among investors
the arrival of fresh management and its prospects of turni
the company round.

Slatter itemizes six sets of factors determining the 'generic str
egies' to be used by turnaround companies. They are: the cau
of decline; the severity of the crisis; the attitudes of stakehold
involved in the turnaround process; the firm's historical strate;
the characteristics of the firm's industry; and, the firm's co
price structure.

A major finding of his research was that: 'The average numl
of generic strategies employed in successful turnarounds is cons
erably greater than the average number of factors causing declir
This is important to the practising manager who may well

ooking for 'individual causes and individual generic strategies'.
Decline may have been caused, say, by poor management, or
lack of financial control, or high product costs. On the face of it,
these defects could be simply remedied by new management,
improved control, and cost reductions – respectively. Slatter
argues, however, that the formulation of a successful recovery
strategy requires more than an understanding of previous cause-
and-effect relationships. He illustrates the point with Fig. 24.2.
This shows 'the principal generic strategies connected with each
of the major causes of decline'. It is oversimplified, he warns us,
because 'turnaround crises are brought about by a number of
causes'.

From a study he undertook of forty British turnaround public

Fig. 24.2

Causes of decline	Principal generic strategies required
Poor management ⟶	• New management • Organizational change and decentralization
Inadequate financial control ⟶	• New management • Improved financial control • Decentralization
High cost structure ⟶	• Cost reduction • Product-market
Lack of marketing effort ⟶	• Improved marketing
Competitive weakness ⟶	• Product-market • Cost reduction • Improved marketing • Asset reduction • Growth via acquisition
Big projects acquisitions ⟶	• Asset reduction
Financial policy ⟶	• Asset reduction • New financial strategy

Fig. 24.3 Comparison of successful and unsuccessful
recovery strategies

	Firms using generic turnaround strategy (per cent)	
	Successful recoveries*	Failed recoveries
Asset reduction	93	50
Change of management	87	60
Financial control	70	50
Cost reduction	63	90
Debt restructuring/financial	53	20
Improved marketing	50	50
Organizational changes	47	20
Product-market changes	40	30
Growth via acquisition	30	10
Investment	30	10

* Including both manufacturing and non-manufacturing firms not experiencing
crisis.

companies during the 1970s – thirty of which recovered, and ten
failed – he assembled the information shown in Fig. 24.3.

Slatter comments on, and interprets, what these percentages do
not show: the relationship between combinations (and subsets)
of his generic strategies and successful recovery, or failure. For
instance:

- Almost all successful turnarounds (recoveries) employed
  asset-reduction and new financing for cash generation, as
  against about half of those whose recovery strategies were
  unsuccessful (failures). However, the former were usually
  better placed to obtain additional bank loans or new equity.
- Divestment was the most common cash-generation strategy
  and was used by about half of the recoveries.
- As the figures show, improved financial control systems were
  more typical of recoveries than failures; but often the failures
  did not utilize the data their new systems threw out to impose
  tight control.
- Though improved marketing was introduced equally by
  recoveries and failures, recoveries tended to combine this

with product-market realignment and growth via acquisition.

Failures made few, or no, organizational changes; while those recoveries which succeeded best, decentralized organizationally and in terms of work processes.

Manufacturing firms used essentially the same strategies as other firms; though organizational change appears to be less important to the latter.

Slatter's UK findings – as to the combination of generic strategies used by recoveries – were similar to those he found when he studied twenty 'Californian growth firms'. But, speaking generally, he tells us that – putting strategy differences aside – the major distinction between recoveries and failures is 'in the *quality* of implementation'. The recovery CE is apparently much more ruthless in the way that he sees strategy is carried out.

Bibliography

Stuart St P. Slatter, *Corporate Recovery – A Guide to Turnaround Management*, Penguin Books, 1984.

Index of authors and
authorities

—

Abell, D. F. 91, 92, 95–109, 240
Abernathy, W. J. 122
Alexander the Great 260
Anderson, M. J. 120
Andrews, K. R. 1, 2, 5–14, 21,
    146, 159, 160, 195, 219
Ansoff, H. Igor 1, 2, 10, 15–33,
    81, 97, 103, 159, 193, 195,
    196, 219, 227, 228, 291

Bertalanffy, L. von 1
Barnard, C. 23, 217
Bauron 52
Bell, D. 15
Berle, A. 182
Bibeault, D. 282
Borch, F. 122, 123
Bower, J. L. 2, 14, 91, 92, 110–
    19, 185
Bruchey, S. 178
Burgelman, R. A. 91, 92, 184–92

Campbell, A. 204
Cassano, J. 207, 209
Cauwenbergh, A. van 199
Chandler, A. D. Jr 1, 2, 18, 21,
    26, 34–41, 116, 145, 146, 150,
    151, 154, 179–81, 207
Chang, D. 70
Christensen, C. R. 2, 14, 21

Clausewitz, C. von 73, 260, 262
Copernicus, Nicolas 145
Cyert, R. M. 2, 20, 26

Descartes, René 6, 25, 40
Digman, L. A. 194, 195–205
Drucker, P. F. 2, 15, 95, 219, 228,
    288
Durant, W. 181, 182

Fayol, H. 8
Fink, A. 179
Foch, F. 260

Galbraith, J. R. 58, 84, 194, 206–
    15
Galileo 145
Gluck 52
Goold, M. 204
Gordon, K. D. 120
Gort, M. 156
Grinyer, P. H. 288
Guth, W. 2

Hamermesh, R. G. 67, 91, 92,
    120–30, 159, 224, 225
Hanaan, M. 97
Harrigan, K. R. 271–80
Harris, J. E. 120
Haspelagh, B. P. 122

Hayes, R. H. 122
Henderson, B. D. 57, 67, 72–80, 121, 159, 224
Hermann, C. F. 283
Hirshfield, D. S. 203
Hofer, C. W. 10, 21, 23, 81, 159, 194, 195, 206, 216–29

Jomini, H. Baron 260
Juran, J. M. 200

Kazanjian, R. K. 58, 84, 194, 206–15
Kepler, J. 145
Kepner, C. H. 58, 81
Kono, T. 204
Kotler, P. 96, 222

Learned, E. P. 2, 21, 194
Lenin, V. I. 260
Levitt, T. A. 95, 97, 228
Liddell Hart, B. 260
Lindblom, C. E. 251–3, 255, 263–9
Lindsay, J. 173
Lorange, P. 233
Lynch, H. H. 149

Machiavelli, N. 260
Mao Tse-tung 260
March, J. G. 2, 20, 26, 241
Marshall, A. 216
Martens, R. 199
McDonnell, E. J. 25
McKinsey and Company 52, 121, 122, 163, 224, 225
McNamara, R. 1
Means, G. C. 182
Mintzberg, H. 91, 92, 131–44
Montgomery, Lord B. 260
Montgomery, C. A. 207

Napoleon I, Emperor of France 260
Nathanson, D. A. 207, 209, 213

Pearce, J. A. II 194, 230–37
Phillips, L. W. 70
Porter, M. E. 2, 3, 5, 14, 42–55, 67, 133, 194, 291

Quinn, J. B. 29, 251–3, 255–62

Reed, J. P. 120
Robinson, R. B. Jr 194, 230–37
Rumelt, R. P. 91, 92, 133, 145–54, 156, 207, 212, 213

Salter, M. S. 17, 91, 93, 145, 150, 155–72
Sayles, L. R. 91, 92, 184–92
Scharnhorst, G. J. D. von 260
Schendel, D. E. 10, 21, 23, 81, 159, 194, 195, 206, 216–29
Schoeffler, S. 59, 77
Scott, B. R. 145, 150, 207
Simon, H. A. 2, 114, 174, 180, 181
Slatter, S. St P. 272, 281–97
Sloan, A. P. 182
Smith, A. 33
Smith, W. R. 96
Spender, J. C. 288
Strickland, A. J. III 194, 238–49
Sun Tzu 260

Tawney, R. H. 110
Thompson, A. A. Jr 194, 238–49
Tilles, S. 95, 96

offler, A. 142
egoe, B. B. 58, 81–9, 209

einhold, W. A. 91, 93, 155–72

Williamson, O. E. 91, 92, 173–83, 207
Wrigley, L. 145–8, 151, 207

Zimmerman, J. W. 58, 81–89

Subject index

—

olute market share 68
defined 67
uisition 32, 87, 93, 129, 146,
  155, 158, 159, 161, 167–9,
  172, 182, 188, 208, 213, 282,
  287, 292–7
uisitive conglomerate 150
defined 149
ptive learning 24
ptive mode 137, 177
defined 143
hocracy 134, 142–4
defined 142
ninistration 2, 34, 53, 180, 188,
  268
defined 37
ninsitrative decision class
  19
defined 18
hual objectives 235
ti-trust measures
  EC decisions 279
  US legislation 73, 99
et reduction strategy 293
et-specificity 174–80
defined 173

otlegging 186
defined 185
ston Consulting Group

(BCG) 57, 67–9, 72, 75, 95,
  120, 163, 164, 224, 225
bounded rationality 174–7, 180,
  181
defined 174
branch method of decision
  making (successive limited
  comparisons) 264–9
defined 264
bureaucracy 134–8, 140–42, 144
business portfolio 171
business definition 92, 95–100,
  103, 104, 106–8, 240
defined 47
business planning process 113
business policy 1, 20, 110, 112
defined 6–7
business strategy 61, 73, 92, 95,
  108, 128, 226
defined 9, 126, 222, 243, 244
business systems concepts 52
business unit 60–62, 65–8, 85, 87,
  88, 108, 121, 122, 125, 127,
  196–8, 201, 225, 243, 244,
  279
defined 60, 108, 125, 225
see also strategic business unit

capability 7, 8, 13, 23–5, 84, 87,
  233–5

capability – *contd*
  defined 10, 23, 96
capital budgeting 110–12, 123, 203
  defined 110
Cartesian approach 6
case histories 36, 256
case studies 5, 120
cash cows 77, 125, 164
  defined 78
cash flow 64, 78, 111, 121, 123–7,
    163–71, 273, 293
  defined 63
centralized structure 291
centre of gravity 209, 211–14
  defined 210–211
chief executive (CE)/chief
    executive officer (CEO) 7–9,
    59, 81, 120, 122–4, 128, 134,
    135, 197, 199, 204, 233, 243,
    244, 286–90, 297
common thread 21, 227
  defined 22
competences 201, 202, 246, 256
  defined 218
competitive advantage 28, 50–55,
    77, 152, 170, 197, 208, 222,
    223, 243, 287
  defined 22, 51, 196, 221, 247
competitive position 60–62, 65,
    225, 235
competitive strategy 43, 46, 120,
    122
  defined 28–9
components of strategy 10, 13, 20,
    21, 195–6, 221
concentric diversification 32, 223,
    235
  defined 20
concept attainment 136
  defined 135
concept of the business 135

concept of the firm's business 22
conglomerate diversification 11,
    32, 145, 149, 150, 157, 159,
    181, 182, 183, 221, 223
  defined 20, 149, 235
context
  strategic 186, 189–91
    defined 185
  structural 111, 113–19, 185,
      186, 190, 191
    defined 114
corporate competence 10, 12
corporate crisis 124, 282–7, 289–
    94, 296
  defined 283
corporate objectives 8–10, 18, 20,
    21, 23, 26, 28, 32, 37, 81, 83,
    108, 113, 115, 126–8, 159,
    160, 176, 181, 195, 196, 198,
    201–3, 206, 218–21, 223, 229,
    230, 232, 233, 234, 235, 238,
    241–4, 248, 256, 261, 264,
    265, 266, 267
  defined 21, 160, 176, 195, 218,
      235, 241, 256
corporate strategy 6, 7, 12–13, 21,
    61, 112, 126, 127, 189, 196,
    221, 222, 226
  defined 9, 10, 126, 196–7, 221
cost behaviour 75, 97, 105
cost-reduction strategies 293, 295,
    296
court ordering 176, 179
  defined 175
critical issues 89
  defined 88
critical mass 33, 75
culture 10, 24, 30, 50, 62, 185,
    190, 214, 236, 246–8, 289,
    290
  defined 23

ustomer functions 97, 100–102,
    104, 105, 107
  defined 101
ustomer groups 97, 100, 101, 104,
    105, 107, 240, 291
  defined 101

ecentralization 34, 138–40, 142,
    211, 213, 260, 290, 291, 295
ecision class concept 17, 26
ecision classes 17, 18, 108
ecision space 18
ecision rules 17, 28
ecision making 6, 27, 58, 111,
    112, 160, 163, 174, 197, 198,
    199, 200, 207, 230, 233, 241,
    251, 252, 255, 259, 263, 265,
    266
eclining industries 271, 274, 279,
    288
efinition sub-process 114–19
  defined 113
ifferentiated marketing 102
  defined 97
ifferentiated strategy 104–6
  defined 102
ifferentiation 44, 47–51, 54, 64,
    96, 99, 100, 103–6, 134, 277,
    292
  defined 29, 44, 48, 97, 102
iscrepancy 115, 116
  defined 113
istinctive competence 92, 161,
    170, 197, 223, 228, 247, 261
  defined 96, 196, 221
istribution 44, 45, 52, 64–6, 84,
    99, 105, 107, 157, 210, 212,
    214, 221, 222, 243, 246, 277,
    278
iversification 11, 30–32, 93, 99,
    103, 107, 145, 147, 151–3,

155–9, 161–9, 172, 184, 191,
    196, 208, 209, 211–13, 223,
    224, 227, 235, 241, 258, 271,
    279, 291
  defined 19, 20, 40, 146, 155–6,
    293
divestment (divestiture) 88, 124,
    182, 208, 213, 235, 258, 271,
    273, 296
Divisionalized Form 134, 138–40,
    142
  defined 138
dogs (cash traps) 77
  defined 78
domain 187, 219
  defined 195, 221
dominant business firms 147–9
  defined 147
dominant-constrained firms 149,
    151, 152
  defined 148
dominant-linked firms 150, 154
  defined 148
dominant product firms 147, 224,
    227
  defined 146
dominant-unrelated firms 150,
    154
  defined 148
dominant-vertical firms 153, 154
  defined 149
downstream 51, 157, 184, 209–11,
    214
  defined 45, 218
driving force 58, 84–9, 209
  defined 84

earnings per share (EPS) 12
economic strategy 10
economies of scale 44, 69, 104,
    140, 177

economies of scope 178
effectiveness 24, 59, 104, 207, 221,
    222
  defined 23, 217
efficiency 24, 82, 104, 105, 176,
    178, 221, 222, 286, 287, 293
  defined 23, 217
elasticity of demand 98, 156
endgame strategies 272-9
  defined 272
enterprise (industrial) 2, 7, 35-40,
    145, 161, 179-82, 259, 261
  defined 36
enterprise strategy 199, 201
  defined 196
entrepreneur 135, 138
entrepreneurial decision class 23,
    24
  defined 17
entrepreneurship 30, 135, 184,
    240
entry barriers 44, 46-8
eras
  mass manufacturing 15
  mass marketing 15
  post industrial 15
ethics 10, 247
exit barriers 44, 272, 274, 275,
    278-80
experience curve 48, 57, 67, 68,
    72, 75-7, 79, 95, 120, 121,
    163, 164
  defined 75-6
extended rivalry 43
FIFO/LIFO 65
firm as resource-converter 18, 26
focused strategy 104-6, 291
  defined 102
formulation of strategy 10, 11, 13,
    20, 30, 37, 50, 85, 88, 89, 136,
    137, 143, 144, 160, 190, 199-
    204, 216, 218-20, 230, 232,
    236-7, 242, 246-8, 255, 257,
    260, 264, 295
  defined 202
functional area strategy 222, 223,
    224
functional strategies 236

Gause's Competitive Exclusion
    Principle 76
general management 1, 5-9, 111,
    113, 117, 123, 150, 154, 157,
    171, 182, 187, 194, 198, 204,
    243
  defined 7
general systems theory 7
generic categories 52
generic competitive strategies
  differentiation 47-51, 54, 291,
    292
    defined 48
  focus 47, 49-51, 54, 102, 104,
    291, 292
    defined 49
  overall cost leadership 47-51,
    291, 292
    defined 48
geographical expansion strategy
    11, 40
geographical growth 28, 29
geographical growth vector 28
goals 9, 10, 37, 38, 40, 113-15,
    125, 140, 143, 145, 146, 181,
    201, 202, 219, 221, 223, 232,
    241, 260, 261, 264, 285
  defined 195, 218, 256
government policy effects 44, 46
grand strategy 234
  defined 235
growth/share matrix 57, 77, 120,
    121

owth vector 18, 22, 28, 30, 227
defined 19, 20

form structure 181
defined 180
erarchy of strategy levels 106,
107, 196, 199, 201, 221–4,
232, 242, 243, 260
listic standpoint 51, 232
rizontal diversification 157,
158, 235
defined 20
rizontal integration 235

ology 33, 72, 246
petus sub-process 113–19, 185–
8, 191
defined 113
plementation of strategy 10, 11,
17, 25, 29, 37, 50, 88, 89, 136,
137, 143, 199, 203, 208, 213,
230, 233, 236, 247–9, 262,
281, 297
ound logistics 52
lustry attractiveness 121, 122,
161, 225, 242
ormation systems 11, 101, 137
novation 36, 44, 141, 142, 153,
160, 163, 180, 185, 190, 210,
235, 288
titutional strategy 127
titutionalizing the strategy 234,
236
egrative management 24
ermediate diversification 213
ernal corporate venturing
(ICV) 92, 190–92
defined 185
ernal development 32, 213
ernationalization 30–33
ue management 25

Japanese strategic planning 25,
204

key profit influences 65, 66
key success factors 157, 245–7
defined 245

labour 46, 65, 115, 134, 167, 212,
224
leadership 11, 129, 134, 135, 144,
197, 236, 241, 248, 261, 289
linkages between strategy and
performance 65–71
logic 10, 199, 252
logical incrementalism 29, 251,
257–60
defined 259–60
long range planning (LRP) 83, 89

M-form structure 180–83
defined 180
Machine Bureaucracy 134–8,
140–42, 144
defined 135–6
management hierarchy 7, 13, 37,
115, 123, 134, 136, 137, 141,
187
margin 50, 163
defined 54
market boundaries 98–100
defined 99
market development 222, 235,
291
market differentiation 28
market geography 28
market heterogeneity 156
market need 28, 186
defined 28
market segmentation 96, 97, 107,
258, 277
market share 29, 60, 61, 66–71,

market share – *contd*
  76, 77, 95, 99, 120, 122, 124,
  125, 127, 163, 164, 170, 223,
  225, 241, 277, 283
market share rank 67–9
  defined 67
market structure 64, 65
maximizing 114, 174–8
McKinsey/GE business screen
  121–4, 127, 163, 224, 225
mission 28, 85, 87, 196, 202, 223,
  232–6, 238–42, 244
  defined 19, 195, 201, 233, 238
mobility barrier 278
motivation 50, 204, 289, 292
multidivisional structure 34, 36,
  40, 134, 138–40, 142, 147,
  150, 151, 180, 207, 291
multinational enterprise (MNE)
  179, 181–3

natural competition 74, 75
  defined 72
Neo-Darwinism 216
net present value 110

objectives 8–10, 18, 20, 21, 23, 26,
  28, 32, 37, 74, 75, 81, 83, 108,
  112, 113, 115, 126–8, 145,
  159, 160, 176, 181, 185, 196,
  198, 201–3, 206, 218–21, 223,
  228, 230, 232, 233, 234, 238,
  241–4, 248, 261, 264, 265,
  266, 267
  defined 195, 218, 235, 241, 256
operating decision class 23, 27
  defined 18
operations 16, 54, 61, 82, 83, 116,
  117, 127, 138, 152, 165, 197,
  249
  defined 52

opportunistic reaction 144
organic development 292, 294
organizational championing 186,
  189, 191
organizational imperative 176
organization's basic purpose 21,
  81–2
outbound logistics 52

Pareto principle 77
partial ignorance 16, 17, 19, 28
  defined 16, 17
pattern recognizers 144
personal values 11, 12, 261
planning mode 136, 137
planning staff 204, 233
policy 8–10, 13, 62, 79, 111, 115,
  160, 178, 224, 227, 253,
  263–9, 276, 283, 295
  defined 16, 204, 222, 236, 256,
    263
portfolio planning 12, 28, 29, 32,
  57, 61, 75, 87, 92, 93, 95, 108,
  120, 122–30, 157, 159, 163–
  71, 194, 196, 223–6, 233, 271,
  279
  defined 120
private ordering (governance) 17,
  177, 183
  defined 176
product differentiation 44, 99, 10
product championing 186, 187
product life cycle (PLC) 100, 222,
  272–4
product-market 18, 21–3, 96, 98–
  100, 103, 115–17, 143, 146–8,
  152, 155–8, 163–5, 258, 287,
  290, 293–7
  defined 98–103
product-market/portfolio model
  159

product-market scope 22
product portfolio 57, 75
product/service differentiation 29
product/service technology 28
Professional Bureaucracy 134,
    140–42
  defined 140
profit centre 60, 211
Profit Impact of Market Strategy
    (PIMS) Programme 57, 59–
    65, 67–9, 71, 77, 99, 121, 163

quality assurance 53
quality management 53
question marks 77, 164
  defined 78

recipe 288, 289
related business firms 11, 149, 150
  defined 149
related-complementary
    diversification (R-CD) 158,
    161, 162
  defined 157
related-constrained firms 150–52,
    154
  defined 148
related-linked firms 150, 213
  defined 148
related product firms 221, 224, 226
  defined 146
related-supplementary
    diversifiction (R-SD) 158,
    161, 162
  defined 157
relative market share 164
  defined 67
relative quality 60, 68–71
  defined 68
research and development (R &
    D) 52, 64, 97, 183, 210

resource allocation 85, 92, 110,
    112, 117–20, 123, 125, 126,
    128, 171, 181, 207
return on investment (ROI) 12,
    19, 21, 63–6, 68, 139, 235,
    241
  defined 62
return on sales (ROS) 62–4, 68
  defined 62
risk 10, 12, 19, 28, 74, 75, 112,
    160, 165–72, 178, 189, 198,
    201, 231, 247, 261
  defined 16, 17, 165–6, 169
risk premium ratio (RPR) 152
risk/return model 93, 160, 165–72
root method of decision making
    (rational-comprehensive
    method) 263, 264–7, 269
  defined 264

satisficing 114
scope 51, 82, 84–7, 96–8, 100,
    102–6, 147, 178, 191, 219,
    221–3, 225, 227, 228, 240, 244
  defined 11, 195, 221
served market 65–7, 99
  defined 60
Simple Structure 135, 138
  defined 134
single product firm 11, 60, 147,
    224
  defined 146
single business firm 147, 149, 214
  defined 149
sociobiology 74
specialization ratio (SR) 147
  defined 146
stages of product-market
    evolution 225
stars 77, 164
  defined 78

strategic building 186, 189
  defined 188
strategic business area (SBA) 28
strategic business unit (SBU) 62,
    63, 232, 233
  defined 60
  see also business unit
strategic competition 74, 75
  defined 72
strategic context determination
    189, 190
  defined 185
strategic decision class 17
strategic decisions 10, 26, 37, 181,
    197–9, 201, 204, 233, 259
  defined 18, 23, 197, 242
strategic fit 161
  defined 160
strategic flexibility 28
strategic forcing 186–9
  defined 187–8
strategic framework 84–6
  defined 85
strategic groups 99
  defined 278
strategic management 9, 10, 13,
    22–4, 26, 27, 32, 191, 194,
    201, 231, 233, 234, 236–7,
    238, 246, 247, 249
  defined 6, 23, 24–5, 87–8, 200,
    230
strategic management process
    (SMP) 13, 233–7
strategic mandate 122
strategic neglect 188
strategic planning 22, 25, 122, 126,
    203, 237
  defined 23, 200
Strategic Planning Institute 59,
    77, 121
strategic portfolio strategy 28

strategy 6, 7, 9–13, 15–18, 20–23,
    25, 27–30, 38–41, 43, 46–51,
    54, 59–62, 64–6, 70, 72–6,
    82–5, 87–9, 95, 96, 98, 102–8,
    112, 116, 118–20, 122–4,
    126–9, 131–7, 143–7, 151,
    152, 155, 157, 159–62, 165,
    169–71, 187, 189–92, 195–7,
    199–204, 206–8, 214, 216–24,
    226–36, 238, 239, 242–9,
    255–63, 274, 276, 278, 281,
    285–8, 290–97
  defined 16–17, 37, 61, 75, 81–2,
    131, 132, 133, 134, 195,
    206, 217–18, 220, 230, 238,
    256
strategy model 93, 159–62, 165,
    169, 170
strategy statements 220, 227
structure 2, 10, 18, 19, 23, 24, 27,
    30, 34–6, 38–42, 46, 88, 98,
    111, 116, 117, 119, 134–6, 138,
    141, 142, 144–6, 150–52, 154,
    178–83, 184, 188, 192, 198,
    203, 206–8, 211, 214, 222,
    225, 236, 248, 258, 285, 290,
    291
  defined 38, 114, 207
structure follows strategy 11, 39,
    116, 145
structural context determination
    191
  defined 190
structural determinants 43
stuck in the middle 50
substitute products 42–9, 98, 156,
    273, 277, 278
  defined 44
sustainability 50–51
switching costs 45, 46
  defined 44, 278

synergy 26, 28, 32, 219, 221–3,
227, 228
    defined 22, 158, 221

tactics 64, 132, 133, 204,
232
    defined 37, 256
transaction cost economics
(TCE) 173, 175–8,
180–83
turnaround
    company 281–97
        defined 281, 282
    strategy 235, 281, 288–97
two-step discontinuity 32

U-form structure 179, 181
    defined 180
uncertainty 28, 111, 112, 135, 153,
166, 173
    defined 16

undifferentiated strategy 103, 104,
106
    defined 102
unrelated business firms 148–50,
154, 156, 293
    defined 149
unrelated-passive 150, 153
    defined 149
unrelated product 147
    defined 146
US Federal Trade Commission
(FTC–LB) 62, 68

value chain 52–5
    defined 51
value enhancement 63
value system 51–2
vertical integration 11, 61, 66,
99, 158, 194, 209–11,
235
    defined 20, 40, 157

Discover more about our forthcoming books through Penguin's FREE newspaper...

Penguin Quarterly

It's packed with:

- exciting features
- author interviews
- previews & reviews
- books from your favourite films & TV series
- exclusive competitions & much, much more...

Write off for your free copy today to:
Dept JC
Penguin Books Ltd
FREEPOST
West Drayton
Middlesex
UB7 0BR
NO STAMP REQUIRED

FOR THE BEST IN PAPERBACKS, LOOK FOR THE 🐧

In every corner of the world, on every subject under the sun, Penguin represents quality and variety – the very best in publishing today.

For complete information about books available from Penguin – including Puffins, Penguin Classics and Arkana – and how to order them, write to us at the appropriate address below. Please note that for copyright reasons the selection of books varies from country to country.

In the United Kingdom: Please write to *Dept JC, Penguin Books Ltd, FREEPOST, West Drayton, Middlesex, UB7 0BR.*

If you have any difficulty in obtaining a title, please send your order with the correct money, plus ten per cent for postage and packaging, to *PO Box No 11, West Drayton, Middlesex*

In the United States: Please write to *Dept BA, Penguin, 299 Murray Hill Parkway, East Rutherford, New Jersey 07073*

In Canada: Please write to *Penguin Books Canada Ltd, 2801 John Street, Markham, Ontario L3R 1B4*

In Australia: Please write to the *Marketing Department, Penguin Books Australia Ltd, P.O. Box 257, Ringwood, Victoria 3134*

In New Zealand: Please write to the *Marketing Department, Penguin Books (NZ) Ltd, Private Bag, Takapuna, Auckland 9*

In India: Please write to *Penguin Overseas Ltd, 706 Eros Apartments, 56 Nehru Place, New Delhi, 110019*

In the Netherlands: Please write to *Penguin Books Netherlands B.V., Postbus 3507, NL–1001 AH, Amsterdam*

In West Germany: Please write to *Penguin Books Ltd, Friedrichstrasse 10–12, D–6000 Frankfurt/Main 1*

In Spain: Please write to *Alhambra Longman S.A., Fernandez de la Hoz 9, E–28010 Madrid*

In Italy: Please write to *Penguin Italia s.r.l., Via Como 4, I-20096 Pioltello (Milano)*

In France: Please write to *Penguin France S.A., 17 rue Lejeune, F-31000 Toulouse*

In Japan: Please write to *Longman Penguin Japan Co Ltd, Yamaguchi Building, 2–12–9 Kanda Jimbocho, Chiyoda-Ku, Tokyo 101*

FOR THE BEST IN PAPERBACKS, LOOK FOR THE 🐧

PENGUIN BUSINESS AND ECONOMICS

Almost Everyone's Guide to Economics
J. K. Galbraith and Nicole Salinger

This instructive and entertaining dialogue provides a step-by-step explanation of 'the state of economics in general and the reasons for its present failure in particular in simple, accurate language that everyone could understand and that a perverse few might conceivably enjoy'.

The Rise and Fall of Monetarism   David Smith

Now that even Conservatives have consigned monetarism to the scrapheap of history, David Smith draws out the unhappy lessons of a fundamentally flawed economic experiment, driven by a doctrine that for years had been regarded as outmoded and irrelevant.

Atlas of Management Thinking   Edward de Bono

This fascinating book provides a vital repertoire of non-verbal images that will help activate the right side of any manager's brain.

The Economist Economics   Rupert Pennant-Rea and Clive Crook

Based on a series of 'briefs' published in *The Economist*, this is a clear and accessible guide to the key issues of today's economics for the general reader.

Understanding Organizations   Charles B. Handy

Of practical as well as theoretical interest, this book shows how general concepts can help solve specific organizational problems.

The Winning Streak   Walter Goldsmith and David Clutterbuck

A brilliant analysis of what Britain's best-run and most successful companies have in common – a must for all managers.